TEACHING THE CULT OF LITERATURE IN THE FRENCH THIRD REPUBLIC

Teaching the Cult of Literature in the French Third Republic

BY

M. Martin Guiney

First published 2004 by
PALGRAVE MACMILLAN™
175 Fifth Avenue, New York, N.Y. 10010 and
Houndmills, Basingstoke, Hampshire, England RG21 6XS
Companies and representatives throughout the world

PALGRAVE MACMILLAN is the global academic imprint of the Palgrave Macmillan division of St. Martin's Press, LLC and of Palgrave Macmillan Ltd. Macmillan® is a registered trademark in the United States, United Kingdom and other countries. Palgrave is a registered trademark in the European Union and other countries.

ISBN 1–4039–6518–8 hardback

Library of Congress Cataloging-in-Publication Data

Guiney, Mortimer
    Teaching the cult of literature in the French Third Republic /
    M. Martin Guiney.
        p. cm.
    Includes bibliographical references and index.
    ISBN 1–4039–6518–8
        1. French literature—Study and teaching—France.
    2. Education—France—History—19th century. I. Title.

PQ63.F8G85 2004
840'.71'044—dc22   2004041686

A catalogue record for this book is available from the British Library.

Design by Newgen Imaging Systems (P) Ltd., Chennai, India.

First edition: September 2004
10 9 8 7 6 5 4 3 2 1

Printed in the United States of America.

For my father

CONTENTS

Acknowledgments

The writing of this book was made possible in large part through the generosity of Kenyon College in the form of sabbaticals and research grants. Many colleagues and friends have given selflessly of their time and energy by reading drafts of chapters and, in some cases, the entire manuscript. I especially want to thank Ralph Albanese, Jr., for his careful reading and numerous suggestions, corrections, and references. Without the benefit of his expertise in the field of literary pedagogy in the French Third Republic, this book may never have seen its way to publication.

Among the many people who have helped make this a better book than I could have managed on my own, I want to thank all of my current and former colleagues who have provided advice, support, and encouragement, especially Jean Blacker, James Carson, Mary Jane Cowles, Juan De Pascuale, Ellen Furlough, and Deborah Laycock.

Eckhard Georgi, Louise Guiney, Mortimer Guiney, Jay Lutz, Stamos Metzidakis, and Tim Raser have all been generous readers of the many interim projects that have led up to the final draft. Stéphane Gerson and Frédéric Viguier invited me to the Institute of French Studies at New York University to present my research, and I thank them and the students at the Institute for their incisive and original questions. I am grateful to Farideh Koohi-Kamali of Palgrave for her faith in this project. Finally, I could not have completed it without the support, understanding, and love of Amy Mock.

PREFACE

There are many reasons for writing a book on French education. In my case, one of the reasons is personal. My own experience of the French educational system was brief, fragmentary, and is deeply buried in the past. Nevertheless, I learned a lot from this experience, and some of what I learned is relevant to the ideas and arguments in the chapters ahead. In small part this book is an attempt to understand, by uncovering their historical origins, some of the forces that operated in a handful of French classrooms in which I happened to sit at various times during the late 1960s and early 1970s.

From October 1967 to June 1969, I was enrolled at the *Cours Elémentaire Albert Camus* in Mont-Saint-Aignan, a suburb of Rouen. I spent the fall and early winter of 1971 in a *Collège d'Enseignement Général* on the rue Cler, in the seventh *arrondissement* of Paris. The "CEG" as it was known was the contemporary avatar of *enseignement spécial*, instituted by the minister of *Instruction Publique* Victor Duruy in 1865–66 as a less demanding and more practical (technical, preprofessional) alternative to the Classics-based curriculum leading to the *baccalauréat*. Finally, my French education culminated with a year in the class of *première A (c)* at the Lycée Jeanne d'Arc in Rouen in 1976–77. *Première* is the penultimate year of secondary education and ends with a sort of "pre-*baccalauréat*" exam called the *épreuve anticipée de français*, and the year was formerly called *année de rhétorique* (as distinct from *année de philosophie*, now *terminale*, the year of the "bac" proper). In 1976, as best I can recall, the "A" meant that our class specialized more generally in the humanities, and "(c)" meant that it specialized more specifically in modern languages.

French education has changed since the 1960s and 1970s, and every year, or at least every new government, seems to come with its own list of fundamental reforms. The recent regime of Education Minister Luc Ferry is no exception. The principal change that I noticed during my childhood, however, consisted of the replacement of the *porte-plume*, a wooden stick with a steel nib, with the more manageable fountain pen. In the 1960s, the teacher would still regularly go from desk to desk replenishing our inkwells with ink stored in an old wine bottle, a ritual that must have existed for centuries. In the years following the Revolution of May 1968 the accepted instrument of writing had been modernized since the nineteenth century more, it seemed, than the methods or content of instruction. The feeling that curricular change between the 1880s and the 1960s, at least in the fields of French language and literature, had been largely superficial made me wonder later in life what really separated the *Education Nationale* I encountered from that of Jules Ferry, or even of earlier founding figures. While researching the French school system of the nineteenth century, I have been so often struck by recognition that it no longer comes as a surprise. Of course this is an illusion, as schools in France have changed enormously since that time. The dominant theme of this book is not change, however, but continuity, and more precisely: continuity disguised as change.

Some of the traditions that my research has uncovered strike me as familiar simply because they are part of the universal experience of every schoolchild who has ever lived; others, I believe, are dependent upon a specific time and place. One of my claims is that the institutional practices I examine in this study are unique to France, specifically to the French Republic, in the attempt to exploit national education as a basis for its legitimacy. Such a claim does not imply that no other nation has ever used the institution of public education, or even the teaching of literature, in order to perpetuate itself, but only that the modern French nation has developed its own special way of doing so. There is no doubt that for the English-speaking world, for example, Shakespeare plays a role in the educative process that is analogous to what I describe here. Schoolchildren learn that it is more important (and much easier) simply to worship Shakespeare's plays than to understand them. Clearly, Shakespeare's status as author has given way to his status as icon representing the ultimate potential of the English language, a potential that few people will ever realize. The popularity of Shakespeare's plays, on stage and at the movies, in my opinion far exceeds the size of the public that is trained to understand the language spoken by the characters. That gap—between what an individual understands and appreciates, and what he or she is told to appreciate whether or not he or she is able—is where the realms of the sacred and the political merge. In a sense, Shakespeare stands for the entire institution of literary studies, and raises the question of their ultimate purpose. Do we control literature by understanding it, or does it control us by resisting our attempts to understand?

Literature is not the only field in which the ostensible purpose and actual result of the pedagogical process collide. In order to illustrate this, I describe some elements of continuity between the schools of the Third Republic, which I have studied, and the schools that I attended as a child and adolescent. Generally, they tend to fall under the categories of: a catechistic model for the transmission of knowledge, especially— though not exclusively—literary knowledge; a tendency to use apparently logical methods to arrive at illogical conclusions; and a strong moral value attached to academic success or failure, to the degree that inability to perform academically is judged not simply as intellectual inferiority, but as a violation of a sacred trust. In the first category, nothing quite conveys the ritualistic and mechanical acquisition of cultural lore than the time-honored tradition of *récitation*. Jean-Jacques Rousseau in Book I of *L'Emile* alludes to this practice in his well-known criticism of the mystifying, Latinate syntax of Jean de La Fontaine: "*Qu'est-ce qu'un arbre perché?*" [What is a perched tree?] because in his poem, La Fontaine wrote that the crow was "on a tree perched" (which sounds in French like "on a perched tree"), instead of "perched on a tree." Indeed, I was often perplexed by the beautiful-sounding verses that we memorized, presented to us like valuable objects to hold briefly in our hands: in another of La Fontaine's most often recited fables, "*La Cigale et la fourmi*," what exactly does the ant mean when she tells the cricket "*j'en suis fort aise?*" What is a "*langueur monotone*" in Verlaine's undeniably musical but, to an eight-year old, mysterious "*Chanson d'automne?*" And, in the realm where the secrets of high culture and sexual taboos coexist: "*Luxe*" and "*calme*" are clear enough, but what is "*volupté*" (yes, today Baudelaire's *Invitation au voyage* has even found a place in the primary school curriculum)? Although some effort was spent on explicating these texts even in the earliest classes, words and sometimes entire stanzas were swallowed whole and unprocessed, not only by me, who could blame these mysteries on my lack of familiarity with the language and culture, but by my native-born classmates as well. The American equivalent of this ritual is the daily recitation of the Pledge of Allegiance, which children notoriously fail to understand and, according to those who have actually listened to their recitations, misquote. In both cases, understanding and analysis are unimportant; some other goal is being achieved, one that the vast literature on good educational practice does not explain, because the goal cannot be justified according to valid pedagogical principles.

As to the logical means of arriving at illogical conclusions, let me give two examples: while studying the Hundred Years' War in our class of *onzième* at Albert Camus (roughly equivalent to second grade), the teacher explained that the English had successfully invaded most of France because they had bows and arrows, while the French used crossbows: in the time it took to shoot one arrow with a crossbow, one could shoot several with a bow. Therefore, the technological superiority of the French forces (a crossbow being far more accurate and powerful than a bow), instead of giving them an advantage in combat, put them at a disadvantage. In fact, it was responsible for the series of military defeats that only Joan of Arc would eventually redeem. If I remember this detail from our class thirty-five years ago, it is because I was reminded of it only ten years afterward when the History teacher at the *Lycée Jeanne d'Arc* made a strikingly similar argument. This time, the conflict was the Franco-Prussian War, the outcome of which, ironically, was supposed to have had such a determining impact on the educational reform policies of the Third Republic. Our teacher explained to us that Antoine Chassepot, a weapons manufacturer, had invented a revolutionary rifle that was purchased by Napoleon III for the imperial army. The officers were so confident in the superiority of their new weapons that they neglected to put as much effort into field strategy as they should have, leading to their quick and humiliating defeat. It is important here to point out that there is nothing illogical about either of these arguments when taken individually and in context. Technological innovation can backfire, so to speak, and it is entirely possible that most historians agree with my teachers (though I doubt that the factors mentioned above bear as much of the responsibility for defeat as they claimed). What is important is the *structure* of both arguments, which is in the figure of a paradox. The obvious last term of the syllogism: (a) better weapons help to win wars (b) the French have traditionally had better weapons than their adversaries, therefore (c) the French win most wars is, in these cases, reversed, because the first term is revealed to be a false premise, a pseudo-axiom. Again, what is significant here is not whether such a logical move is valid. What I want to emphasize, and what this book tries to show in a more objective fashion, is that the dependency on paradox, the deceptive emphasis that the school places on reason, only to snatch the reward of rational thinking away at the end, is part of a larger strategy. It is part and parcel, I argue, of the state-mandated educational system's attempt to advance a crypto-theological ideology modeled on the mysteries of the Roman Catholic Church, under the deceptive guise of a rational, universalist, and scientific antithesis of the theology it seeks to replace.

The third aspect of the educational system I mention here is the moral dimension imposed upon academic achievement. The first illustration of this argument is once again anecdotal, but I hope it is more substantially borne out by the evidence exposed in the course of this study. As an American child in a French school, I was astonished at the degree of moral indignation that accompanied the teacher's public humiliation of a pupil who failed to perform a task according to standard. I am not talking about discipline for unruly behavior, which no doubt takes on the appearance of forced atonement for sin in every school in the world. Rather, I am talking about *academic* lapses: poorly recited poems, spelling errors, compositions that are too short, failure to master the multiplication table, and so on. Admonishment for these errors was always public: the culprit was made into an example for the others, and his sins were not viewed as isolated *acts* but rather as symptoms of an inherent deficiency that only a radical change in character, a *conversion*, would correct. The counterpart to such moral condemnation was the ritual distribution of small cardboard tickets, called *bons points*, to every pupil who did something well: a flawless *dictée*, a well-formed answer to a question, mastery over the diabolical *porte-plume* evidenced by the absence of ink spots on one's *cahier du jour*, and so on. The desire for *bons points* generated a compulsive, pavlovian pattern of behavior, especially among the better pupils, who could exchange ten *points* at the end of the week for a small color reproduction of a famous scene in French history.

I end this autobiographical prelude by guarding the reader against the impression that the view of the French educational system that informs this book is overly critical or negative. That is far from the case. If I describe the School of the Republic as an institution based partly on deception and bad faith, I also believe that *every* educational enterprise is fundamentally at odds with its openly expressed purpose. One cannot escape the fact that absolute values of beauty, knowledge and truth are also the very terms that society appropriates in order to serve the interests of its more powerful members. One also cannot deny that virtually every educational institution ever created is complicit in this appropriation. Finally, there is no such thing as perfect, or even good pedagogy, literary or other. There is only better and worse pedagogy, and I could only judge the value of the French solution to the pedagogic challenge by comparing the Third Republic's national education to the systems developed by other societies. Such is not the purpose of this book. I will, however, take this opportunity to say that one of the best teachers I ever had taught literature under the French Republic. Her name is Sylvie Morel. She spent the last part of her career in Paris, but I had her at Jeanne d'Arc in Rouen, where she prepared us for the *épreuve anticipée de français* using the *Lagarde et Michard* anthologies and a handful of *Classiques Larousse*. Madame Morel did not "teach to the test," however. As genuine a believer in her mission as any graduate of any *école normale* of the last two centuries, she showed us by example what living in God's light truly meant. By constantly exceeding the boundaries of the *programme*, taking her students to speak with writers, directors, actors, and to view art exhibits, plays, and movies on almost a weekly basis, she succeeded in actually *demystifying* the tradition of sacred knowledge in which she was born and raised (like many teachers, she was herself the child of an *instituteur*, and she taught the three subjects that have traditionally been the foundation for higher learning in the French educational system: Greek, Latin, and French). To this day, she serves as a model to which I can only aspire in my own attempts to convey the value of French literature to new generations of students.

INTRODUCTION
LITERATURE VERSUS SCRIPTURE

The focus of this book is the functional similarity of two separate characteristics applied to texts within their respective institutional frameworks: sacredness and literariness. At first glance these terms are distinct, since what qualifies a text as sacred is specific to Scripture, and what qualifies one as literary is specific to literature. Such difference is made evident by the occasional practice of writing "Scripture" with an upper case "S," as a proper name referring not to a genre, but to an identifiable, definitive body of texts. In Scripture, what is important is the recognized divine origin of the text and its status as revelation; in literature, the text is not sacred except figuratively at best. Producers of literature, according to tradition, normally do not take dictation from God, nor do they partake of the divine, except in the figurative sense that their activity evokes the ancient, Orphic ideal in which there was no clear distinction between literary and sacred discourse. The literary author has long been secularized, and as a consequence, what qualifies certain texts as "literature" is the subject of unending debate.

Literature nevertheless exists, even in the absence of an adequate definition of the term. One proof of its existence is the continued prosperity of institutions that depend on it, such as the publishing industry, the field of literary criticism, and the teaching of literature at all levels of education. I argue that such institutions tend to equate sacredness and literariness: from a sociological perspective, the function of sacred texts within a spiritual tradition is similar to the function of literary texts within secular institutions such as the ones enumerated above. Even one of the foremost concerns of the guardians both of spiritual and literary institutions is practically identical: the legitimacy of the practice of determining which texts are authentic, that is, truly sacred or literary, and which ones are not. One way to explain this similarity is to say that "sacred" is a metaphor for "literary," a means of gaining some purchase on a term that has no clear referent. Sacredness works as a metaphor for literariness because it accounts for many of the ways in which literature behaves in its institutional settings. Though not all literary authors, critics, and pedagogues would like to admit it, the importance to society of what they do is largely dependent on faith: specifically on a belief, shared by the larger group of consumers of literature, in the existence and value of literariness, whether such value is considered absolute, according to a religious model, or relative, according to an economic one.

From a structural standpoint, however, the questions of literary value and sacredness are similar. The difference is one of essence: the mysterious, elusive, and above all specific nature of the quality that defines a text as sacred or literary, but not in the effect that such qualities have, or the functions they serve, in the institutions to which they give rise. This book investigates how literature, regardless of how distinct it may be from Scripture in its essence, nevertheless functions in a manner similar to Scripture. The investigation focuses on a particular time and place: the public primary and secondary schools of the French Third Republic.

I stated above that separation of canonical texts from the mass of discourse is one of the functions both of religious and literary institutions. There is another, less obvious (though related) function common to both institutions on which I want to concentrate: assimilation. From the perspective of canon formation, the question of which texts deserve the designation of Scripture is largely settled in the Roman Catholic Church. Such relative stability is absent from the literary field, in which the question of what texts, past, current, or future are authentically "literary" is always open. The complex process of inclusion and exclusion represented by literary canon formation is similar to assimilation, understood as the never-ending constitution of a collective identity, such as the nation. It is on this similarity that a large part of my thesis depends.

When the term "assimilation" is used in a social context, such as the granting of citizenship or other, less official means by which an identifiable group recognizes individuals as its own, a particular dynamic is implied by which the individual must sacrifice whatever part of his or her identity is intolerable to the group. A typical example would be the history of Jews in Europe and their relationship to the legal entity of the nation. Jews born in France under the *ancien régime* were considered foreigners unless they converted. Religious conversion as a condition of naturalization constitutes an extreme example of the process of assimilation, and of the extent of the sacrifice demanded of the one petitioning for membership in the national community: Jews are out, Christians in. Under the laws of the Republic, Jews could become citizens without converting.[1] These famously progressive laws did not, however, affect means of acculturation other than religious conversion. Citizenship, a form of assimilation that does not depend on conversion, is relatively easy to attain since in theory it is possible in most modern democracies, including France, for the individual to join the national community while retaining "foreign" cultural characteristics such as religion, language, and mores.[2] Still, the issue of whether one nevertheless has to sacrifice such particular characteristics in order to achieve recognition from the larger society—and to what extent—continues to be relevant in every society, even those that do not require religious conversion as a precondition to citizenship.

The institution of literature operates on a similar principle. To be recognized as "literary," what aspects of a given text must adhere to a collective model? Is there such a thing as "conversion" in the literary field, meaning access to the realm of literature? The question in the literary field (and fields of cultural production in general) is complicated by the tendency, especially since the advent of modernism, to value what is particular about a work, its originality or "difference," traits that are akin to "foreignness." However, the paradox that originality or "difference" in art may enable rather than inhibit assimilation into the collective (the canon) does not mean that the process is fundamentally different from what happens when individuals negotiate their membership in a group. First, there is the fact that "difference" when elevated to a *sine qua non* of canonicity can become a type of conformity, as the history of modernism in the twentieth century abundantly illustrates: the injunction to be new, to transgress established boundaries, itself becomes a matter of artistic convention; second, the history of culture outside of the modernist canon, especially of literature, in France as well as (and perhaps relatively more than) elsewhere has traditionally placed a high value on adherence to preexisting norms, specifically to classical high style, as a condition for inclusion. In that sense, the term "assimilation," in all its sociological richness, can apply to the history of national identity as well as the evolution of a national literature.

It is possible that the intersection of the themes mentioned above—the relationship between sacredness and literariness, the function of assimilation in the construction of national identity as well as of literary tradition—has never been more dominant in the public sphere than it was during the first half of the French Third Republic. The establishment of political authority on lay principles, the struggle between Church and state[3] for control over the educational process, and the gradual replacement of Latin by French as the medium for the transmission of literary value, all occurred contemporaneously, creating conflicts that continue to exert a determining influence on the French literary field and French society in general.

While this book focuses on French national education from the 1870s to World War I, it touches on the more distant past, especially the years immediately following the French Revolution, and also on issues such as social and cultural assimilation that are more relevant to French society today than ever. The revolutionary past and the multicultural present are privileged vantage points for examining the Third Republic debate over the cultural and educational responsibilities of the state. It is an axiom in French Studies that the educational laws promulgated by *ministre de l'Instruction publique* Jules Ferry between February 1879 and November 1883 constitute a critical stage in the history of the official construction and promotion of French national identity. This book examines the theory and practice of literary pedagogy of the period, two areas that lead to speculation on the nature of literature itself.

More than most academic subjects, the field of literary studies struggles with the question of what, exactly, is being taught. As long as literariness eludes definition, the suspicion that something other than literature takes its place in the classroom will never disappear. Another theme of this book is therefore pedagogical substitutes for literature, methodological stopgaps that allow literary studies to exist despite the absence of an adequate definition of literariness. The success of literary history as an academic discipline in the late nineteenth century is in part a result of the apparent truth of which pedagogues have long been aware, that literature *per se* cannot be taught except indirectly.

The paradox of teaching a subject by teaching something else in its place is especially characteristic of, but not unique to literary pedagogy. Part III of this book is about primary education, in which literacy is a more important concern than literature. Common sense dictates that every primary school must transmit the rudiments of reading and writing, if nothing else; and yet primary education, for much of its history, has in fact been teaching "something else" in addition to and even instead of literacy, as the following example illustrates.

There is a French colloquialism that refers to the absolute basics of a particular skill or body of knowledge, what we in English call its "ABC": "*le b-a ba.*" The expression comes from old-fashioned primers. Such texts, which multiplied as a result of the increased attention to popular education during the Reformation and Counter Reformation, typically consisted of an abecedary that presented the letters of the roman alphabet; a syllabary that combined those letters into syllables (the "*ba*" of "*b-a ba*"); and finally, the most common prayers and other elements of the Latin liturgy that all Catholic children needed to know by heart (Julia 1984: 470). Already, the use of a foreign language, Latin, to teach children how to read French raises questions as to the true purposes of such education. Even disregarding the substitution of Latin for the vernacular, however, one can legitimately ask whether literacy was truly the goal of primary education under the *ancien régime*. In practice, the teaching of reading (which at the time occurred separately from and prior to the teaching of writing) seems to have been a kind of charade, explaining why the level of literacy among the population was even lower than the level of school attendance. Dominique Julia quotes a revealing passage from Nicolas Rétif de la Bretonne's memoirs in an article on prerevolutionary primers included in the massive, beautifully printed anthology *Histoire de l'édition française* (1984). Nicolas recounts an early classroom experience, probably from around 1740, when the teacher asked him to read the *Pater noster* from his *syllabaire*. The word "*tuum*" in the phrase "*sanctificetur nomen tuum*" had been partly erased by the greasy thumbs of all the schoolchildren who had used that particular text, and appeared on the page as the two separate words: "*tu in.*" Nicolas, reading the words as he saw them, and believing in the authority of what he perceived to be the actual printed text, kept repeating "*tu in*" instead of "*tuum*," and the teacher (who evidently did not bother to check what was on the page) grew more and more angry. What is especially significant in this anecdote is that Nicolas's classmates were all trying to help him by whispering "*tuum!*" yet he stubbornly continued to read what he saw on the page rather than the word that he and his classmates already knew by heart. Julia draws the logical conclusion from this anecdote that Nicolas was the only one in the room who was actually reading; the other children were simply using their purely aural knowledge of the text to participate in a simulation of the act of reading: "les enfants . . . ne lisent pas, mais se contentent de reconnaître dans leurs livres des prières déjà apprises par coeur" [children . . . do not read, but merely recognize in their books prayers already learned by heart] (473).

The failure to teach reading continued at every stage of the standard course of popular education, up to and including the preparation for the First Communion, which consisted in learning the *grand catéchisme*, a term referring both to a text and to a process of rote instruction. The simpler *petit catéchisme* was for smaller children, and served as a bridge between the *syllabaire* and the *grand catéchisme*. During his research, Julia discovered that very few individual *catéchismes* were actually printed during the seventeenth and eighteenth centuries compared to the number of *syllabaires*: while the more elementary primer was widely disseminated, the more advanced one was not. Also, the actual texts of the *catéchismes* that made it into print varied tremendously, often depending on the diocese in which they were to be used; so while the word "*catéchisme*" referred to a large variety of different texts, there were by contrast very few actual copies of each one. He concludes that children rarely held a *catéchisme* in their own hands, but depended instead on purely oral instruction (as indeed the etymology of "catechism" implies): "le catéchisme est donc d'abord exercice de mémoire" [catechism is therefore primarily an exercise of memory] (478), even though it was nominally part of the process of instruction in reading. Reading was simply not a big part of most popular education before the nineteenth century, writing even less so.

The absence of "reading" from the school experience persisted in spite of the fact that, ever since the Reformation, *all* of Christianity, not just the reformed variety, viewed the ability to read as "une voie essentielle pour assurer son salut" [an essential means of ensuring one's salvation] (Julia 1984: 468). The catechism simply became the Catholic substitute for the actual Word of God upon the direct knowledge of which Luther had mounted his challenge. The fact that children often did not learn to read during their usually brief and cursory exposure to formal education is not nearly as important, for our purposes, as the countervailing fact that the goal of literacy had never officially been deposed as the ostensible justification for primary education. Julia therefore presents us with an important theme that recurs throughout the following chapters: how does national education hide the true nature of what it teaches? To put it another way, how does one *not* teach language, or literature, while claiming to be doing nothing else? The partial answer that I attempt to formulate will depend on the argument that the type of "non-teaching" that took place under the dual (religious and linguistic) pedagogy of the *ancien régime*, both at the popular, primary level and the elitist, secondary level, survived under a different guise after the reforms of the French Republic. In the nineteenth century, while most of the population was well on its way to achieving basic literacy (as François Furet and Jacques Ozouf have demonstrated in *Reading and Writing: Literacy in France from Calvin to Jules Ferry* (1977, trans. 1982), the practice of "non-teaching" survived, that is, the practice of claiming to teach language and literature exclusively and disinterestedly, while actually pursuing different goals.

If the purpose of popular education before 1789 was to subordinate literacy to personal salvation, the revolutionary reaction was to subordinate it to civic salvation, that is to say membership in the newly created nation. The fact that both enterprises have much in common was not lost on the early proponents of republicanism. The history of republican educational policy is often presented in mythic terms, as in the claim by republican pedagogues that they had a precursor in Charlemagne,[4] who encouraged the creation of schools partly in order to evangelize the population. While meaningful similarities between Charlemagne and Jules Ferry are hard to discern, in one respect the legend of Charlemagne is appropriate for the Third Republic: it provides a historical precedent, and hence a justification for the true purpose of public education, which is evangelic. The suggestion of distant origins in time for the educational mission of the Third Republic, extending well beyond the French Revolution and even beyond the origin of the French monarchy, functions diachronically, as the inaugural phase of a *tradition*, with the authority that common law allocates to that term. It also functions synchronically, as one of the two coordinates of eschatological time—in other words, as prophecy. The fulfillment of prophecy is the triumph over historical time, a process that is itself the pretext for ritual, or the regular commemoration of that victory. The republican interpretation of history depends on the evolution of evangelism from its literal sense of conversion to Christianity by preaching the Gospels, to the figurative sense of assimilation into French collective identity through teaching: specifically, through textual practices applied to a well-defined linguistic and literary heritage.

The role of linguistic and literary pedagogy in founding the authority of the state has already been compared to the relationship between the Gospels and the institution and expansion of the Church. In fact, the founders of the Third Republic and their precursors explicitly identified their enterprise both with the Protestant return to Christ and with the Enlightenment project of placing religion on a rational basis.[5] Jules Ferry's principal biographer, Jean-Michel Gaillard, points out the messianic role that Ferry consciously adopted, both politically and spiritually, first by leading France out of its cycle of historical convulsions with the advent of the Republic, the one and only legitimate form of government; and second by reestablishing the tradition, begun during the Enlightenment, of a polity founded upon *laïcité*, civic salvation, or religion without God (134).

The idea of a "republican catechism" that would serve as the instrument of the new evangelism had been around longer than the Republic itself: in 1781 d'Alembert had the *Académie Française* sponsor a contest to reward the best catechism for the teaching of morality without reference to the Bible (Gaillard 1989: 149). The republican state's political self-legitimization as the spiritual guide of the nation was the basic structure within which French literature was about to play a decisive role. That structure had two principal components: the teaching of the French language as a tool of universal salvation defined as membership in the nation, and the teaching of literature—first predominantly Latin, then predominantly French—as a means of controlled access to the realm of the sacred. In fact, literature had performed the latter function since early Christianity, when the study of classical texts was not an end in itself but the path towards a better understanding of Scripture.

In the pages that follow, I therefore propose to show how the French literary canon operated as a type of scriptural authority for the secular power of the state. Inherent in literature is a tendency to bring into question Scripture's exclusive claim to divine inspiration. The theory and practice of literary pedagogy during the Third Republic go even further, demonstrating the need to eliminate the distance between religion and nation, Scripture and literature, not so as to discredit Scripture and the institutions that arise from it, but rather to accredit literature and the state.

The grounding of literature in the sacred would seem to guarantee its function as a legitimizing force by those in society who claim it as their own. Indeed much sociological work, especially that of Pierre Bourdieu and his disciples, explores the relationship between literature, education, and power. One sociological critic, Edgar Tripet, shows the relationship's complexity in an important essay titled "Langue, littérature et pouvoir" [Language, Literature and Power] (1975) that warns against the easy tendency to view culture as a vector of power, as if great art and literature were the justification for world dominance. One problem with this model, Tripet points out, is that it ignores the fact that political hegemony can more easily be the basis for the "greatness" attributed to cultural artifacts than the reverse. Of the seventeenth century, the period that has come to symbolize the apex of both the artistic and geopolitical dominance of the French language, he wrote: "c'est parce que le français est la langue de la Grande Nation constituée politiquement que sa littérature rayonnera au-delà de l'aire du pouvoir politique—une aire qui n'a pas à être nécessairement identique à celle de la langue même" [it is because French is the language of the politically constituted Great Nation that its literature shall radiate beyond the area covered by political power—an area that is not necessarily the same as the one covered by the language itself] (202–3). Tripet reverses the more traditional explanation, made repeatedly in pedagogical texts since the nineteenth century, that the great authors reinforced the political prestige of the monarchy by producing literature that justified France's domination in world affairs. Tripet in effect denies literature the claim to transcendence that it shares with Scripture and defines its claim to universal significance, perhaps too narrowly, as an effect of political prestige rather than its cause. His stark formulation of the subservience of culture to historical circumstances is a salutary reminder, however, of the arbitrariness of the claim that political power derives legitimacy from the same source that literature (for example) draws its literariness. Tripet exposes two centuries of abuse of the literature of the seventeenth century, "une littérature à qui on reconnaît un droit à l'universalité parce qu'elle parlerait la langue limpide de la raison—une fois occulté le rapport de force, entre la France et l'Europe, qui a produit avec cette universalité le droit de dire la raison" [a literature granted the right to universality because it speaks the transparent language of reason—once the power relation between France and Europe, that produced along with universality the right to speak reason, has been hidden] (205).

The extreme version of Tripet's conclusion is that the value of "great" art, whether the reason and transparency associated with classicism, or some other "universal" qualities associated with cultural products of a different time or place, is simply the values imposed by elite groups for the purpose of maintaining and extending their dominance, often beyond the geographical limits of the nation. The antithesis of this conclusion is the ideology subtending the teaching of language and culture in the school: that artifacts such as canonical literary texts exist as embodiments of eternal truth, unrelated to the affairs of the world. I argue that the best way to analyze the cult of literature as it was practiced by the pedagogues of the Third Republic is in light of Tripet's radical skepticism toward culture's claims to transcendence, itself a reflection of modern skepticism toward religion's claims to transcendence. It is further evidence of the similarity between sacred and literary texts that the ideologies in which they operate are subject to the same critique.

The Church can therefore be said to be evangelical in the literal sense, the Republic, figuratively. However, the means by which textual authority, in the Church as well as in the Republic, translates into spiritual authority are similar: a professional caste (priests, teachers) assumes the responsibility of converting individual human beings into members of a collective founded upon words. One can argue that the difference between the two sorts of text, Scripture and literature, distinguishes republicanism from Catholicism enough to justify the claim that republicanism is not a religion. Also, scriptural authority presents the text and the institution built upon it as one: the Church attempts to make manifest the underlying nature of a single, immutable text. The secular state can be said to have a similar relationship of identity with its Constitution, but not with something as unwieldy, heterogeneous, and evolving as a national literary corpus. However, literary texts possess "literariness," a quality on which legal documents do not depend in order to function; because of that quality, literary texts produce an impression of transcendence of the circumstances of their creation, and a claim on truth, to which legal documents as such do not. The term "literariness," precisely because it is impossible to define, brings the concept of faith into the realm of secular education. Third Republic literary pedagogy does not set out to demonstrate or prove the literariness of texts; instead, literariness is a given, an absolute origin which it is impossible, or rather forbidden, to explore.

In literary criticism there have been many explorations of the relationship between the terms "literary" and "sacred." I allude here to two of them: early-twentieth-century formalism (especially the Prague School) attempted to establish "literariness" as a distinct category; more recently, René Girard has explored literature as a manifestation of the sacred. Both approaches help to define the literary pedagogical context.

It is widely acknowledged that the term "literariness," designating the one true object of literary studies, first emerged from the work of the Russian Formalists (see, e.g., Cuddon 1991: 498 and Bertens 2001: 33). "Defamiliarization," Victor Shklovsky's term for the property that distinguishes the literary from the nonliterary, and a cornerstone of twentieth-century structuralism, started the search for a theory on the distinctiveness of literature, a feature that Roman Jakobson was the first to name "literariness." The first scientific inquiry into the nature of the literary began with a catalog of techniques that distinguish the literary text by privileging the self-referential, ambiguous, noncommunicative aspects of language. Formalism was the theoretical expression of the recently achieved autonomy of the literary field, summarized by the maxim: "*[a]rt is a way of experiencing the artfulness of an object; the object is not important*" (Shklovsky 1965: 12). Ironically, the earliest systematic attempts to arrive at a definition of "literariness," that is, to demystify the sacred nature traditionally ascribed to literary texts as distinct from other modes of discourse, actually contributed even further to literature's institutional autonomy, and hence to its magical aura. Much of the critique of this stance by Marxist sociological critics of literary pedagogy is that the formalist inquiries into the separate nature of literary texts were actually perversions of science, strengthening rather than dispelling the mystifying properties of literature, especially as they operate in the pedagogical context. Shklovsky's "defamiliarization" (the most commonly used equivalent of "*ostraneniye*") is certainly akin to the more pejorative term "mystification"; I would add that its kinship with the term "foreignness" (or more precisely: "making/becoming foreign") is also important. The concept of assimilation that I have already invoked, and that reappears throughout this study, is part of the exploration of "foreignness" as yet another metaphor, along with "sacredness," for the literariness of a text.

The sacred aura of literature that allowed the pedagogues of the Third Republic to enlist it in the cause of nation building is largely a matter of tradition. I begin with one aspect of this tradition: the assimilation of literary inspiration to divine revelation. One characteristic of Scripture is that it escapes categorization as a literary genre. It is "above" literature, and putatively devoid of the ambiguities and gratuitous embellishments, in short: of the *artifice* that characterizes the literary text. It is divine, in other words, because on a fundamental level it is not man made. If one has faith in Scripture, then unlike all other utterances (including literary ones), it escapes from a structuralist definition of meaning according to which signs signify in relation to other signs, and not to the extratextual, the "*hors-texte*" whose existence Jacques Derrida famously denied. The meaning of a religious text is superior, exceptional, according to René Girard's analysis of the origins of language in religious ritual in *Things Hidden since the Foundation of the World* (1978, trans. 1987). Instead of the structuralist theory of meaning arising from binary opposition, Girard proposes an even more basic model:

> [T]he model of the exception that is still in the process of emerging, the single trait that stands out against a confused mass or still unsorted multiplicity. It is the model of drawing lots, of the short straw, or, of the bean in the Epiphany cake. Only the piece that contains the bean is truly distinguished; only the shortest straw, or the longest, is meaningful. The rest remain indeterminate. (100)

Girard goes on to characterize games of chance, lotteries, and other processes by which a random entity is arbitrarily distinguished from an indeterminate group to achieve sacred status. It is the combined emergence, in religious ritual, of the process of identification of the sacrificial victim ("drawing lots"), and of the primordial signifier. The "one" to have been chosen at random becomes the medium for access to the divine.

Girard's theory on the origins of meaning is a direct descendant of his earlier theory on the origins of religion in *Violence and the Sacred* (1972, trans. 1977). The banishment or sacrifice of the ritual victim is a unanimous collective act. It literally (and, because of its ritualistic nature, repeatedly) *founds* the community. Religion, like language, is at the same time everything—the source of all meaning—and nothing. The "nothingness" derives from Girard's scientific claim to be searching for a "real" (not divine) origin of religion, an origin in the mobilization of collective violence against a randomly chosen victim:

> A delusion concerning its own factual basis—*not* the absence of that basis—is characteristic of religion. And the source of this delusion is none other than the surrogate victim; or rather, the fact, which remains unperceived, that the surrogate victim is arbitrarily chosen. (1977: 103–4)

The theory that an arbitrary singling out of an individual from an otherwise undifferentiated mass is the "real" origin of religion raises many questions. Girard's primary challenge, for our purposes, is the claim that the foundation for belief is a collective act of differentiation, and that the distinction resulting from this act does not exist except as a result of the act itself. In other words, the religious ritual does not commemorate a revelation of the divine, but repeats a process whereby the divine is merely created by the decree of chance: fate chooses the sacrificial victim (who, in myth, will carry many names, including Oedipus and Jesus), who in turn allows the community to forget the arbitrary nature of its own identity.

Girard's theory, despite its deeply speculative nature, contains a formidable challenge for teachers and students of literature: that our belief in the value of literature, though perhaps not exactly akin to belief in God, is just as arbitrary. When he extends his anthropology of the sacred into the realm of signification in *Things Hidden since the Foundation of the World*, Girard invites us to think in those terms. If "the simplest symbolic system" (1987: 101) accounts for the origins of all language, and accounts as well for the most exalted function of language—to refer to and to render accessible (albeit indirectly) a transcendent signified—then how is the community of readers any different from other societies united by the delusion that their religion is based on truth instead of on chance? What is important here for our purposes is that the sacrificial victim who is also the Word, the "chosen one," the vehicle for access to the divine, is in reality random, common (in his words: *quelconque*); there is nothing to distinguish it from the mass of possible signifiers except for the mere fact that it has been chosen. The fact that it has been chosen, and the process by which it has been chosen, make all the difference. Girard shifts the burden of the term "sacred" (which he also relates to the term "literary") away from its ostensible reference to an inherent property of a text, and toward a process: the ritual act that constitutes the reception of the sacred text within a community. That ritual act is named literary pedagogy.

Another important theorist of the sacred function of literature is Pierre Bourdieu, whose book *The Rules of Art: Genesis and Structure of the Literary Field* (1992, trans. 1996) compares the autonomy of the literary field to the autonomy of religious institutions: both depend on a perceived absence of direct connection to the physical universe that is understood as a transcendence of physical and temporal boundaries. The irony here is that their success in claiming independence from the world, such as their putative independence from economic and political forces, or "disinterestedness," makes them into very effective vectors of political power. Like all parliamentary democracies, the French Republic claimed to be more than a compact between state and society founded upon reason and the common good, and hence mandated to govern. Such more-than-contractual claims to legitimacy require the support of myth so as to appeal to the citizen's faith as well as reason. I claim that the French Republic relied on the disinterested institution of literature in its own process of self-legitimization. It did so by promoting blind faith as the primary guarantor of truth, in conscious contradistinction to the French Revolution's traumatic, threatening, and antiliterary call for lucidity. The simultaneous invocation and distortion of the revolutionary call for a nation founded on a regenerated and transparent French language, which I discuss in part I, therefore defined the concept of literary value on which literary pedagogy in the Third Republic depended.

There is also a discussion of the relationship between "sacredness" and "literariness" from a broader historical perspective in John Guillory's important study on the relationship between literature and pedagogy: *Cultural Capital: The Problem of Literary Canon Formation* (1993). Guillory criticizes the fetishization of individual texts that is common to both sides of the still-current debate over the literature curriculum: the right-wing view that great literature is part of a homogeneous culture that transcends time and place, and the left-wing view that affirms the existence of an "other," unrecognized and marginalized canon which, according to Guillory, simply mirrors the deified Western tradition. What remains unexamined and even unacknowledged on both sides of the culture wars is the dependence on a tautological definition of the "cultural" (artistic, literary, esthetic). Whether "culture" is defined as the physical embodiment of a transcendent law applicable to all humans (the right-wing position), or of the particular value-set of an identifiable community at a given point in time (the left-wing position), its definition calls for an act of faith. Where there is faith, one has left the domain of science and entered the domain of the sacred, of the eternally elusive meaning that we can only talk about, but never adequately express.

One of Guillory's corrective measures is to historicize the concept of "literary canon" in a way that reveals the meaning of terms such as "sacred" and "secular" as applied to texts. If one looks at the Middle Ages, for example, the relationship between sacred and secular texts in the school, up to and including the university, was not figurative ("literature is like Scripture") so much as it was literal: "The medieval pedagogic canon was selected according to the criterion of *truth*" (72), whether the text in question was religious or secular, biblical or classical. All texts worthy of study, therefore, were sacred—though not quite in the same way, since Aristotle's writings, for example, no matter how "true" they may have been, could not be confused with the Gospels. While the distinction between sacred and secular, Christian and pagan texts was of utmost importance, the overriding criterion of truth as the validating feature of *all* canonical (religious or secular) texts made them equivalent as far as their function in a pedagogical setting was concerned: Virgil was not only equivalent to Scripture from a pedagogical point of view, but the very term "literature" had no meaning in such a context: "The medieval *scriptorium* had no need for such a category" (72).

When an autonomous literary canon began to emerge from the shadow of medieval pedagogy, states Guillory, it did so in conjunction with the rise of vernacular languages and the concurrent development of national identities. In short, the clergy no longer had a monopoly on culture. The High Latin of the Church and the classical languages of canonical texts gradually ceded ground to a "vernacular High Culture" (73). While for many years the word "culture" applied to the clerical monopoly over both classical and Christian texts and their dissemination, a more complex picture emerged around the twelfth century: the nobility and middle classes ratified their social domination by separating vernacular culture into a "High" culture that required a long, formal apprenticeship in order to master, and a "low" culture that did not. The crucial point that Guillory does not emphasize enough is that the vernacular "High" culture was itself modeled on the amalgamation of Christian and classical culture over which the clergy had once exercised complete authority.

The consequences of modeling "High vernacular" culture on scriptural and classical models are many, and I concentrate on two. First, the split of vernacular culture into a higher and lower register challenges the superiority of the Christian and classical corpus by presenting an alternative: such is the case when the vernacular is said to be as capable of containing cultural—and therefore spiritual—value as Latin, Greek, or other ancient languages (Joachim Du Bellay's *Défense et Illustration de la langue française*, the "*Querelle des anciens et des modernes*," and Luther's translation of Scripture into German being examples). Second, under different historical circumstances, the continued emphasis on the Latinate qualities of the "High" vernacular culture—what Guillory calls a "fetishization of grammar" (75)—intensifies the aura of sanctity surrounding the *echt-Hochsprache*, if one will: the classical, theological, and scriptural models to which the vernacular canon is compared, usually insofar as it tries to measure up to its sacred predecessor. In the school of the Republic, we will see evidence of both consequences.

Guillory argues against one of the strategies I have adopted: the figurative use of the term "Scripture" applied to texts belonging to the national literary canon. While acknowledging "that 'literature' [claims] for itself a 'truth' which communicates and competes in some fashion with [scientific and philosophical writing]" (76), and that "the very fact that the body of literary works can be analogized to the scriptural 'canon' betrays the fact that vernacular writing must borrow the slowly fading aura of scripture as a means of enhancing and solidifying its new prestige" (76), Guillory states that it is nevertheless a mistake to view "the emergence of the vernacular 'canon' [as] a process like the formation of scripture," which would "confuse the institutions of the church and the school" (76). Guillory's conclusion presumably derives from his valid claim that "the vernacular canon belongs to the nationalist agenda" (76), and a nationalist agenda is not to be confused with the universalist aspirations either of Christianity or of Renaissance neoclassical humanism. Indeed, nations always construct themselves against other nations, and therefore national ideologies are always particular, interested, and nonuniversal—hence, in part, the inadequacy Guillory perceives in the analogy between (national) literary canon and Scripture.

Guillory, however, does not pay much attention to the fact that nation-states regularly claim universalism as their own. One could even say that national identity depends in part on the belief, shared by the majority, that national values transcend the particular historical and geographical limits of the state.[6] Even religions, which are universalist by definition, construct themselves in opposition to other belief systems. The fact that they typically deny any legitimacy to these other systems except on a very limited basis (such as Christianity's dependence on Judaism) does not make them fundamentally different from nations forced by international law to acknowledge and respect the legitimacy—boundaries, sovereignty, even cultures—of other nations. To say that the universalist aspirations of religion are different from those of nations is to give religion too much credit, and to create a distinction between sacred and secular where none exists. This is not to say that Scripture and literature are by nature indistinguishable, only that they are not different in the way Guillory claims that they are.

My objection to Guillory's dismissal of the scriptural metaphor applied to literature is also culturally based: he focuses on the English-speaking world, and would perhaps have needed to adjust his claims in order to take into account other cultures, especially French. Simply put: French literary canon formation must be studied differently, if only by virtue of the fact that it has been the result of a specifically French grounding of national identity in universalist principles. Naomi Schor, in her recent posthumous article "The Crisis of French Universalism" (2001) makes the case that "French national discourse has for centuries [particularly since the Revolution] claimed that France is the capital of universalism and, though often challenged, that claim has remained largely secure" (43). The cultural identity that France developed through the interaction of state apparatuses and the cultural field does not valorize distinctiveness (of language, style, ethnicity), but rather homogeneity and the right to speak for all humanity. While Britain, the United States, and other nations with an imperialist past have invoked universalism as the basis for national culture, the French state is unique in the *degree* to which it has merged its political role with the development and dissemination of a literary canon under the banner of universalism. Literature and Scripture may not be adequately analogous in many national pedagogical models, as Guillory claims, but I argue that France is a special case. This may sound like an appeal to "exceptionalism,"[7] akin to the claim that Christianity is the only true religion, but it is a description of that aspect of French culture that one can justifiably term both particularist and universalist: the promotion and dissemination of French culture during the nineteenth and twentieth centuries modeled on Catholic evangelism. France has arguably taken the identification of a national community with a utopian homeland for all of humanity to an extreme, in its political, social, and cultural institutions.[8]

Girard's radical skepticism with regard to the inherent value of the word, whether sacred or literary, is very useful for understanding the social uses of literature. He does not deny literature its value, but rather says that we can learn more about the nature of such value by concentrating on the text less as sacred object than as the pretext for a particular ritual.[9] Like any teacher of literature, I am eager to accredit it with unique properties that elevate it above all other productions of language. The subject of this book is, however, the *teaching* of literature or, more precisely, the role of literature in primary and secondary pedagogy, and I discuss men and women whose faith in literature's inherent value has led to abuses of the pedagogical situation. For the time being, radical skepticism as to literature's sacredness is in order. We see at the conclusion of this study if there is any room to reintroduce the concept of literariness as something other than the ideological purpose to which certain texts are assigned.

The alleged divinity of Scripture places it rather paradoxically in a position of utter subordination to its evangelical purpose: it is the embodiment of a higher principle, the physical door to the spiritual realm beyond time and place. As the only real medium for divine truth accessible to humankind, Scripture is both exalted and limited by its subordination to a higher reality "beyond words" (a subordination that eternally condemns it to hide the truth it is meant to reveal), and stands in this world for the eternally elusive God, the immediate presence of Whom in this world would make the Word superfluous. In stark contrast to Scripture is the corpus of literature, condemned always to be nothing more than the words of individual human beings, yet because of its mundane origin, free of the burden of constant subordination to divine truth. In certain extreme literary enterprises (e.g., Mallarmé), literature comes close to being a form of heresy, claiming to be an end in itself that excludes the divine by denying the capacity of writing to refer to anything outside itself or, worse yet, claiming that literature is itself the revelation that Scripture purports to be.

Nevertheless, Scripture and literature are also forever associated, first in the empirical difficulty of clearly differentiating between the two (Scripture seems to avail itself of much the same rhetorical, narrative, and formalistic devices as literature) and second, in the attempt by writers and readers of literature constantly to play the role of priests and worshipers, claiming for literature, intentionally or not, a significance beyond its contingent status. In nineteenth-century pedagogy, the sacredness of Scripture and the literariness of literature were both equated with morality. Critic Ralph Albanese, in an article on the role of La Fontaine's fables as a "lay catechism" for the republican school, states that the sacredness of literature was perceived as indistinguishable from the "*morale laïque*" that emanated from individual texts (1999: 829). Indeed, republican theorists of pedagogy such as the philosopher Alfred Fouillée (see part III) even solved the problem that only a few works of literature such as those by La Fontaine explicitly contain "morals," by positing a morality inherent in the grammatical and stylistic qualities (order, transparency) of canonical literature in general, similar to Guillory's "fetishization of grammar" cited above. Yet such attempts to ascribe the sacredness of literary texts to a supposed morality of content (La Fontaine) or of form (classicism) are ultimately deluded: the reduction of sacredness to morality was the republican pedagogues' way of justifying the exalted status of literature, and their attempt to replace the indefinable category of "literary" with something definable. The argument I follow depends on resisting the temptation to give either literariness or sacredness a different name, and to understand these forces structurally, as they determine the institutional uses of canonical texts.

The barrier between Scripture and literature, upon which Scripture depends in order to function, is difficult to maintain. One might say that the two institutions are linked forever in struggle, since the divine (Scripture) must always differentiate itself from the secular (literature), while the secular always strives for exactly the opposite: literature in a sense "wants" to be taken as seriously as the Bible, and thereby constantly challenges the distinction that places Scripture in a separate category. The attempt in the nineteenth century to construct a "lay morality" is therefore an example of Girard's "mimetic rivalry," pitting the word against the Word, the world against God. Where the religious–secular distinction is perhaps hardest to maintain is in the fact that faith exists as a common element in both. Just as Scripture constitutes a means of access to that which exists beyond the realm of language (God), literariness requires the reader to believe that the words of great literary works are imbued with significance beyond the range of syntactically and lexically determined meanings.

So, does not literature also call for an act of faith? To an extent, yes: if there were no such thing as a widespread belief in the capacity of literature to "mean" more than what any mere human being, no matter how gifted a writer, is capable of intending, then I wager there would be no such thing as literary criticism, or even an autonomous literary field. True, the buildings and institutions within which the activities of literary criticism and pedagogy take place are not churches or temples, except metaphorically. But one must ask: "What is the difference?" It is because that question is so hard to answer that the parallel between Catholic (universal) Church and republican (also universal) regime is so revealing. The abstract universal term "Catholic" refers to the "whole," the concrete universal "republican" refers to the "people"; the former proceeds towards transcendence deductively, positing an a priori unity (*holos*) emanating from God, and the latter proceeds inductively, deriving an a posteriori unity (*res*) from the multiplicity of human subjects (*publicus*). Both Catholicism and republicanism, in contrasting ways, adequately fit the etymological meaning of "religion" in the verb *religare*, "to bind (people) together," whether based upon the premise of an already existing covenant with God as symbolized by the Church, or upon that of a constantly reenacted covenant with one another made manifest by civil discourse: Communion or community.

The irony of this scheme is that it inverts the relation between literal and figurative. Normally, the figurative begins from the purely denotative (e.g., the word "wine" in the figure of speech "the wine-dark sea") to arrive at the "higher," connotative level by doing violence to the denotative: we know that, strictly speaking, the sea does not consist of wine, and it is precisely such knowledge of the literal falsehood of the statement that allows the figurative and, some would say, the literary dimension of the utterance to emerge. Literature, sometimes defined as the realm of language in which the figurative predominates over the literal,[10] enjoys a perverse relationship with Scripture, because of the "exception" that applies only to Scripture, among all forms of discourse. Whatever the rhetorical means (literal/denotative, figurative/connotative), Scripture refers ultimately to God, the one word in our language that has no clearly denotative function: it is impossible to "know" what "God" means *except* indirectly, through the figurative (metaphoric, parabolic, etc.) aspects of His Word. Nevertheless, the reference to God in Scripture is not a metaphor: God is God is God. When I suggest that literature is Scripture's figurative shadow, therefore, I am well aware of the statement's contradiction: Scripture is necessarily figurative, because it reveals that which is hidden from human cognition. By striving to be like Scripture, literature takes on the appearance of the veil covering the sacred. To put it simply: in Scripture, the word "God" designating the hidden cause of all things is to be understood literally; in literature, it can only be understood figuratively. The figurative meaning of "God" (and of the sacred in general) in literature as opposed to Scripture constitutes, for our purposes, the principal difference between the two types of discourse.[11]

The argument is presented in four parts. In part I, I examine the eighteenth-century roots of the cult of literature from the perspective of nineteenth-century academics, such as Gabriel Compayré, who gave the reforms of the Republic a historical justification. The late eighteenth century is a crucial period for the history of literary pedagogy because of the tension between the elevation of the "man of letters" to the status of lay spiritual authority during the Enlightenment, and the revolutionary distrust of literary language such as it was perceived. I examine the advent of the author as a source of spiritual authority (as described by Paul Bénichou in *The Consecration of the Writer, 1750–1830* 1973, and 1996, trans. 1999), the French Revolution's subsequent initial rejection of literature and suspicion of the written word, and the gradual rehabilitation of both in the debates over national instruction.

Religious conflicts—first between Catholics and Protestants, and then between the secular and the divine—influenced conceptions of pedagogy throughout history, and provided the Third Republic with one of its major arguments: that after centuries of trial and error, the time had come to move away from sectarian oppositions and make room for the true pedagogy. By claiming to put an end to the religious appropriation of education, the Republic attempted nothing less than to place itself in the role of absolute authority that the Church had traditionally claimed. In order to understand the process by which national literature became the textual basis for the state's claim to spiritual dominion over the population, I contrast the different attitudes toward literature of various legislators and polemicists of the First Republic. The dominant, radical revolutionaries of the time successfully argued that literature, like religion, needed to be expelled from the public realm, and for similar reasons: the appeal to the imagination, the strong hold over the mind of superstition, myth, fiction and figurative speech interfered with the cultivation of reason, which was the state's primary pedagogical role.[12] The Revolution put forward the myth that language in its regenerated state could serve as a perfect vehicle for communication. The rejection of literature took the form of a rejection of rhetoric as a basis for separating literature from the rest of human discourse, and as a basis for the elitist Jesuit pedagogy that monopolized the institution of literary studies at the time. Opposed to this briefly dominant, antiliterary group were more moderate figures such as Condorcet who believed that literacy and access to literature could become nation-building tools, in the way that the Word of God served as the means for establishing the authority of the Church. Both groups, the radical faction that wanted to exclude literature, or at least the literary tradition from the public forum, and the moderate one that wanted to include it, survived in the Third Republic under the guise of a pragmatic, left-wing faction that claimed adherence to utilitarian values, and a moderate faction favorable to the educational policies of Jules Ferry, respectively.

Part II focuses on the Third Republic's implementation of the educational promise made by the First. I do not intend to analyze Jules Ferry's reforms and the struggles over educational policy that led up to them, a field well covered by historians. Rather, I propose to examine literary threads in the fabric of Third Republic ideology, such as the foundation of a secular canon through the pedagogical selection, editing, and treatment of French literary texts. I begin with the birth of the science of literary pedagogy in works by Ferry's cadre of academics such as Ferdinand Buisson's monumental *Dictionnaire de pédagogie et d'instruction primaire* (Dictionary of Pedagogy and Primary Education) published between 1882 and 1887, and proceed with an examination of several primary school textbooks created for the purpose of implementing the new republican pedagogy, ranging from relatively forgotten literary anthologies to more famous works such as G. Bruno's *Le Tour de la France par deux enfants* (The Travel around France of Two Children; 1877).

The above examples will help to explain the role of literature and language in the political question of the legitimacy and control of state power. In simple terms, the leaders of the Third Republic had painted themselves into a corner. By pressing for the democratization of society through education, they provided their adversaries on the left with powerful, antielitist arguments. Why, for example, should literary culture continue to be the cornerstone of public education, when in the modern world science and engineering are clearly more direct means of achieving success on an individual as well as a national level? The focus of the ensuing debate was the mandatory status of Latin on the national *baccalauréat* exam. It seemed that the state was promoting elitism by preserving a tradition that prevented those who did not have the means or motivation to study a dead and difficult language, that is, the lower classes, from moving up in society. The Republic responded to this attack on its democratic principles by shifting emphasis away from Latin and onto French. Language and literature still served as a means for social distinction. But since the language and the literary corpus that represented it were now French, their elitist function was hidden under the guise of assimilation into an abstract, homogeneous national unity.

Part III examines positions in the debate over the relative importance of French versus Classical literature in the secondary school curriculum and the broader debate over the importance of cultural versus utilitarian goals in education; I argue that, just as literature took over the role of Scripture, French took over the role of Latin in conveying the sacred mysteries that undergird worldly authority. The state's use of literature as a means of achieving national unity by transcending individual (and regional) idiosyncrasies reinforced the belief that the French tradition is rooted in abstraction and purity of form. The seventeenth century had been crowned the greatest age of French letters long before 1882, but the interests of the Republic required that classicism be elevated even higher in the national scale of values. Anti-republican sentiment fed a growing reaction to the state's co-option of the literary heritage.

Finally, I attempt to draw conclusions as to the effect that the long process of building an official monument to and *of* French literature has had upon the literary field itself. There are examples throughout literature of the late nineteenth and early twentieth centuries of the increasing importance of the school in the consciousness of the time. The classroom became not only the site of conflicts over the role and status of the national literary heritage, but the very subject of literature itself. The concluding chapter returns to the concept of "literariness" as a function of the educational uses of literary texts, a subject that happens to have been very much in vogue in modern literary criticism, especially during the structural–sociological debate that peaked in the 1970s in France. In the wake of such influential works as Pierre Bourdieu's *La Reproduction* (1970, trans. 1990) and *La Distinction* (1979, trans. 1984) sociological critics, often with a Marxist orientation, thoroughly analyzed the literary pedagogy's complicity with the interests of the "dominant class": Renée Balibar, Marc Fumaroli, Charles Grivel, to name a few. At roughly the same time, proponents of structuralism such as Roland Barthes, Gérard Genette, and A.J. Greimas weighed in on the debate surrounding literary pedagogy. The historic conference at *Cérisy* in the summer of 1969 on *L'Enseignement de la littérature* (The Teaching of Literature, published by Serge Doubrovsky and Tzvetan Todorov in 1971), and the issue of the journal *Littérature of* October 1972 titled *Le Discours de l'école sur les textes* (The Discourse of the School on Literary Texts) are among several important milestones in the history of structuralist criticism's attempt to take the practice of teaching literature into account. The whole story of the sociological and structuralist analyses of Third Republic literary pedagogy and its effects over time would constitute the material for an entire book in itself. The School, both primary and secondary, continues to loom large in the ongoing debate over what constitutes the ends and the means of institutionalized practices of reading, in France more than anywhere else.

PART I

ORIGINS: THE REVOLUTION AND THE REPUBLICAN CULT OF LITERATURE

CHAPTER 1

THE TABOO AGAINST LITERATURE IN THE SCHOOL OF THE REPUBLIC

Under the *ancien régime* education, especially literary study, was a privilege. Under the Republic education, including literary study, became a right. During the French Revolution, the principle of universal access to primary school and of equal opportunity of access to secondary school was high on the legislative agenda, as the debates over national education between 1791 and 1795 attest. Members of the Legislative Assembly and National Convention not only were concerned with the logistics of state control over education, but also with content and methodology. Clearly, in a country where according to the survey by Abbé Grégoire six million citizens did not speak French, six million spoke it badly, and three million spoke it well, national education would be first and foremost an initiation into a common language, into a community of transparent signs that conveyed laws and decrees, allowed citizens to exercise their right to free speech, and united the population under a national culture. It was immediately apparent, however, that these goals were contradictory; for if legal and political efficacy depended on transparency, that is, on universal agreement as to the true meaning of texts, national culture did not. In fact literature, the highest linguistic manifestation of culture, was under suspicion not only as the idle pastime of the aristocracy, but as a forbidding tissue of useless subject matter and obscure rhetorical devices, in brief: the antithesis of a national patrimony accessible to every citizen. In 1794 the *bibliophages* even proposed the destruction of all books; they were the avant-garde of a widespread suspicion of the written word.

Even the more moderate proponents of national education in the First Republic believed that without a complete transformation of the language and repudiation of the traditional definitions of literariness, the schoolchild could easily metamorphose into a sorcerer's apprentice. In 1793, the *Bureau de Consultation des Arts et Métiers* issued the following warning concerning the risk of teaching literacy to every citizen in the making: "[E]n mettant cet instrument [l'écriture] dans la main de l'homme, craignons d'introduire dans son esprit l'idée du mot tracé sur le papier, au lieu de l'idée de la chose que ce mot doit rappeler" [By putting this tool [writing] into man's hand, let us beware lest we introduce into his mind the idea of the word drawn on the paper, rather than the idea of the thing that this word must recall] (Lavoisier 1793: 12).

The Convention wasted no time in applying the notion that reading and writing were dangerous. Here is an excerpt from article 2 of the decree of November 17, 1794 calling for a specific curriculum for primary education (and, as such, an ancestor of the curricula of the 1880s, discussed in chapter 5, to which it provides a basis for comparison):

[O]n enseignera aux élèves:

1. A lire et à écrire, et les exemples de lecture rappelleront leurs droits et leurs devoirs;
2. La Déclaration des droits de l'homme et du citoyen et la Constitution de la République française;
3. On donnera des instructions élémentaires sur la morale républicaine;
4. Les éléments de la langue française, soit parlée, soit écrite;
5. Les règles du calcul simple et de l'arpentage;
6. Les éléments de la géographie et de l'histoire des peuples libres;
7. Des instructions sur les principaux phénomènes et les productions les plus usuelles de la nature.

On fera apprendre le recueil des actions héroïques et les chants de triomphe. . . .

[Students shall be taught:

1. To read and write, and reading samples will remind them of their rights and responsibilities;
2. The Declaration of the Rights of Man and Citizen and the Constitution of the French Republic;
3. They shall receive elementary instruction in Republican morality;
4. Elements of the French language, either spoken or written;
5. The rules of simple calculation and land measurement;
6. The elements of geography and the history of free peoples;
7. Instructions on the principal phenomena and most common productions of nature.

They shall learn the compilation of heroic acts and songs of triumph. . . .]

(Quoted in Palméro 1958: 259)

Just as in the curricula from the 1880s that I discuss in part II, the topics are in rough order of priority. While the ability to speak French is part of the fifth item of the curriculum, the ability to read and write is the first, most fundamental and most important skill, one that is indistinguishable from the school's mission as moral guide to the student's "rights and responsibilities." In fact, all of the first four topics are virtually inter-changeable: clearly, rights and responsibilities are codified by the Constitution and the Declaration of the Rights of Man, and form the basis for "*morale républicaine*," and "elements of the French language" are merely the formal term for the knowledge required to read and emulate in writing the founding texts of *laïcité*. Finally, scientific instruction as instituted by the 1880 laws is almost identical to its 1794 archetype: though the nineteenth-century curriculum no longer specifically mentioned "*arpentage*," this particular application of mathematics was to survive as a symbol for the proper role of science in republican educa-tion.[1] As for item seven, it remained enshrined in the official primary curriculum of the Third Republic as "*leçons de choses*." The importance of having initiation into science occur through measuring land and instruc-tion on the "most common productions of nature" (to which the Third Republic added man-made objects), even if it occupies the last place on the list of essential topics, is that it preserved the quintessentially revolu-tionary valuation of *things* over abstractions. It allowed the republican pedagogues to continue to argue that they promoted an education based entirely on empirical knowledge, even as the priority given to language and moral education in their curricula undermined such a claim.

The taboo against literature arose paradoxically at a point in time when the spiritual authority of the writer was at its peak. A major state-ment on the parallel between literature and Scripture, and its role in the evangelic aspects of French national culture is Paul Bénichou's *The Consecration of the Writer, 1750–1830* (1973, trans. 1999), which describes how literature came to assume a spiritual function that orga-nized religion had lost in the years leading up to the French Revolution. Bénichou argues that while literature had close ties with the state and with dominant religions at various times in antiquity and the Middle Ages, the social function of the author never attained the level of spiri-tual authority before the middle of the eighteenth century.

According to Bénichou, the spiritual void caused by the political decline of the Church meant that sacred terms increasingly came to designate traditionally secular realms such as literature, beginning with the authors themselves: "from about 1760 until the Revolution, the apologia of the man of letters becomes a veritable glorification whose exalted tone is associated with a general doctrine of emancipation and progress" (14). Bénichou's first chapter, titled "In Quest of a Secular

Ministry" leaves no doubt as to the absolute primacy in status that writers sought and eventually received. But what brought about this apotheosis? Bénichou argues for nothing less than a paradigm shift in France (with repercussions throughout Europe and beyond) from belief in the authority of the priest to that of the author. The divine inspiration of the poet, instead of being a mere imitation of the mediumistic function of the priest, actually replaced it: "the man of letters in the sublimity of his calling at the moment when inspiration descends. . . ." (14–15), committing his gift to the general good of humanity, became the guide to salvation. Unlike Catholic priests who are merely human intercessors and imitators of Christ the Savior, each author individually and collectively *is* the savior. The Godhead, under this new paradigm, is no longer a principle under which the enlightened caste exercises its authority, but rather the product of its inspiration: the texts themselves, to which the authors are not subordinate, but with which they are identified. No longer does the divine stand above a fallen humanity, but among and within a humanity that holds the key to its own salvation: "the lightning bolt leaps from earth to heaven" (20). The age of the consecration of the author (Bénichou speaks also of his "ministry") coincides with the cult of reason, as well of deism and the revolutionary cult of the Supreme Being. The basis for the elevation of the function of the man (or, increasingly, woman) of letters lay precisely in skills enabling him to bring out the "divine" capacities of both reason and sentiment from the human body. Salvation, or "[t]he happiness that sensibility takes as its object is of a sort rationally reconciled both to itself and the truth of things" (17), leading to a radically new type of spirituality: "When a person of this time says 'celestial' or 'divine,' it is almost always a question of human things, insofar as they suddenly appear as measureless . . ." (20).

An interesting complement to Bénichou from the realm of psycho-analysis is provided by Jean-Claude Bonnet ("Naissance du Panthéon" 1978), who described the filling of the void left by the gradual disappearance of God as a form of transference, in which a pantheon of writers was built to receive the devotion that, after the death of the Father, had been left without an object. "A travers la célébration du père, c'est à son propre sacre que le fils contribue, car l'écrivain s'impose comme le véritable héros du siècle" [Through the celebration of the father, the son contributes to his own consecration, since the writer asserts himself as the true hero of the century] (47). The worship of the writer was a variation of the worship of the father, since the writer embodied the (pro) creative function that Bénichou designated as the writer's new status as legislator for humanity: the Father creates people, but the writer founds society. To some extent, this phenomenon was characteristic of its times. Bonnet draws attention to the multiplication of images of fathers and fatherhood in Enlightenment literature; Diderot's play *Le Père de famille* (The Father; 1758) being a perfect example, as the clinical symptom of a collective crisis. By assimilating the cult of the father to the consecration of the writer, however, the eighteenth century left an important legacy: it became just as important, if not more so, to give homage to the deceased writer by making a pilgrimage to his tomb or monument, as to read his work. The mediumistic powers of the writer-father are ultimately more important than the words that those powers bring forth, a phenomenon that we will see repeated in the school.

The promise of happiness in this world rather than the next is a political one. It is a promise that makes modern political life possible, since it gives people (or citizens) the idea that happiness is attainable through organized political action, revolutionary or not. Since worldly happiness only existed as a promise, however, it became necessary to make it plausible, to endow it with form, in order to use it as a means of political change. The sacralization of literature, or what Bénichou and Pierre Bourdieu both call "consecration" (Bénichou's "*sacre*," Bourdieu's "*consécration*"), that was to become the condition of educational reform under the Third Republic, helped to focus attention on the newly rediscovered "immeasurability" of human, rather than divine truth.

The culmination of the role of the man/woman of letters in the new order, according to Bénichou, is the description in Rousseau's *Lettres morales, pour Madame d'Houdetot* (Letters on Morality, to Madame d'Houdetot; 1757–78) of the writer-legislator-educator as the member of a new caste: "it is they who bring humanity into being [*instituent l'humanité*]" (30). For the first time, literary production became a qualification for assuming political responsibility in a society, and literature was expressly linked to a pedagogical function. Both outgrowths of the writer's role, the political and the pedagogical, were a direct consequence of the newly acquired spiritual status of literature and its practitioners.

The Revolution itself, Bénichou concedes, almost derailed the progress of the author toward his exalted status: "[W]hen events are at the highest pitch of intensity, the revolutionary power is seen placing all of literature in a suspect category . . ." (39). In the next chapter we see various forms of this suspicion of literature, from the creation of civic ceremonies purged of language altogether, to the radical call for the moral regeneration of French language and literature. The problem, according to Bénichou, was political, since freedom of thought and its "incarnation in power" (40) are incompatible, and it was spiritual as well: there simply was no role for literature to play in the creation of a revolutionary cult to replace Catholicism, in spite of the fact that the bases of the new cult—"nature, virtue, human sublimity" (41)— actually derived from prerevolutionary, preromantic literary sources. But the cult of the Revolution did not succeed, a failure that Bénichou blames on the lack of a supernatural element: a religion without God, both "religion . . . and . . . counterreligion" (43), unable or unwilling to resolve its fundamental contradiction.[2]

Bénichou's thesis on the role of the author helps to explain the reasons for literature's future importance for the founders of national education: for if the cult of the Revolution (and its concrete manifestations as cult of the Supreme Being or cult of Reason) failed because of its lack of an adequately transcendent dimension, the cult of national literature suffered from no such problem. If nature, mankind, reason, and liberty all proved to be inadequate substitutes for God, literature did not. The belated attempts by the First Republic to enlist literature in its support are signs that people recognized poetic inspiration as a fundamentally religious, and therefore legitimizing force. Consequently, literature was given the task of supporting and celebrating the revolutionary enterprise, an avenue that, of course, proved to be a dead end. Bénichou's statement that poetry during the Revolution "is relegated to the celebration of values whose principal source is elsewhere [outside of poetry]" (46) holds true for the many attempts since the French Revolution to subordinate literature to secular political goals, which we recognize today as a totalitarian, and therefore doomed impulse (e.g., the term "socialist realism" has become synonymous with cultural bankruptcy). The First Republic failed to recognize that, if the institution of literature is to function properly as a guarantee of political legitimacy, then it must exist above, not within the political realm. The solution was to depend on an important modification of republican cultural policy: to enlist literature in the service of the state, rather than authors. The Third Republic, by recognizing the autonomy of the literary field, and placing emphasis upon the nation's literary inheritance rather than on the current conditions of literary production, was able to achieve what the First Republic could not.

In order to make my point clear, it is necessary to state an obvious difference between the phenomenon to which Bénichou draws our attention and the function of the author (via the literary work) in Third Republic pedagogy. Bénichou wrote about the status of the actual, living author in French society. The years he examines are those during which society looked to authors for guidance, and for an alternative to the weakened authority of organized religion. In the Third Republic, by contrast, one has to speak of the authority primarily of dead authors. In fact, the systematic promotion of French classicism and, through it, the persistent aura of authority conferred upon "real" (Greek and Latin) classicism, ensured that the consecrated authors would all be very dead indeed. A large portion of this book will be devoted to the argument that the role of literature in the school is in fact a clandestine return, via the text, of the "*pouvoir laïque*" of the man/woman of letters that Bénichou saw as actually declining in the course of the nineteenth century. The spiritual authority of the writer, as Bénichou demonstrated, ran aground on its own propensity to threaten the order of society. Having once been taken by surprise by the sudden rise in influence of the author, the state, whether monarchist, bonapartist, or republican, was not going to encourage its resurgence.

The state did, however, promote the cult of literature, though not of contemporary literature, and I argue that its ability to do so depended on the paradigmatic shift from priest to author that Bénichou ascribes to a clearly delimited period in French history. Often, the Third Republic is said to have finally realized the ambitions of the First, merely by moderating them and making its social reforms tolerable to its principal ideological enemies, almost to the point of cravenness. Nowhere is this analysis more prevalent than in the history of republican pedagogy, such as this passage from a 1975 article by Claude Désirat and Tristan Hordé on the revolutionary-era attack on Jesuit rhetorical pedagogy by the founders of the republican educational enterprise, and the subsequent refusal by members of the Third Republic to carry it further:

> [L]a Troisième République, en imposant la réconciliation nationale et l'union sacrée, estompe les traits trop marqués de ces modèles [de la Première République], quitte à accepter une image négative de la première révolution et à redorer parfois les blasons de l'ancien régime.

> [The Third Republic, by imposing national reconciliation and sacred union, tones down the exaggerated features of these (First Republic) models, at the price of accepting a negative image of the first revolution and, at times, of restoring some luster to the coats of arms of the *ancien régime*. (50)

But what if the story of the institution of national education were not merely one of compromise, of the false completion, in a minor key, of a process undertaken during the First Republic? The difference between the First Republic and the Third, in other words, especially in the area of cultural and educational policy, might not have been one of degree, but of kind. The repeal of the author as saint to a period in time that is irretrievably remote, together with a strategy of concealing that unbridgeable distance with an ideology of national literature that claims eternal relevance of ancient texts to the concerns of the day, represents a vastly different and more sophisticated public project than anything that had preceded it. The founders of the First Republic who concerned themselves with matters of education and cultural policy, contrary to common wisdom on the subject, would not merely have been disappointed by their Third Republic heirs: they would not have recognized them.

The eighteenth-century canonization of the author took place in conjunction with another historical development that contributed to the emergence of the school as a quasi-religious institution. In the Introduction, I mentioned that the manner in which text is transmitted in the republican school is closer to the function of Scripture in the Roman Catholic Church rather than the individual access to the Word that is fundamental to Protestantism. This represents a reaction on the part of Third Republic pedagogues to the potential dangers of granting the population at large the ability to read and write, and therefore to become agents of "high" culture and not simply its passive recipients. Learning to read is not unlike taking responsibility for one's own salvation: an inherently subversive attitude.[3]

The members of the Third Republic understood that the conflict between Church and state was much more complicated than the Revolution had shown it to be. Whereas the First Republic had denied, not only the power of the Church, but also the means by which the Church perpetuated its authority (by proclaiming itself guardian of the Word), the Third Republic realized that it needed instead to recognize the validity and effectiveness of the means (worshipping the Word), and then to appropriate it for its own ends. In simpler terms: the First Republic sought to overthrow the Church by rejecting both its dogma and its institutional practices, and the Third pursued an entirely different goal: to wrest control of the seat of spiritual authority away from the Church, without fundamentally altering its specific hegemonic practices. The sacredness of the literary canon, though it needed constantly to be reaffirmed, already existed in principle, as a result of the long process which Bénichou describes: "the new society established its belief upon a spiritual recasting of ideas that had established themselves violently" (337).[4] The Revolution, then, arose from a set of ideas (the Enlightenment version of happiness as a specifically literary synthesis of sentiment and reason) that it had failed at first to declare as the basic foundation for the justification of its own existence. It was only when the Third Republic, the first republican regime not to arise out of revolution,[5] succeeded in making use of the spiritual value that had been ascribed to literary productions, that the Revolution, such as it had become, reached fruition as a legitimate, positive moral force, and not simply as the end of an old and no longer legitimate order.

The manner in which the Third Republic claimed for itself the work of the First has received much attention from historians: a recent issue of the journal *Revue du Nord* was devoted to the interpretations of revolutionary-era debates on education by Ferry and his academic allies. A recurring theme is that the fact education was such an important topic in the early 1790s provided the Third Republic with an opportunity and a problem. The opportunity—to find historical roots for the reforms they were about to propose—was undermined by the danger of the radicalism so often contained in those roots (if I can be forgiven the pun). According to one of the contributors to the *Revue du Nord*, Claude Carpentier, the *Revue pédagogique* (created in 1878 as a vehicle for the new discipline of the science of pedagogy) published 53 articles on the educational proposals of the First Republic, and 17 additional articles that touched indirectly upon the Revolution, all but a handful appearing between 1883 and 1914. The content of those articles, however, tends to mitigate any assumption that the journal's contributors were seeking to establish a direct genealogical link between the two periods. Carpentier selects three articles as typical of the journal's ideological stance: one by Alexis Bertrand on the *Déclaration des droits de l'Homme et du Citoyen*, an adulatory piece on the great symbolic achievements of the Revolution; an extremely favorable analysis of Condorcet's proposals for national education by Francisque Vial; and an aggressive attack on the proposals put forth by less moderate figures, including the partially realized institution of *écoles centrales* proposed by Lakanal, or the more extreme appeal to Spartan tradition of Lepeletier de Saint Fargeau, who proposed to remove children from their families so that the state could have full control over them during their years of mandatory education (953–65). In another analysis of Third Republic revisionism, Jean-François Chanet (1996) shows how the commemorations of the educational enterprise of the Revolution, culminating in the centennial celebrations of 1889, tend to return to its more distant origins by foregrounding the "rural subject" represented in the *Cahiers de Doléances*, bypassing the First Republic altogether (990–5).

The most important article for our purposes in the *Revue du Nord* (1996) special issue is by Charles Coutel, who describes the fascination of Third Republic pedagogic theorists with the educational proposals of

Condorcet. In addition to the edition of Condorcet's educational writings put out by Hippeau in 1881 and the more complete and authoritative edition compiled by Gabriel Compayré in 1883, there is the famous statement by Jules Ferry himself that the reading of Condorcet had been a revelation, a conversion experience into the faith of *laïcité*. Coutel explores the Condorcet–Ferry filiation and discovers that Ferry had actually read very little of Condorcet, a fact that he came close to admitting when he said that he had studied Condorcet's writings "*de haut*" [from above] (970), implying a supercilious attitude toward the man who, along with Auguste Comte, was supposed to be Ferry's great inspiration. Coutel's article is therefore valuable in its attention to the distance Ferry maintained between himself and Condorcet, at the same time as he attributed to the reading of Condorcet the status of revelation. In particular, Ferry completely ignored Condorcet's notion of the emancipatory role of scientific reasoning, favoring instead an authoritarian, conformist model of education; furthermore, Ferry's belief that the laws governing education had a "sacred" status was incompatible with Condorcet's notion that law had to be based upon scientific principles (970–3).

When Ferry was a member of the republican opposition during the Second Empire, he gave further evidence of his ambivalent relationship to the founding fathers of the Republic, as demonstrated by François Furet in an article on the polemic that occurred in the press between Ferry and a radical member of the Jacobin revival, Alphonse Peyrat, over Edgar Quinet's book *La Révolution française* (1865). Quinet's thesis was that the First Republic failed because it shrank from its historic obligation to found a new religion on the model of the Reformation in the sixteenth century. Peyrat attacked Quinet's thesis from a materialist, antireligious point of view, accusing him in particular of dividing the anti-Bonapartist opposition into conflicting interpretations of the Revolution, thereby playing into the hands of the Empire. Ferry wrote a series of rebuttals of Peyrat's attacks in which he argued that the Revolution had in fact succeeded: although the Empire was not democratic, the society over which it ruled benefited from all of the freedoms promised by the Revolution, and Peyrat and his camp were simply apologists for the reign of Terror. Ferry did not touch upon the question of the founding of a new religion, the original thesis of Quinet's book; instead, he concentrated on discrediting the Jacobin claim of guardianship of the true spirit of the Revolution, echoing a common middle of the road argument (associated with Guizot, among others), that it was the profound changes in the farthest reaches of French society (and

French territory) that proved the success of the Revolution, not the makeup of the current government (Furet 1985: 19–20).

Although these articles on the interpretation of the revolutionary legacy show that the Third Republic academic establishment contained many perspectives, it agreed that only Condorcet was worthy of the mantle of precursor; yet even his moderate though resolutely materialistic (one might even say prepositivistic) view of education was ultimately incompatible with the desire of Third Republic theorists, Ferry included, to view both the Law and the institution of national education as sacred, in the sense that they operate without any justification beyond themselves. This is a significant step backward from the Enlightenment belief, ostensibly reaffirmed in the positivist nineteenth century, that the justification for authority derives from its origins in, and fidelity to, the physical structures in which it operates (society, nature, matter).

By focusing on the more moderate voices in the education debates of the Revolution, therefore, the republican intellectuals found plenty of material to support a revisionist view of history. Compayré's publication in particular of Condorcet's *Ecrits sur l'Instruction Publique* during the height of the conflict over the laws establishing mandatory public education was the implementation of a strategy. Part of the Trinity of moderate, rational educational visionaries that also consisted of Talleyrand and Daunou, Condorcet provided the perfect means to escape from the radical concreteness of so much of the Revolutionary debate that threatened the very existence of the humanistic tradition. Indeed the Girondins, the faction to which Condorcet belonged, with their simultaneous championing of parliamentarianism and bourgeois hegemony, were the clear ascendants of the Third Republic elite, and it is through him that Compayré promoted an interpretation of the First Republic's struggle with the issue of national education as plain and simple prophecy: as the question was settled by Condorcet's proposal in 1792, so shall it be in 1882. Compayré's editing job was therefore an exercise in theological exegesis, whereby the restitution of the words of the prophet promotes the evangelical mission of his heirs. As we have just seen, however, the reading of prophecy by those individuals who claim to embody its realization, no matter how scientific they claim to be, is fraught with problems of objectivity. It is also true that Condorcet's work on education was not all of a piece, as a closer examination of it will show.

In order for the Republic to develop a coherent policy of linguistic and literary pedagogy, it had to make the case that the roots of its legitimacy are inseparable from the printed word. Such an argument indeed underlies Condorcet's proposal in *Rapport sur l'instruction publique* (Report on Public Instruction; 1792). The badge of literacy and of reason that validates the vote cast by the citizen can only be earned through education, and that education is both practical *and* literary, neither quality overshadowing the other. If in antiquity, political power was measured by the spoken word, with greatest influence accorded to the most eloquent citizens, the invention of printing has changed the arena to that of the written word, which he terms "*écriture*" (I: 112). The term, as Condorcet uses it, is therefore akin to the classical concept of eloquence, which it replaces.

The shift of emphasis from speaking to writing is not only one of the unacknowledged debts of Third Republic pedagogy toward its revolutionary origins; it is also one of the factors that allow for the broad comparison made in this study between the political authority of the state and its self-assigned role as new spiritual power. The traditional foundation of the discipline of rhetoric in the sphere of oral communication, and the historical tendency (most characteristic of Jesuit education) to view the classical literary tradition as a model for eloquence, perpetuated an increasingly outmoded definition of literariness in the form of the cult of the spoken word. Condorcet's secret contribution to the truly substantive changes later enacted by the Third Republic may well have been the notion that language, in a truly democratic society, had to be made accessible *in its highest form* to the greatest number; consequently eloquence could no longer stand for the highest form of language, since by tradition and presumably also by nature, eloquence was not only associated with privilege, but also was accessible primarily to privilege.[6]

Between 1870 and 1911, Gabriel Compayré edited and published many of the major texts on education from the Revolutionary period, not just those of Condorcet. His explicit purpose was to commemorate the Revolution around the time of its centennial by restoring to public attention the words of several of its founding fathers. The story of the Revolution that Compayré presented, therefore, was the prehistory of and rationale for contemporary laws that became the belated realization of the vision of republican heroes. Compayré elevates to the status of myth the conflicts that opposed, before and during the First Republic, radical and conservative members of the *Assemblée* and the *Convention*.[7] Condorcet, who was to be one of the many victims of the Revolution's increasing radicalism, was the perfect hero for his story.

Several characteristics of Condorcet's proposals were especially useful for the republican educational agenda. To begin with the obvious: just as Martin Luther made literacy into a tool for direct, individual access to the Word of God, and put his disciple Melanchthon in charge of creating the universal pedagogy that would make it possible, Condorcet made literacy into a condition for good citizenship. In Compayré's words, the *homo suffragens* is predicated on the *homo cogitans* (I: 13). Politically, the purpose of education is twofold: it is emancipatory, to make the citizen capable of holding the reins of power, since the printed word, in the eighteenth century, had taken over the function that the spoken word once had in the agora; conversely, it limits the autonomy of the citizen simply by the fact that education serves the state in a system where, paradoxically, the individual's ability to understand and participate in public debate establishes the legitimacy of the government's control over him.

Not surprisingly, given the ambient antielitism in which he carried out his duties as member of the National Convention, Condorcet did not promote the cult of the writer that Bénichou identified as central to the Enlightenment. While he opposed the universal teaching of Latin and Greek, which he identified as the linchpin of the Jesuit schools' complicity with the aristocracy (consistent with the anti-Jesuitism that would continue to characterize republican views on education), he was also very cautious concerning the inclusion of literature of any kind in public instruction, because of its tendency to embellish upon, or hide entirely, the truth:

> [Le maître] enseignerait à ses élèves, en les exerçant sur des exemples, à démêler l'erreur au milieu des prestiges de l'imagination ou de l'ivresse des passions, à saisir la vérité, à ne pas l'exagérer, même en se passionnant pour elle.

> [[The teacher] would instruct his students, by having them practice on examples, on how to distinguish error among the marvels of the imagination and the ecstasy of passion, to capture truth and not to exaggerate it, while nevertheless being passionate for it.] (I: 113)

Literature, after all, appeals to the imagination and distracts from the pursuit of truth (echoing Plato's *Republic* in this respect), a fact that does not, however, place it beyond redemption. Condorcet grants some legitimacy to the teaching of literature, while placing it in an ancillary position relative to history and science.[8]

By teaching its citizens to read, the Republic proves its legitimacy but also runs a great risk. By opening up literature to the people, the government might awaken them to a realm of unlimited possibility. The immediate need to present literature in a manner that constrains its applications within the citizen's physical and affective existence is an aspect of republican pedagogy the importance of which cannot be exaggerated. Condorcet seized upon the central paradox that was to continue to dominate the use of literature by the Republic. Quite simply, literature is truly revolutionary. It does not, by and large, heed the call to reason that Condorcet and other moderate delegates proffered in their search for a legal basis for the alliance of representative government and public education. The solution to this paradox, therefore, is fundamentally to misrepresent the literary tradition. If the school were to present only works that embodied republican virtues, the literary canon would obviously be truncated, and nobody would take it seriously. A far better, yet much more challenging solution would be to present a convincing appearance of an integral literary canon, yet to do so *in such a way* as to defuse its revolutionary aspects.

Condorcet nevertheless ventures a pro-literary stance when he says that instruction of literary texts must be free of state (or other kinds of) censorship, unlike certain other subjects of instruction that he had discussed earlier, such as history: "[I]l ne faudrait pas ici, comme nous l'avons proposé pour les vies des hommes illustres, destinées à l'éducation morale, retrancher ce qui ne tend pas directement à l'instruction, et on doit y laisser tout ce qui caractérise l'auteur ou le siècle" [Here one must not, as we proposed doing in the case of the lives of famous men that are destined for moral education, eliminate [passages that do not] contribute directly to instruction: one must leave everything that characterizes the author and his century] (I: 175). Respect for the integrity of the literary text is the *sine qua non* of its transformation into republican monument. Such integrity distinguishes instruction in literature from history, the "*éducation morale*" derived from lives of great men, which in contrast to literature *is* subject to censorship: one has to distinguish between factual biography and useful, moral history, and choose the latter. It is no small irony for someone with Condorcet's scientific credibility to state that history, the discipline that deals in actual events, needs to be cut and pasted onto a moralistic narrative, whereas literature, the discipline that is unconstrained by what is real, does not. Literature for Condorcet cannot be made to serve a political purpose except as itself, in an unadulterated state. The educational institution must, at the very least, serve as a convincing guardian of the integrity of the literary corpus.

Comparing the teaching of literary texts to the use of great men's lives for the purpose of moral education, Condorcet only went so far as to say that one should not limit the text to its literal content, or that which is necessary for "instruction." The style that characterizes the author and/or his century is an important consideration as well. Aside from this concession to what one could term "literariness," granting to it an inviolable status that history does not require, Condorcet's work on the subject of national education contains virtually no other references to the teaching of literature. One could interpret this fact as inauspicious when searching for the antecedents of the Third Republic's privileging of literature within the pedagogical field. The answer to this dilemma, as far as Condorcet's importance as a founding figure is concerned, is that literature actually never played that large a role in national education *as such*. What we are dealing with are the various surrogates for literature that make it possible to speak of a "literary pedagogy" during the Third Republic.

There is in Condorcet another means by which the teaching of literature was to become the cornerstone of republican pedagogy. Speaking of the growing universality of the French language, Condorcet states:

> [D]éjà plusieurs nations ont adopté les formes plus simples, plus méthodiques de nos phrases, en sorte que leurs langues ne diffèrent presque plus de la nôtre que parce qu'elles emploient des mots différents et différemment modifiés.

> [Several nations have already adopted the simpler, more methodical forms of our sentences, such that their languages differ from ours almost only in that they use different words, differently modified.] (176)

In other words, the other languages of Europe were gradually turning into simple codes of French, progressing toward an ideal in which substantive differences in expressive potential, and therefore in meaning, will some day be erased. Condorcet did not explain why French was able to achieve this exalted status among languages (though its mere status as a European *lingua franca* was empirical evidence in support of his claim), nor did he try to prove this characteristically overstated universalist affirmation. However, with the gradual ascendancy, after the end of the revolutionary era, of the French seventeenth-century corpus as the ideal congruence of language, civilization, and literary expression, Condorcet's fears will ultimately become irrelevant. What he defined as the danger inherent in literariness—the potential of language to exaggerate and distort truth through the exercise of the imagination and the passions—are precisely the qualities which Republican pedagogy will, if not suppress, at least relegate so far to the margins as to render them harmless.

CHAPTER 2

BEYOND CONDORCET:
THE REVOLUTIONARY ATTACK ON
LITERATURE

There were a few founders of the First Republic besides Condorcet who rose to defend literature, however mildly, against the dominant antiliterary forces within the Convention. One of the many stillborn projects for a national education under the First Republic was by Claude-Laurent-Louis Masuyer, a deputy to the National Convention whose *Projet de décret sur l'organisation de l'instruction publique* (Proposal for a Decree on the Organization of Public Instruction) appeared in 1793. Masuyer was a left-wing critic of the projects of Condorcet and Romme but, as we will see, there were others who were far more radical. Masuyer still believed that the written word, in the appropriate context, could serve as the foundation for the nation better than any other medium of expression. The edition of his project published by the *Imprimerie Nationale* contains a letter from Masuyer to his publisher, referring to a trip the two men had made to Venice, and in which he says that national education is important, because words have greater power over people than any other mode of representation:

> [T]u sais que l'on a remarqué que c'est à la magie des inscriptions qu'il fallait principalement attribuer le charme des jardins chinois, mal-à-propos nommés jardins anglais; tu te rappelles l'impression que t'ont causée les statues, les inscriptions éparses avec tout l'art des hasards dans ces monumen[t]s du luxe et de la délicatesse nationale; tu sais enfin comme on a dit avec raison que l'impression que causent les inscriptions est plus vive que celle que causent les statues: si celles-ci émeuvent le sentiment & les passions, celles-là éveillent la pensée, agrandissent l'âme, l'instruisent & la portent à la réflexion.

> [You know that it has been said that the attraction of the Chinese gardens, referred to improperly as English gardens, is to be attributed to the magic of inscriptions; you remember the effect on you of the statues, of the

inscriptions scattered with all the artistry of chance upon these monuments of national luxury and refinement; you know finally that one rightly says that the impression caused by the inscriptions is stronger than the one caused by the statues: if the latter excite sentiments and passion, the former arouse thought, enhance the soul, instruct and lead it to reflection.] (8–9)

Masuyer apparently envisioned a nation in which the edification of the public would take place through inscriptions in streets and parks, just as in the Chinese (or English) gardens in Venice. But the purpose of national education clearly is not simply so that the state can cover walls and monuments with official inscriptions. Its purpose and its rationale, as the above anecdote illustrates, lie in the inherent superiority of the written word over other art forms, specifically when it comes to founding a collective national identity outside of the esthetic and moral authority of the Church. Imagery, here under the guise of plastic form rather than rhetoric, is to be sacrificed in favor of the word, stripped of any decorative function.

Masuyer expanded on this belief in the sacred mission of France to provide a secular, textual foundation for the salvation of all of humanity in a speech on the floor of the National Convention during the debate over the national education proposals of Condorcet and Romme:

> Représentan[t]s du peuple français . . . vous tenez en quelque sorte dans vos mains les destinées de toutes les sociétés; vous êtes appelés à dicter *la constitution universelle*, et tous les peuples de la terre, toutes les générations béniront à jamais votre mémoire.
>
> [Representatives of the French people . . . you hold in your hands, so to speak, the destinies of all societies; you are called to dictate *the universal constitution*, and all the peoples of the earth, all the generations will forever glorify your memory.] (3–4)

And later:

> [A]ffranchissez les citoyens du joug des prêtres, en leur offrant des fêtes et des cérémonies civiques, plus attrayantes, plus sentimentales que les *liturgies* gothiques de Pierre, de Luther ou de Mahomet.
>
> [Liberate citizens from the yoke of the priests by offering them civic ceremonies that are more appealing, more sentimental than the gothic *liturgies* of Peter, Luther, or Muhammad.] (18)

Another member of the Convention, Bertrand Barère de Vieuzac, had called for emancipation from "l'emprise des prêtres" by the teaching of

French language. Masuyer refers instead to the wholesale substitution of the range of liturgical practices found in Christianity and even Islam, of which words are only a part. Or, if words do belong to those liturgies in any fundamental way, they do so in a "gothic" manner, a term that in the eighteenth century was full of pejorative connotation that could be summarized as the perversion of style away from the ideal of adequacy between form and content, signifier and signified. In Masuyer's vision, one senses a desire to engage religion on its own terms. In the first quote above, he makes the logical connection between a written constitution as the cornerstone of the state, and scripture as the cornerstone of religion. The second quote, in which he mentions the secular equivalent of "liturgy," or actual devotional practices designed to demonstrate the legitimacy of the Republic, the parallel is less clear. What, exactly, can take the place of the esthetically and emotionally outdated ("gothic") traditions of Peter, Luther, and Muhammad? If one takes into account the letter concerning public monuments, then it is fair to assume that the "civic ceremonies" Masuyer envisions will involve words, not images. Since the context of his argument is a debate over the form to be given to national education, it is also fair to assume that the site of these ceremonies will be the school, and not the outdoor commemorations which were already a part of republican myth-making, and which emphatically did not rely on words, or at least not on their figurative meanings, as demonstrated in Mona Ozouf's book *La Fête révolutionnaire* (1976), to which I will return shortly.

Masuyer's vision, extreme compared to Condorcet's, was yet exceeded by other members of the Convention. The split between otherwise allied factions of the Left over matters of education, so characteristic of the Third Republic (*la Question du latin* discussed in part III, chapter 7, gives ample evidence of this), was not foreign to the First. Michel Edme Petit, a member of the far left (*Montagne*), argued vehemently against all of those who had proposed plans for education that valued the literary tradition. Although I found no evidence that he ever attacked Masuyer's proposals, his opposition to those of Condorcet and Romme was stronger than that of his colleague. His own projects for public education clearly restricted the role of language to the practical, scientific disciplines, and he was an example of the kind of revolutionary who, as Bénichou wrote, wanted to institute national literature on a radically new basis.[1] His contribution to the debate, with its extreme suspicion of the literary use of language, serves clearly as an example of the challenge faced by the Third Republic in its attempt to find a source in republican tradition for

its own cultural policy:

> Le républicain abhorre le mensonge, la fausseté, la dissimulation; car il sait que la vérité seule peut en tout produire le bien absolu . . . car il craint toujours de ne pas pouvoir faire assez pour une patrie qui lui est plus chère que lui-même. . . . Il cultive moins les belles-lettres qu'il ne soigne sa conduite, & préfère les bonnes actions qui lui font connaître les hommes vertueux aux beaux livres qui ne lui montrent que des auteurs. . . . [Il] déteste naturellement tous les petits hommes dont l'insolente loquacité met toujours des mots à la place des choses. . . . . Il secoue et brise tous ces brinborions élégan[t]s, ridicules joujoux dont nos petits républicains monarchisés chargent encore leur personne et leurs habits.
>
> [The republican abhors lying, falseness, dissemblance; for he knows that truth alone can in all things produce the absolute good . . . for he constantly fears not being able to do enough for a fatherland that he loves more than himself. . . . He does not cultivate literature so much as he attends to his conduct, and prefers good acts that acquaint him with virtuous men over pretty books that only show him authors. . . . [He] naturally detests all little men whose insolent loquacity always puts words in the place of things. . . . He shakes off and breaks all those elegant baubles, ridiculous playthings with which our little monarchicized republicans still decorate their body and their clothes.] (5–6)

A major split between members of the Left occurred over the issue of national education, and whether language and literature were the appropriate content of such a project. Petit's austerity, in which he compares literature ("*beaux livres*") to the ridiculous fashion accessories of the nobility and of the "*républicains monarchisés*,"[2] has its counterpart in the "utilitarian" arguments of the Left in the late nineteenth century.

Those who, like Petit, denied any authority to the written word that might be of relevance to the founding of the Republic, were able to dominate the discussion for a time and then quickly found themselves on the margins of the debate. The real issue surrounding education, from a political standpoint, in the eighteenth just as in the nineteenth century, is not whether the book should be the main object of the national cult, hence, the process of canonization, but rather *which* book. The brief period during which orators such as Petit attacked the very status of French literature, such as it had been inherited from the past, was nevertheless to leave a profound mark on future debates. The linguist Michel Bréal (1872), when he advocated educational reforms in the wake of the defeat of 1871, echoed Petit and other revolutionaries, for example, when he attacked the secondary school exercise of *thème* (translating a French text into Latin or Greek) because "[il a] le tort de tourner sur les mots l'attention que nous devrions avant tout tourner sur les choses" [[it has] the fault of turning to words the attention that one must above all turn to things] (quoted in Weill 1921: 157). As we will see in Part II, the attempt to accredit a pedagogy of things as opposed to words was to dominate educational policy during the final third of the nineteenth century, though in a far more muted and subtle manner than the polemics of the late eighteenth century from which it derived a good deal of its strength.

The educational proposals put forward by the First Republic mostly did not materialize, but they express a conundrum that was to resurface during the debates on education in the 1880s, and had perhaps never been far removed from the realm of *éducation laïque* in the intervening years: how does one teach literacy without letting out the genie of rhetoric, of the word *for its own sake*? To put it differently, how can one teach literacy as a prerequisite for citizenship without simultaneously teaching literature, and all the elitist mystification the term invokes?

Just because the tendency to place the real above the symbolic dominated the discussion of pedagogy during the Revolution, and survived into the Republic, it did not follow that literature itself was to be excluded from the curriculum. What was meant by the term "literature" was the subject of official concern, more or less openly expressed. If literacy was to be made universal, and if it was to grant access to literature conceived as the highest goal of the apprenticeship in reading (two logical assumptions in any discussion of the right of the citizen to education), then literature itself would first have to be reinvented. As Mona Ozouf points out, no better explanation can be found for the apparently paradoxical return to the worship of antiquity, classical literature especially, during a period in history so closely identified with a radical modernism: Ancient Greece, just like the hoped-for French nation, was "[une] société toute neuve, innocente, où l'adéquation des paroles et des actes est entière" [(an) entirely new, innocent society, in which the adequacy of words to actions is complete] (1976: 460). These radical ideas could not be more alien to the cadre of intellectuals and politicians who collaborated on founding the school of the Third Republic, for whom the extreme materialism and hatred of mystification evidenced by the First Republic was simply no longer relevant.

For a time, the need for a new national literature overshadowed the question of the transmission of the literary heritage such as it already existed. Indeed, what did it matter *how* literature was taught in the schools, when the very corpus of literature such as it was at the end of the eighteenth century had been largely discredited? The attacks on the institution of literature were contemporaneous with the dismantling of the Church, and the two phenomena were not unrelated. The return of literature to the forefront of republican educational policy in the 1880s was evidence of a far more complex (and therefore less antagonistic) relationship of the state to the esoteric aspects of both organized religion and "high" literature.

Those who, like Michel-Edme Petit, denied any authority to the written word that might be of relevance to the founding of the Republic, dominated the discussion for a time and then quickly found themselves on the margins of the debate. The real issue surrounding education, from a political standpoint, in the eighteenth just as in the nineteenth century, is not whether the book should be the main object of the national cult, but rather *which* book. The brief period during which orators such as Petit attacked the very status of French literature, such as it had been inherited from the past, was nevertheless to leave a profound mark on future debates.

Such anxiety was in part a holdover of the *ancien régime* attitude that learning to read and write encourages peasants and workers to aspire to conditions above their birth. When education was a privilege, the question of literature's lack of reference to reality simply does not arise as a social problem. When it became a right, however, it was understood that for citizenship to succeed, each person must live in the real world, and not a virtual one. Consequently, methods of instruction throughout the nineteenth century returned obsessively to the subordination of abstract language to concrete phenomena, whether through "*leçons de choses*" [object lessons], in which students at the primary level studied everyday objects as part of their apprenticeship into language and science, or through the adoption of a more active pedagogy than the traditional one based on the catechism, a modern pedagogy in which language is presented in context (what foreign language specialists now refer to as "communicative" methodology).

One of the cornerstones of the history of French national education is the argument that the defeat of 1871 was due to inadequate schools, and specifically to an inadequate subordination of word to thing: it became known as "La défaite des instituteurs" [the defeat of the teachers]. Ernest Renan's 1871 book *La Réforme intellectuelle et morale* (Moral and Intellectual Reformation) called for a regeneration of education, as did the linguist Michel Bréal in 1872 in *Quelques mots sur l'instruction publique en France* (A Few Words on Public Instruction in France). The pedagogues of the Third Republic also feared the potential of education to cut men loose from their moorings in concrete existence. Emile Durkheim, who in 1902 inherited the Chair of Pedagogical Science from Ferdinand Buisson at the Sorbonne, hinted at this complexity when he pointed out that the Enlightenment, in its Revolutionary guise, emphasized *things* as opposed to words: "les humanités . . . réduites à la portion congrue . . . [furent] dépouillées du plus clair de leur vertu, puisqu'on n'y pouvait puiser l'art d'écrire, ni celui de penser" [the humanities . . . reduced to their simplest form . . . (were) stripped of most of their virtue, since one could not draw from them the art of writing, nor the art of thinking] (quoted in Françoise Mayeur 66). As a consequence of this philosophical *parti pris des choses,* First Republic pedagogues were forced into the difficult position of challenging the supremacy of humanistic studies in the school curriculum, and claiming that the activities of "correct" reading and writing, reduced to their proper subordinate position in a science-based pedagogy, had yet to be invented (Mayeur 1985: 65–6).

This resurgence of revolutionary pragmatism influenced the cadre of intellectuals responsible for the justification of Jules Ferry's reforms. In 1889, the *Ministère de l'Instruction publique* published an anthology of pamphlets on national education as a way to promote the controversial educational policies of the Third Republic. The celebration of the centennial of the Revolution, the use of the 1889 World's Fair to propagandize, domestically and internationally, on behalf of the policies of the regime, made of this anthology a kind of manifesto for national education, a version of the pedagogical science created by Gabriel Compayré and Ferdinand Buisson adapted for mass consumption. It contains an article by M.I. Carré on "Le Certificat d'Etudes primaires élémentaires" in which he discusses spelling:

> On attache évidemment à l'orthographe une importance exagérée dans les écoles primaires. Ce qu'on y apprend d'abord à l'enfant, c'est la manière dont les mots s'écrivent; ordinairement ensuite on les explique, c'est-à-dire qu'on tâche de lui en faire comprendre le sens; troisièmement enfin, mais trop rarement, on remonte du mot à l'idée qu'il exprime. C'est juste le contraire qu'on devrait faire. La raison, qui n'est ici que le bon sens, ne dit-elle pas qu'on devrait d'abord placer l'enfant en face des objets et des faits et lui donner des notions, des idées? puis, lui apprendre les mots qui expriment plus exactement ces idées; enfin, mais accessoirement, lui enseigner comment ces mots s'écrivent . . . ?

> [One clearly grants to spelling an exaggerated importance in the schools. One first teaches the child the way that words are written; one normally then explains them to him, that is to say one tries to make him understand

their meaning; thirdly and lastly, but too rarely, one goes back from the word to the idea it expresses. One should do exactly the opposite. Does not reason, which is here nothing other than common sense, say that one should first place the child in front of objects and facts and give him some notions and ideas? Then teach him the words that express those ideas more precisely; finally, but secondarily, teach him how these words are written . . . ?] (493)

Carré proposes a reversal of the tendency in primary pedagogy, inherited from the *syllabaires* and catechisms of the past, to place the child immediately in the realm of abstraction, which was also the realm of faith. A pedagogy without God needed to be a pedagogy of the *real*, and words are nothing by themselves: it does not even matter if children ultimately never learn to spell—correct spelling, after all, is a sign of social distinction, not of good citizenship—as long as they can correctly connect words to their experiences.

Another article in the 1889 anthology is by Félix Hémon, a professor of *rhétorique* at the *Lycée* Louis-le-Grand and a successful author of pedagogical works, most notably *Cours de littérature* (1909). His contribution is a history of the role of literature in primary education, *Les Auteurs français de l'enseignement primaire* (French Authors in Primary Education). During and after the period of the French Revolution, wrote Hémon, literature played no role in public primary education: "la grammaire est partout, la littérature nulle part" [grammar is everywhere, literature nowhere] (3: 382), a comment that deliberately echoes the ancient definition of God, cited by Montaigne and Pascal, as a circle of which the center is everywhere, the circumference nowhere; the few texts widely used in primary education in the first half of the nineteenth century that carried actual content, as distinct from grammar and spelling manuals, were considered to be devoid of literariness, meaning that they were created for pedagogical purposes, or at least were presented as if pedagogy were their sole purpose: they included Catholic catechisms, Fénelon's *Aventures de Télémaque*, and a series of stories by Laurent de Jussieu about a pedlar, *Simon de Nantua ou le Marchand forain* (60), to name the most popular examples. When literature, meaning texts that were not written for the edification of children, began to appear in primary textbooks around 1850 it was, according to Hémon, for very specific reasons. In addition to literacy, two new goals for primary education appeared: to transmit "une idée nette du génie français" [a clear idea of French genius], for the promotion of national identity, and "des idées générales humaines" [general human ideas], meaning the foundations of lay morality (3: 390–8). Both in the concrete (creation of a community) and the abstract (teaching morality), the school began to take over the function of the Catechism. The contradiction of simultaneously transmitting "génie français" and "idées générales humaines" can be resolved in one of two ways: either by claiming that the two are really one and the same, and that it is the *specificity* of French literature to convey general human ideas (with the consequent assumption that literatures of other cultures are characterized by some other quality), or by claiming that the pedagogical canon must consist of a relatively small number of authors who manage to combine the a priori unrelated qualities of French genius and universal human virtues. Both solutions to the universal/particular paradox are quite different, and both would continue to subtend the integration of literature into the primary curriculum.

Hémon therefore makes two very important claims in his history of primary school pedagogy, the first of which is only relatively problematic: that literature was virtually absent from the primary school curriculum before mid-century, with the exception of texts written for an audience of children (*Télémaque*, La Fontaine's *Fables* were not considered literature in the context in which they were used; this is a definition of literariness that is not intrinsic—a text either is or is not literary—but extrinsic: a text is not literary if it is not read as such). Literature appeared in the classroom by the decree of Victor Cousin, minister of public instruction during the Thiers government in 1840 (50–1).

The French literary canon, Hémon claims, consists of two levels: distinct from the mass of authors from every century who can legitimately claim the status of national treasure, there are "quelques écrivains privilégiés" [a few privileged writers] (3: 398) who deserve inclusion in the curriculum, and whom future *instituteurs* and *institutrices* must therefore study in preparation for the *brevet de capacité*, the certification required to become a teacher. Practically all of the "écrivains privilégiés" are from the seventeenth century, a fact that Hémon justifies as follows:

> [Q]uoi de plus humain à la fois et de plus national que cette littérature . . . où tout est tourné à l'étude de l'homme? . . . Et quoi de plus intelligible aussi que des chefs d'oeuvre dont la vertu essentielle est la simplicité?

> What is more human and at the same time more national than this literature . . . in which everything is turned toward the study of man? . . . And what is also more intelligible than these masterpieces of which the essential virtue is simplicity? (3: 385–6)

For their expression of moral values both in content ("l'étude de l'homme") and form ("la simplicité"), therefore, the works of the French classical period set the standard for inclusion into the primary school canon.

At the same time as Hémon published his essay, A. Philibert-Soupé, a professor at the *Faculté des lettres* in Lyon, published a guide for candidates to the literature exams required for various diplomas (*certificat, brevet, baccalauréat,* etc.) in which he gave a different justification for the primacy of the seventeenth century: "Le dix-septième siècle marque l'apogée de notre littérature classique. . . . Ce fut pour les lettres, les arts, et même les sciences une époque privilégiée, où la raison, le bon goût, le beau style égalèrent et parfois surpassèrent le génie et l'inspiration" [The seventeenth century marks the highpoint our classical literature. . . . It was a privileged time for letters, arts, and even sciences, during which reason, good taste, and beautiful style equalled and at times surpassed the genius of inspiration] (34). In other words, the specificity of French literature is its ability to free itself from excessive dependence on "genius and inspiration." The dispensation from inspiration accorded to French national authors has two immediate consequences: the first is to distinguish French literature from the Anglo-Germanic tradition, characterized by irrationality and obscurity, the results of unchecked "inspiration"; the second and more far-ranging consequence is to distinguish French literature from Scripture (which is always "inspired"), replacing a divine moral basis with a worldly one. Works from eras of French literature other than the seventeenth century, measured against this standard, will also attain canonical status by virtue of their independence from the mostly foreign and biblical traditions of poetic and divine inspiration, by virtue of their simplicity and intelligibility, as well as of their moral (human-centered) content.

Returning to Hémon: his second important argument in favor of seventeenth-century authors, after their "humanity" and "intelligibility" is that they place the ancient classical period, distant from contemporary France both geographically and chronologically, at the center of French literary specificity:

> [N]e pouvant toujours puiser directement à la source inépuisable de l'antiquité, les candidats de l'enseignement primaire doivent s'adresser de préférence à la littérature "suggestive" [d'idées générales] entre toutes, à celle du dix-septième siècle, héritière de l'antiquité, que fait revivre, en la rajeunissant, son imitation créatrice.
>
> [Unable always to draw directly from the endless wellspring of antiquity, the candidates [for the certificate] of primary education are better off

devoting themselves to the literature which is most "suggestive" [of general ideas], that of the seventeenth century, the heir of antiquity that its creative imitation brings back to life.] (3: 399)

The process Hémon describes above is a type of assimilation. Classical literature, for all of the contemporary educated person's supposed familiarity with its characters and plots, reveals itself on closer examination to be inalterably strange. There are two main obstacles preventing the modern reader from taking possession of the classical past: linguistic, since the "candidats à l'enseignement primaire" are not required to read Latin or Greek; and intellectual, since the mode of thinking of classical authors remains to some degree alien to us, even when we can read them in the original. Both of these facts militate strongly against the myth that classical literature is somehow at the center of the cultural identity of the nineteenth-century French citizen. The seventeenth century solved this problem by appearing to provide access to the classical past (according to Hémon) but in fact, replacing it. This myth of assimilation of the foreign and ancient source of moral authority, for which seventeenth-century French "classicism" played such a crucial role, was one of the ideological functions of national education.

By claiming that the plays and poems of the seventeenth century could somehow "stand for" classical texts, Hémon presents us with a number of assumptions. First of all, there is the obvious objection that texts of the French classical period cannot serve as translations or adaptations of Greek and Latin texts in any valid sense of those terms. Whoever goes to Corneille and Racine hoping to learn about ancient myths and tragedies will encounter serious problems, a fact of which Hémon was no doubt well aware. I believe that he was in reality making a different claim, but one that could not be spoken aloud: that French literature, especially (but not exclusively) as exemplified by the seventeenth century, is every bit as meaningful and valuable as the classical literature that preceded it. This is a revival of the *Querelle des anciens et des modernes*, but with a twist: classical literature had enjoyed a monopoly on culture for centuries, primarily because nobody could claim to be educated if they had not received extensive instruction in reading and especially in speaking and writing classical languages. Literary pedagogy was a matter of *noblesse oblige*. The Third Republic officially declared an end to the classical monopoly. For the first time, knowledge of (or at least instruction in) one's national literature was claimed to be a sufficient standard of what it means to be "cultured."

Hémon was fearlessly explicit in excluding from the primary school canon those more recent authors who did not fit the standards he described: because of his "vagueness" and preoccupation with Christianity, "[Il] faudra veiller de très près au choix des morceaux de Lamartine (3: 426)" [One must choose very carefully the passages from Lamartine], for example. On Vigny: "[J]amais il ne sera largement populaire; en ces poèmes délicats ou profonds, jamais la foule ne verra clairement ce qu'y voit l'élite. Or les candidats au brevet sont légion" [He will never be widely popular; in those delicate and profound poems, the crowd will never clearly see what the elite sees. And the candidates for the *brevet* [the diploma required of all primary school teachers] are legion] (3: 427). On Musset: "La nature, la famille, la patrie, la liberté sont absentes de cette oeuvre profonde, mais sans largeur d'horizon et sans sérénité" [Nature, family, fatherland, liberty are absent from this profound body of work, yet one that is narrow in scope and devoid of serenity] (3: 428). Hugo, however, transcends his era because of "[sa] forte précision . . . rendant sa pensée toujours intelligible" [his strong precision . . . making his thought always clear] (3: 428). One may well question this characterization of Hugo, and Hémon's reasons for making him the glaring exception among nineteenth-century writers in terms of his importance in the school curriculum deserve an entire book by themselves. For our purposes, it is enough that Hugo was far more popular than his contemporaries, *de facto* more accessible, and hence ready to belong to the republican canon in which "intelligibility" was paramount.

The authors belonging in primary education therefore needed to meet certain standards: a concern with moral topics and issues (where Musset falls short), clarity and intelligibility (not Vigny's strong points), and, finally, access to the classics, which seventeenth-century authors provide with their "creative imitation" of antiquity.

Tristan Hordé (1985) points out that French texts were absent for so long from the curriculum because their meaning was considered self-evident, and only Latin texts required *explication* (50). Ironically, it is precisely the attribute of self-evidence ascribed to French literary texts that eventually made them so valuable to the school. Literary concerns, which inevitably lead one away from the "self-evident" and toward the discovery that, for example, La Fontaine's *Fables* are not nearly as moral and unambiguous as they appear at first glance, have absolutely no place in the school. The value of literature for primary education depends on a perpetual deferral of specifically literary concerns. What, therefore, does literary pedagogy consist of? An examination of some concrete examples is in order.

As mentioned above, Hordé asserts that Victor Cousin, during his stint as *ministre de l'Instruction publique* in the Thiers cabinet in 1840, was the first public official to question the assumption of transparency of French literature and to recognize the challenge it offers by introducing it into the curriculum (50–1). Even then, very little progress occurred until the reforms of the 1880s (Fayolle 1979: 8), and the definition of *"Belles Lettres"* as consisting of the imitation of Latin (and some Greek) texts with an emphasis on grammar and rhetoric—the hallmark, in other words, of Jesuit education—continued to stand for the "real" discipline of literary studies long after initial challenges to its monopoly.

When the study of French literature finally established itself in primary and secondary schools, it did so not only slowly and gradually, but also indirectly. The study of the history of French literary pedagogy is a burgeoning field, but one that has already reached important conclusions. One of the most significant is that the school of the Third Republic, while marking the "triumph" of French literature as academic discipline, nevertheless did not practice literary studies in any current sense of the term. Part of the reason for the suppression of literature at the very moment that its position in the primary curriculum was confirmed rises out of the fear that we saw among legislators during the First Republic of the dangers of substituting words for things. The quiddity of literature—that which makes it distinct from other phenomena, and leads to the analysis of literature on its own terms—was precisely the characteristic that literary pedagogy could not afford to recognize.

As for the clarity and intelligibility of the consecrated texts, one can of course argue that not only are they not transparent, upon examination, but that here as well, the disinterested reason given for valuing such qualities (ease of assimilation by the schoolchild) overlies a far more pragmatic political reality. As Rachael Langford (1999) argued in a recent article, the practices of the republican primary school centered around the standardization and organization of time and space, so as to ensure that no student would be left to his or her own devices at any point during the school day (92–9). The requirements that students be visible to the teacher at all times (requiring something as obviously simple as the installation of the *estrade*, or raised platform on which stood the teacher's desk), and that every schoolteacher account for the activities of each day with a *journal de classe* available to the inspectors,[3] not only contribute to the utilitarianist, "panoptical" function of the national education system, but find their corollary in the subject matter of each lesson. In the case of French literature, texts that make up the primary school curriculum must appear to be consistent with these disciplinary values of transparency and standardization in order to direct attention away from their function as means of social control, and to elevate them to the status of absolute values in their own right.

The effect of using literature as a means of justifying the practice of social control and political legitimization is complex. On the one hand, literature becomes reduced to serving a utilitarian function. Literary texts in the school are, in a sense, nothing other than illustrations of sound moral and civic principles, sugar to coat the pill of republican civic instruction. The subordination of literary texts to secular principles is not a way, one presumes, to present literature as the physical manifestation of the sacred. On closer examination, however, one can see that this practice does serve to support the institution of literature as an autonomous and sacred entity, if one simply inverts the terms. The primary school textbook appears to subordinate literature by making it an incidental *aide-mémoire* for the assimilation of civic morality, but one can just as easily see that it functions so well in this capacity precisely because it embodies absolute value. The myth that one can extract moral benefits from transparency, standardization and harmony, posited as essential qualities of literary texts, serves in turn to validate the texts themselves. The moral authority of literature, as of Scripture, is still fundamentally a matter of faith. Nobody can say for sure how or why the regular ritualistic contact with the Word results in living a better life. It suffices that it does, and in so doing, that it reinforces the power of the Word.

PART II
LANGUAGE AND LITERATURE IN PRIMARY EDUCATION

CHAPTER 3

THE EVANGELISM OF NATIONAL EDUCATION

Jules Ferry's title from February of 1879 to November 1881, January to August of 1882, and February to November of 1883, was *ministre de l'Instruction publique, des Beaux Arts et des Cultes*. According to Dimitri Demnard, "*cultes*" remained associated with the ministry until 1906, when it was definitively eliminated from the portfolio as a result of the 1905 law on the separation of Church and state.[1] The creation of a "*ministère de l'Instruction publique*" dates from 1828, replacing the titles of "grand-maître de l'Université" (created by Napoleon in 1808 and first assigned to Louis de Fontanes) and "ministre des Affaires ecclésiastiques et de l'Instruction publique" (created in 1824 and first assigned to Denis Frayssinous). It only became *ministère de l'Education nationale* in 1932, and has remained so ever since except during the Vichy regime, during which it temporarily reverted to *ministère de l'Instruction publique* in order to symbolize more effectively the historical and ideological break with the Third Republic (Demnard 1981: 534–8). For most of the nineteenth century, therefore, the state's involvement in education and its relationship to organized religion (codified in the *Concordat* signed by Napoleon and Pius VII in 1801) were part of the same portfolio. An even stronger bureaucratic connection links education to the "*beaux arts*," since the latter were under the purview of the education ministry from Jules Simon's tenure in 1870 all the way to 1958, when the constitution of the Fifth Republic led to the creation of the first autonomous post of minister of culture, held by André Malraux.[2]

Without making too much of the purely administrative conjoining of religion, art, and national education, one can at least wonder at the persistence of their coexistence under one ministerial roof. In the early nineteenth century, when primary education was largely the responsibility of religious orders, and part of the salary of priests came from the government's budget, it made sense to have public instruction and religion share the same portfolio. The fact that religion continued to be under the responsibility of the education ministry well into the Third Republic is surprising, however. The controversy surrounding legislation in the area of education was analogous to the one over the state's right to intervene in the autonomous realms of religion and culture, realms in which the principle of personal freedom had long been fundamental. Such was the opinion of a large part of the French public, for whom the issue of the school's autonomy from the state was related to the issue of the autonomy of the Church and the autonomy of art. Keeping that similarity in mind helps to explain the negative conservative response to the Republic's educational reforms, many of which only ratified developments that had already taken place.

The important laws passed during Ferry's mandate were the ones establishing national education as lay (March 12, 1880), free (June 16, 1881), and mandatory (March 28, 1882). The principle of *laïcité* was further enforced through the requirement that all teachers be certified by the state (a law known as "le monopole de la collation des grades"), whether they serve in public or private schools. The rough balance between central control and local initiative that allowed teachers from religious orders to continue their functions, but required them to meet standards of training and to teach subjects determined by the state, was reflected as well in the very important area of production of school materials. Since 1880, teachers from individual schools could select whatever textbooks they preferred, but then had to submit their list to a government committee, formed at the level of the *département* and made up of *inspecteurs primaires* and administrators of *école normales* (teacher training schools), which had the power to veto any item (Déloye 1994: 211).

The long list of initiatives undertaken by the ministry at various points since the Revolution include the tradition of establishing the *programme*, or list of items to be taught in the various disciplines. An important precedent for this tradition at the secondary level, going back to 1801, was the state-mandated curriculum of the *"Prytanée français,"* a school founded by the state for the sons of military officers that later became the *lycée Louis-le-Grand* (Bernard 1978: 671). The curriculum of the *Prytanée* became the basis for those of the first lycées established by Napoleon (Françoise Mayeur 459), and is therefore also the classical curriculum that was to become the subject of intense polemics discussed in part III. This particular aspect of the minister's authority is fundamental: by defining the topics and even the texts necessary to learn in order to obtain the certification that one has completed one's mandatory education, as well as the content of all further diplomas such as the *baccalauréat*, the state in effect holds a monopoly on education: even private schools had to use many of the same textbooks and methodologies as the public ones. Although it is ironic that the mass of scholarship on French education deals almost exclusively with public education when Catholic schools in the nineteenth century taught 50 percent of all students (Weiss 1969: 160), one can see that the study of public education during the Third Republic *is* the study of French education.

Because the school of the Third Republic is so often associated with the person of Jules Ferry, it is important to take into account his own expressed views of pedagogy. Most of the literature on Ferry, not surprisingly, emphasizes his role as a moderate and a healer of national divisions, rather than a rabid "*bouffeur de curé*," the epithet applied to many advocates of lay national education. For example, Ferry wanted to maintain the "*régime concordataire*" of 1801 according to which the French government administered a budget for priests' stipends, nominated bishops, and generally recognized Roman Catholicism as a "protected" religion if not an "official" one (Chevalier 1972: 186–7). The *Concordat*, in effect until 1905, ceded spiritual authority to the pope at the same time as it gave the French state an important role in ecclesiastical affairs, creating an interesting balance between fidelity to Rome and the tendency towards Gallicanism that had characterized French Catholicism over the centuries. Whether Ferry supported the Concordat because he did not believe in the separation of Church and state, or only wanted to postpone the separation until after the ideological battles of the Republic had been won, is still a matter of debate (Jean-Marie Mayeur 1985: 149–52). What is more certain is that his ideal of a "*morale laïque*" (for which he quoted Kant as a source, much to the dismay of right-wing nationalists who deplored the substitution of an authority based in Rome with one based in Königsberg[3]) was not to be understood as having religious overtones, not even the "religion" of Comtian positivism that he claimed was so influential on him. Just as he was hostile to religion in even its most "natural" form, arguing that he did not want teachers to constitute "a corps of fifty thousand *vicaires savoyards*" (quoted in Françoise Mayeur 1985: 154), he was profoundly hostile to the Jacobin materialism that had reemerged on the left wing of the republican coalition (156).[4]

The fact that the institution of public education exhibited similarities to, and at times even seemed to parody the dissemination of ecclesiastical (specifically papal) authority was itself a part of the propaganda for the republican school. In 1885 Melchior Duboys published an *Exposé de l'Instruction publique en France: son histoire, son état actuel* [*Survey of Public Instruction in France: its History and Present Status*] that served as a defense of the new legal status of education in the form of a thorough description of its organization and methods. He begins with the chain of command, dominated by two bodies: the ministry of Public Instruction and the *Conseil supérieur d'Instruction publique* consisting of notables (prelates, academics, judges, and politicians who serve *ex officio*), who delegate their power in each of the 17 *académies* through a *recteur*, the ecclesiastically equivalent terms of which would be diocese and bishop, respectively; the *recteur* in turn oversees as many *inspecteurs d'académie* as there are departments in his district (since there were 87 dioceses in France at the time, their geographical areas were similar to those of the departments, of which there were originally 83). The *commune* or municipality would be the equivalent of a parish, and the faculty and administration of each educational establishment were the priests at the bottom of the hierarchy.

Of course hierarchical organizations, whether spiritual, political, or military tend to have similar structures. Duboys continues his exposition by explicitly comparing the administration of education to the Church, however, in his chapter on the daily life of the *école normales* (teacher training schools), which he likened to monasteries and convents. The comparison arose naturally from the tradition according to which orders of priests and nuns supplied the staff of primary education before the autonomous profession of *instituteur* emerged during the Revolution; but the atmosphere and discipline of these teacher-training schools pushed the analogy much further. Every hour of the day was strictly regimented, not just those spent in class. Even a watered-down rule of celibacy prevailed, at least for women: the *Ecole Normale Supérieure* for women at Fontenay-aux-Roses barred entrance to students who were either married or divorced (Duboys 1885: 49). The justification for such a practice was not simply that professional women in the nineteenth century, according to social convention, could not also be wives and mothers. In a speech to a gathering of women teachers in April 1881, Jules Ferry professed that "l'institutrice qui reste fille trouve dans l'éducation des enfants d'autrui la satisfaction de ce sentiment maternel, de ce grand instinct de sacrifice que toute femme porte en elle" [the female teacher who remains unmarried will find in the education of other people's children the fulfillment of the maternal sentiment, of this great instinct for sacrifice that every woman carries within herself] (quoted in Gaillard 1989: 510). A woman who lost her virginity had also lost her ability to transfer to her students her sublimated love for family (or, as Freud would say, her repressed libido). Clearly, the terms "church," "seminary," "monastery," and the richly connotative term "vocation" help convey the solemnity of the pedagogical task. So exalted was the mission of the teachers of the Third Republic that it is not surprising that they were compared to conquering soldiers ("les hussards noirs de la République" [the black hussars of the Republic] in Charles Péguy's oft-quoted phrase[5]) and to early Christian evangelizers ("prophètes éblouis du verbe nouveau" [illuminated prophets of the new word] according to Georges Clemenceau, quoted in Gaillard 1989: 508). The premise that the Third Republic modeled its school on the Church entails a great many consequences, the most important of which, for the present discussion, is the new institutional status of French language and literature.

The idea that republican education secretly took on many of the characteristics of Catholicism while publicly confronting it underlies most historical research on the birth of public education in France, such as Mona Ozouf's highly authoritative *L'Ecole, l'Eglise, et la République—1871–1914* (1963). The Jesuits were the targets of Jules Ferry's famous 1880 decree ("*l'article 7*") that forbade members of "non-authorized congregations" to teach. Police raids literally expelled priests from their classrooms, one of the earliest of many milestones in the history of the gradual takeover by the Republic of the educational role of the Church.[6] In order for the substitution to be successful, would it not make sense for the state, under the guise of republicanism, to appropriate the tools and methods, as well as the function, of Catholicism?

Such an impression is confirmed by a superficial reading of the symbolism of republican education. One cannot help being struck by how naturally the crucifix on the walls of classrooms was replaced by images of Marianne, and by the passions that arose from this transition. Mona Ozouf quotes from the August 10, 1882 issue of *Le Correspondant*, one of many vitriolic attacks on the newly minted concept of *laïcité*: "Le meilleur commentaire de ce vocable, n'est-ce pas la disparition de l'image divine des salles de classe, au profit de la figure si peu artistique et si peu idéale de la Marianne Républicaine?" [Is not the best commentary on that term the disappearance of the divine image from classrooms, replaced by the face, so inartistic and short of ideal, of the republican Marianne?] (Ozouf 1963: 75) The practice of modeling the bust of Marianne on a real woman (in recent years, models included actresses Brigitte Bardot, Catherine Deneuve, and Sophie Marceau) began early, according to an 1872 pamphlet by Ernest Caron, professor at the *Institut Catholique* in Paris. Well before the reforms of the 1880s and the program of renovations of classrooms that allowed for the systematic replacement of the crucifix by busts of Marianne, Caron (1872) wrote: "[P]renons la liberté de jeter un coup d'oeil profane dans le sanctuaire. —Cette chose en plâtre que vous voyez au-dessus du maître, à la place du *Christ*, c'est la déesse Raison, une tête copiée d'après nature dans quelque boudoir enfumé" [Let us dare to cast a profane glance into the sanctuary. —That plaster thing you see above the teacher, replacing Christ, is the goddess Reason, a head modeled after nature in some smoke-filled boudoir] (7). Caron was already well aware that the classroom had become a type of parody of a Catholic "sanctuary," and his suggestion that Marianne was modeled on a prostitute in some "smoke-filled boudoir" (a shrewd comment, that makes one wonder about the current policy of using fashion models and movie stars to model Marianne, and a possible lingering association between those honorable professions and the *cocottes* who, in the nineteenth century, supposedly filled those same ranks), underscores the difference between the crucifix and the symbol of the Republic as well as their essential identity: "real" people (Jesus, a prostitute) whose image stands for something spiritual (God, the Republic).

Yet underneath the defense of Catholicism and its symbols of power in the school, an issue emerges that is far more capable of arousing conservative passion than the weakening of the Church. The editorialist of *Le Correspondant* compares Marianne and the crucifix, not because of what they symbolize, but because of their artistic merit as icons. According to him, the female bust of the Republic cannot attain the status of a work of art, nor can it transcend individual diversity through universal redemption. The story of how Marianne was made to replace Christ is not of a political conflict between Church and state so much as a struggle for artistic authority: for centuries, the Church exercised control over artistic production; now, the French state was poised to assume the authority to judge the validity of art of the past, present, and future, and to be a patron. The level of passion of the debates over educational reform is therefore due in large part to the fact that the school was then, as it is now, the site of the culture wars. It is through literature that the French language would save the national soul, just as God saved mankind through His Son. Ironically, Ernest Caron, the author of the quote above comparing Marianne to a real-life prostitute, unwittingly argued in the same piece that artistic and literary master-pieces are unavoidably *religious* in nature (9), by which he probably meant that they necessarily spring from divine inspiration, if they are not overtly religious in content. The irony, of course, is that the spiritual nature of art, understood in broader terms as its ability to transcend the boundaries of rational inquiry, is precisely what allowed the school of the Republic to enlist literature in the national service: not as a product of Christianity (as European art had traditionally been), but as its rival, a degree of hubris on the part of the state which Caron did not even suspect.

All that the symbolic transition from Christ to Marianne required, at the outset, was some strategy. In November of 1880, Parisian authorities, acting in the name of the recent laws restricting the role of the Church in the schools, abruptly removed the crucifixes (and, in girls' schools, the images of the Virgin) from classrooms. Upon learning of this operation, Jules Ferry became furious, knowing that the public would never stand for such change. He therefore convinced the National Assembly to allocate funds for the gradual renovation of school buildings in each of the *communes*. Whenever the walls of a classroom were replastered, the crucifix that had adorned them would disappear. Ferry hoped, quite reasonably, that nobody would take much notice of the disappearing symbols, as long as they were part of a larger and more protracted change (Capéran 1957–61: 250).

The truly religious aspect of education is not in its administrative structure or in the symbolic décor of the classroom, however, but in pedagogical practice. The next two chapters, as well as all of part III, describe the application of French literature within the pedagogical framework. In order to understand the uses of literature in the school, it is first necessary to place them in the context of the evolving sense of the word "literature" during the nineteenth century. The struggle over the proper method of teaching literature, occurring largely within the confines of the school, reflected the dual meaning of the word, understood both as active (writing) and passive (erudition). "*Belles-lettres*," denoting the exercise of grammar and elocution and the imitation of classical models, as opposed to reading as an end in itself, was an increasingly outmoded term after the Revolution (Fayolle 1975: 9), although the practices to which it referred continued to be an important part of secondary education. "*Littérature*" in the early nineteenth century was not clearly distinguishable from "*belles-lettres*," referring as it did, according to Philippe Lejeune (1969), to "soit . . . une *étude*, nommée aussi rhétorique, soit un *ensemble d'oeuvres* étudiées, c'est-à-dire proposées à l'imitation" [either . . . [a field] of *study*, also called rhetoric, or a *collection of works* being studied, that is to say serving as models for imitation] (26). Both of these meanings of the word are part of an active pedagogy: learning the rules of oral and written style for the purpose of attaining eloquence, and imitating classical authors for the same purpose. Although by the end of the century students were still being asked at times to create written texts in the manner of literary figures of the past, the pedagogical emphasis had shifted dramatically in favor of erudition, the passive reception of literary works, over rhetoric.

The shift in literary study from acquiring a skill to acquiring knowledge correlated closely with the gradual increase of French literature in the curriculum, a phenomenon I study in greater detail in part III. Lejeune, like most historians of literary pedagogy, dates the coming of age of French literary studies with the ministry of Victor Cousin, who first allowed French texts into the curriculum in 1840. For the first time, students in secondary education were required to speak and write about French literature, and the discourse *on* rather than *of* literature began its ascendancy: "le type de langage de l'élève commence à pouvoir n'être plus identique à celui de l'oeuvre étudiée" [the kind of language [used by] the student can start to cease being identical to that of the work being studied] (Lejeune 1969: 30). A new type of discourse came into being in the confines of the classroom, and with it came a very different sense of the word "literature." From being primarily a skill, it became a subject of knowledge, and an initiation into national identity inasmuch as the teaching of literature was always the teaching of a particular literature, the French one. As Lejeune views this long evolution, it is a completely disorienting paradigm shift. Reflecting that the republican school only slowly and reluctantly allowed nineteenth-century writers into the *baccalauréat* curriculum, and living writers almost never, Lejeune concludes that "la littérature, c'est . . . ce qui est *mort*. . . . Est classique ce qui est classé, et seul ce qui est classique peut s'enseigner en classe" [literature is . . . that which is *dead*. . . . What is classical is classified, and only that which is classified can be taught in class] (31–2).

Later in this chapter I describe attempts by the university establishment, in coordination with the state, to develop a theoretical framework for the nascent enterprise of national education. The need for such a framework was twofold: first, the creation of a market, that is to say the increasingly urgent demand for a solution to France's perceived education gap relative to other societies (especially Germany after 1871), a mostly utilitarian goal; second, an enormous faith in the power of education to provide a spiritual as well as an economic and political rebirth. Both needs, the utilitarian and the spiritual, appeared with increasing frequency in the press and in pamphlets, such as Charles Frédéric Robert's *Le Salut par l'éducation et le discours de Fichte à la*

Nation allemande en 1807 (Salvation Through Education and Fichte's Speech to the German Nation in 1807) published by Hachette in 1872.[7] Fichte's 1807 speech on education became a point of reference for numerous calls for the Republic to rejuvenate the nation through education, both because people perceived it as the impetus for the development of German schools that France never had, and because of the spiritual overtones of Fichte's appeal.[8] The theme of spiritual rebirth dominated France, as in Ernest Lavisse's call for a "History of War" in the mandatory curriculum that would teach every schoolchild the redemptive value of the defeat (Dupuy 1953: 30).[9] The promotion of Germany's example as a solution to the French military, social, and cultural crises is of course typical of the postwar era. What is most interesting, however, is the evangelical tone of Robert's plea for a regeneration of the French educational system by the state. His call for an educational system that would save the nation in the spiritual as well as physical sense, while it was consistent with the religious rhetoric that abounded following the defeat, goes even further:

> Que l'école devienne de plus en plus le centre où doivent converger nos regards, nos voeux et nos espérances. Consacrons-lui plus que la dîme de nos loisirs, sans lui mesurer la place qu'elle doit tenir dans nos pensées. . . . Que les hommes d'Etat, ceux auxquels Fichte s'adressait d'une manière si pathétique, s'emparent de cette cause sacrée.

> [May the school become more and more the center towards which our gazes must converge, our wishes and our hopes. Let us devote to it more than the tithe of our leisure hours, without putting a limit on the space it must occupy in our thoughts. . . . May statesmen, to whom Fichte spoke with such pathos, take hold of this sacred cause.] (30)

The rhetoric of salvation was strongest in the years right before Ferry's reforms took place, when it was politically necessary to create the sense of a spiritual void that required immediate attention. The fervor of the Reformation was clearly a model, as in the above passage in which Robert calls upon the French to devote to education more than "la dîme de nos loisirs," a reference to Luther's rejection of tithing as a substitute for true devotion—in other words, "works" as instruments of salvation as opposed to the twin paths of grace and faith.

Ernest Renan saw the defeat as an opportunity to publish a lecture he had already given in 1869 titled "La part de la famille et de l'Etat dans l'éducation" [The Role of the Family and of the State in Education] in his book *La Réforme intellectuelle et morale* (Intellectual and Moral

Reformation; 1871), the title evoking both the "*Réforme*" in the history of Christianity and the "*réformes*" that the Republic needed in order to place France back on top. In contrast to the overtly religious rhetoric of many of his contemporaries, Renan's text reaffirms the distinction between Church and state, and between public instruction (in academic skills and knowledge) and private, moral education (in ethics); only the family, and especially the mother, is qualified to "educate" in this sense:

> L'éducation, c'est le respect de ce qui est réellement bon, grand et beau; c'est la politesse, charmante vertu, qui supplée à tant d'autres vertus; c'est le tact, qui est presque de la vertu aussi. Ce n'est pas un professeur qui peut apprendre tout cela.

> [Education is respect for all that is truly good, great and beautiful; it is courtesy, a charming virtue that compensates for so many other virtues; it is tact, which is almost virtue as well. No professor can teach all of this.] (328)

On one level, Renan clearly denies the state any role in the moral and spiritual growth of the child, which seems incompatible with the call for national salvation, in the religious sense of the term, through education. The state, in his opinion, must simply grant families the freedom, time and space to inculcate a moral (and perhaps even esthetic) sensibility. The great error, both of Jesuit pedagogues and of revolutionaries such as Le Peletier de Saint Fargeau, was to take students away from their families so as to exercise complete domination over their lives.

While Renan's call for a limited, rational state role in education went against the prevailing spirit of the era immediately following the defeat, it was still possible to find in his text plenty of support for education as a means of salvation, connoting much more than renewed economic and geopolitical dominance. He reminded his auditors that education had always been a privilege of the dominant classes who feared that if it became a universal right, then the condition of slave, peasant, and worker, upon which the upper classes depend, would cease to exist:

> La littérature, dans cette manière de voir, ne sert qu'à l'homme de lettres, la science qu'au savant; les bonnes manières, la distinction ne servent qu'à l'homme du monde. Le pauvre doit être ignorant, car l'éducation et le savoir lui seraient inutiles. Blasphème, Messieurs! . . . [S]i la culture de l'esprit est la chose sainte par excellence, nul n'en doit être exclu.

> Literature, from this perspective, is useful only to the man of letters, science to the scientist; good manners, breeding are useful only to the man about town. The poor must be ignorant, since education and

knowledge would be of no use to them. Blasphemy, gentlemen! . . . [If] cultivation of the spirit is the essence of saintliness, no one is to be excluded from it. (309)

It is clear from the passage above that Renan did not, in fact, see the family as the sole purveyor of "respect du beau," "politesse," and "tact." These exclusively nonutilitarian goals were for him a part of the purpose of general education, and while "la culture de l'esprit" is not the same as moral and spiritual development, it nevertheless overlaps with it considerably; and as "la chose sainte par excellence" it may even serve as the privileged path towards salvation. After all, Renan introduced *La Réforme* by saying that Germany's superiority was severely limited: "La grande supériorité de l'Allemagne est dans l'ordre intellectuel; mais que là encore elle ne se figure pas tout posséder. Le tact, le charme lui manquent." [Germany's great superiority is in the intellectual realm; but in this realm also, she must not imagine that she has everything. She lacks charm and tact] (x). The transmission of the same "charme" and "tact" had been labeled as the sole prerogative of the family, in the first quote from Renan above. Given the context of Renan's call for national reform, however, it is safe to assume that in 1871 he no longer felt quite the way he had in 1869, and that the education of "littérature," "science," and "bonnes manières" was at least to some degree an affair of state. Renan joined a growing political trend that wanted to bring matters of national identity that previously belonged in the private realm, such as the transmission of "taste" and "tact," understood as terms for the essence of French particularity, into the public realm governed by the institution of national education. The message is clear: leave religion to the families, but place civic religion, which includes the subtlest norms of behavior and esthetic distinction, under the responsibility of the state.

Renan's polemical intervention in the post-1871 debate, proposing the universal application of a rational, limited public education program may have stopped short of a call for a new religion, but others did not. The rhetorical tenor of such utterances sometimes aimed at simple instinct, such as the cry by Emile Escoffier, a staunch republican lawyer and propagandist: "La France est morte, vive la France!" in *La Régénération de la France par l'instruction et l'éducation républicaines* (The Regeneration of France through Republican Instruction and Education; 1873); at other times it spoke to the soul itself. In 1875 Léon Bourrié, an *instituteur* in Saint-Jean-de-Védas, near Montpellier, wrote in the heroic mode of his vocation as a secular priest indistinguishable from his religious counterpart

in a pamphlet titled *De la Lecture considérée comme exercice de classe* (On Reading Considered as a Classroom Exercise): "continuons avec courage et résignation notre tâche toute de dévouement, d'abnégation, de sacrifice. Nous succomberons peut-être à la peine; mais du moins, en mourant, nous aurons la satisfaction d'avoir contribué, dans notre modeste sphère, à la régénération, intellectuelle et morale, de notre chère patrie, qui en a tant besoin" [let us continue with courage and resignation our work of devotion, self-denial, and sacrifice. Perhaps we will succumb under the task; but in dying, we will at least feel the satisfaction of having contributed, in our small domain, to the moral and intellectual regeneration of our dear fatherland, which needs it so much] (8).

In spite of the priestly persona he projected, Bourrié, like Renan, spoke of sacrifice and regeneration from a still-secular point of view. Yet there also existed after the defeat a much stronger argument that secular morality in education constituted a literal rebirth of the spiritual mission of Christ. An example is a self-published pamphlet titled *Les Principes de l'éducation républicaine pour l'enseignement dans les écoles* (Principles of Republican Education for Teaching in the Schools; 1878) by Jean-Pierre Hureaux, a militant republican who did not hesitate to frame the advent of national education in terms of a return to the true path of Christianity. Hureaux was, admittedly, an unusual case: a pharmacist who became a fervent believer in the regeneration of Christianity through science, he spent his entire life announcing the advent of a new era of which the title of another one of his pamphlets says all: *L'Oeuvre de résolution des temps: Le Code moral de la République ou de l'esprit chrétien passé majeur* (The Work of the Resolution of Time: the Moral Code of the Republic or, on the Attainment by the Christian Spirit of its Majority; 1879).[10] It would be reckless to claim that the leaders of the Third Republic would have recognized themselves in Hureaux's enthusiasm. He is worth mentioning, however, as an example of the phenomenon of republican "mystics" who espoused the heresy that the Republic was the prelude to the Second Coming of Christ, and who therefore give a clear idea of the religious tenor of the public crusade for a spiritual dimension to national education. First, Hureaux presents the problem in the conventional language of traditional, doctrinaire *morale laïque* that, with its Positivist overtones, purported to transcend and even supplant the teachings of Christianity:

> Le but de l'Education Républicaine est d'élever le niveau de la vie sociale par la Liberté, et de former un peuple supérieur dans la crise transformatrice du monde chrétien qui caractérise le dix-neuvième siècle.

[The purpose of Republican Education (*sic*) is to raise the level of society through Liberty, and to educate a superior people in the transformative crisis of the Christian world in the nineteenth century.] (5)

And later: "La fausse morale des sectes va faire place à la morale universelle" [The false morality of sects [religions] will make way for the universal morality] (10). Hureaux's rhetoric then takes a surprising turn, moving rapidly from a critique of the moral bankruptcy of Christianity consistent with the more extreme republican-radical political rhetoric of the time to a kind of renewal of Christianity from within, a return to its origins. At first, he couches his call for reform in terms connoting a general religious ascesis ("l'émancipation humaine . . . est une purification] [human emancipation is a purification] 23) and transcendence ("[l]a liberté est un principe de l'Humanité, c'est une vertu divine" [liberty is a principle of Humanity, it is a divine virtue] 24) and finally, he places the evangelical card face up on the table: "Si vous voulez être les véritables frères du Christ, marchez résolument à la conquête de la Liberté, seule capable de vous conduire à la vie éternelle" [If you want to be the true brothers of Christ, march resolutely towards the conquest of Liberty, she alone can lead you to eternal life] (26); "Les siècles qui séparent l'An I de 1871, la voie de douleurs parcourue de Jérusalem à Paris, du Calvaire au Panthéon, accomplissent l'ère de la Chrétienté Mineure, et nous font arriver à la fin des temps annoncée par le Christ" [The centuries separating year one from 1871, the *via dolorosa* from Jerusalem to Paris, from Calvary to the Panthéon, end the Minority of Christianity, and bring us to the end of times announced by Christ] (32). The coming of age of the heretofore "minor" Christianity, inaugurated on the sacrificial altar of 1871, is an extreme example of confusing socialist and Christian teleologies, but it is one that nevertheless occurred, and that may not be that far different from the more subtle messianism of republican politicians and pedagogues, beginning with Ferry. Hureaux, clearly a mystic of sorts, directed his propaganda at Catholics, a fact that also helps to explain his choice of words; he wanted to convert them by presenting republicanism as the Truth that Catholicism had forgotten.

More generally, of course, references to the divinity of Christ and to eternal life are quite incompatible with the secular religion of positivism so often associated with the institution of national education. While positivism and its ancestors in the ideologues of the Revolution (see Part I) are part and parcel of the justification for Third Republic educational policy, there is clearly more to the picture. In the following discussion of the intellectual groundwork for the state's increased involvement in the educational enterprise, I would like to keep in mind the dual nature of the strategy of the Republic. On the surface, it presented a secular ("lay") alternative to the sectarian values that had dominated education for centuries, according to the positivist dogma that all religions are merely dialects of the "mother tongue," which is to say *morale laïque*. In tandem with this manifest strategy was an occult one, in which Christianity was not the enemy to be assimilated, but rather the model to be imitated. From the perspective of this dual strategy, the creation of national education takes on a different meaning than it has in the past.

The subject of this book is in part the Third Republic's attempt, both in theory and in practice, to enlist literature in support of its claim to legitimacy. In brief: literariness, the quality that is axiomatically inherent to canonical texts, functions as the source of the manifest aura of authority that sanctions the exercise of political power, especially of that political power which had explicitly relinquished the rule of force in favor of representative democracy. To put it differently, in their attempt to promote and to regulate the notion of literariness, the pedagogues of the Third Republic derived political capital from the exploitation and dissemination of the belief that literature is *sui generis*, that it manifests the absolute yet secular value that alone can provide the state with the means to replace the spiritual authority of organized religion as well as the brute, physical authority of tyranny.

While I argue for the importance for the republican state of establishing a cult of literature, with all that the word "cult" implies about literature's status as an autonomous institution, the environment in which this establishment occurred was in many ways hostile. The First Republic radicals' suspicion of the written word, which translated into a denial of value to literary works of the past, and their failed attempt to create a new literary tradition based upon a utopian belief in the transparency of language, resurfaced in somewhat altered form during the Third Republic. Much of the new resistance to literature occurred under the banner of "utilitarianism," as I explain in part III, and was nourished by the strong demand for practical education in the wake of the 1871 defeat, partly blamed on the lack of adequate education:[11] the imperial soldiers may have lacked skills that would have made a difference in the field, such the ability to read maps or understand German, but certainly their inability to read Latin or French literature was not a factor.

The resistance to a literature-based curriculum was well rooted in republican pedagogy, and not simply a temporary aberration of First Republic ideology. In 1874, for example, François Enne produced a

luxurious, illustrated folio entitled *Le Panthéon Républicain*, a hagiogra-
phy of all the secular heroes that the nascent Third Republic could enlist
for its cause. Who is the first and greatest of those heroes? Not, strictly
speaking, a *philosophe*, much less a French classical author. In fact, not
primarily an author at all, nor even a Frenchman: George Washington,
"le héros le plus fameux des temps modernes. . . . On chercherait vaine-
ment parmi les hommes de l'antiquité quelqu'un à qui il pût être
comparé" [the greatest hero of modern times . . . . One would search in
vain among the men of antiquity for one comparable to him] (13).
What is most interesting is not the fact that Washington would be the
greatest republican hero (after all, what better way to avoid objection
from French political factions than by putting forward a person who was
never directly involved in French politics?), but rather the reasons Enne
gave for his position at the top:

> Rien n'est plus simple et touchant que la vie de Washington. . . . Son
> esprit était peu propre à la culture des lettres; il s'appliqua tout de suite
> aux notions exactes de l'arpentage et à l'agriculture. . . . Il s'agissait de
> parcourir le désert, de défricher les savanes, de les mesurer et d'en hâter
> la colonisation.

> [Nothing is simpler and more moving than Washington's life. . . . His
> mind was ill suited to the cultivation of letters; he devoted himself imme-
> diately to the exact sciences of surveying and agriculture. . . . It was a
> matter of exploring the desert, clearing the plains, to measure them and
> to hasten their colonization.] (13)

Washington's skills as surveyor and landowner were in measuring and
cultivating actual, geographical space, not the virtual space created by
the written word; similarly, the history of education in the Third
Republic is full of attempts to place objects before words, reality ahead
of literature. It is not difficult to recognize, in this obsession of republican propaganda and pedagogy with material objects, a descendant of the
old aristocratic fear of education's potential to drive peasants from the
land. What is emphatically not attributable to aristocratic values,
however, is the concomitant denigration of literary sensibility ("son
esprit était peu propre à la culture des lettres"). While literature was
certainly inaccessible to the masses, the associations with literature under
the culture of the *ancien régime* were positive. For the first time perhaps
in French public discourse, literariness took on a negative connotation
during the Revolution and, as Enne's book suggests, among its heirs. It
is time now to look at just how the Third Republic managed this legacy,

and in the process operated a complicated form of redemption upon the literary corpus and the values it represents, first in the primary curriculum.

On March 28, 1882, the law establishing the curriculum for mandatory schooling for girls and boys between ages six and thirteen was passed, and the list of subjects was as follows:

> L'instruction morale et civique; la langue et les éléments de la littérature française; la géographie, particulièrement celle de la France; l'histoire, particulièrement celle de la France jusqu'à nos jours; quelques notions usuelles de droit et d'économie politique; les éléments des sciences naturelles, physiques, et mathématiques; leurs applications à l'agriculture, à l'hygiène, aux arts industriels, travaux manuels et usage des outils des principaux métiers; les éléments du dessin, du modelage et de la musique; la gymnastique; pour les garçons, les exercices militaires; pour les filles, les travaux à l'aiguille.

> [Moral and civic instruction; language and elements of French literature; geography, especially of France; history, especially of France to the present; some common notions of law and political economy; the elements of natural sciences, physics and mathematics; their application to agriculture, hygiene, industrial arts, manual labor and the use of tools of the principal trades; elements of drawing, clay modeling and music; gymnastics; military exercises for boys; needlework for girls.] (Quoted in Palméro 1958: 312.)

The above list closely follows the report produced at the request of Jules Ferry by Paul Bert in 1879, which states that the subjects for obligatory education are listed in order of importance. One can therefore safely assert that this is not simply an enumeration of required subjects, but represents an order of priority that could easily be converted into a *plan d'études*, or practical curriculum.

The amount of time devoted to a subject in the daily schedule of schoolchildren is a complementary way of determining its position in the official hierarchy. In 1871, minister of Public instruction Jules Simon published an *emploi du temps* or class schedule adapted from the influential plan created by Octave Gréard, the *vice-recteur* for the *Académie* of Paris and the rest of the department of the Seine (Giolitto 1983–84: 222–6), which he wanted all schools to adapt to their own local needs and circumstances. Simon's ideal school day begins with 30 minutes of prayer and religious instruction (time that will later be devoted to *Instruction morale* under the new laws[12]), followed by two and one half hours of French grammar, dictation, reading, and recitation. The afternoon is divided among arithmetic (one and one half hours), history and geography (one hour), and, finally, "*leçons de choses*" for a quarter of an hour, with some variation in the schedule depending on the level of the students (Giolitto 1983–84: 227). Although the government generally failed to enforce the adoption of a uniform schedule by every school, and by 1882 had relaxed its requirements in response to local resistance to standardization of the timetable (230), the effort put into the creation of an ideal distribution of required topics over the course of the school day was clear evidence of the relative importance of each topic: religious or moral instruction was the most important topic in terms of the chronology of the school day, and French language and literature the most important in terms of the amount of time they occupied in the schedule.

In the list of required subjects in the 1882 law, civics and morality are first, supplanting the pro-Catholic 1850 "*loi Falloux*" that had mandated religious education, since national education had to present itself both as a means of socialization and as a secular religion; French language and literature are second, for what I would argue are similar reasons. Geography, in the 1882 list, is placed ahead of history, the opposite of the time-honored tradition of designating both disciplines as "*histoire-géo*"; though perhaps considered no more important than history, it might have been placed first due to the belief that the Franco-Prussian War was lost because the Prussians knew the geography of France, whereas the French soldiers did not. Science appears at or close to the bottom of the list; evidently, it was not believed to be on the same level of importance as the other components of the program.

The roughly two and one half hours devoted in primary schools each morning to the study of French, according to Jules Simon's *plan d'études*, required also more precise organization. In the first three years of primary education, in which acquisition of literacy was the primary objective, repetitive exercises dominated the schedule: dictation, recitation, and copying. That does not imply that students were not being initiated into the French literary tradition. Quite the contrary: the use of literary texts even at the most elementary level, and especially at the advanced elementary level, ensured that some "éléments de littérature," in the words of the 1882 legislation, would form the very basis of the students' education. I conclude this chapter with the role of literature in republican pedagogy, as it evolved from the practice of purely repetitive exercises in early education, to more sophisticated, though no less ritualistic practices in the advanced stages of mandatory education.

It was not until January 18, 1887 that a list of required subjects specifically for early primary education, as distinguished from general, mandatory education, was instituted by ministerial decree. The differences between this list and the one in the 1882 legislation are revealing:

> L'instruction primaire comprend: L'enseignement moral et civique; la lecture et l'écriture; la langue française; le calcul et le système métrique; l'histoire et la géographie, spécialement de la France; les leçons de choses et les premières notions scientifiques; les éléments du dessin, du chant et du travail manuel, principalement dans les applications à l'agriculture (travaux d'aiguilles dans les écoles de filles).

> [Primary instruction includes: Moral and civic instruction; reading and writing; French language; arithmetic and the metric system; history and geography, especially of France; concrete instruction and the first notions of science; elements of drawing, singing and manual labor, especially in its agricultural applications (needlework in girls' schools).] (Quoted in Palméro 1958: 320)

The most obvious change in the list is the absence of literature, replaced by reading and writing, and the addition of "*leçons de choses*" in the spot occupied by the sciences. Based on the language of the laws themselves, and upon which the actual pedagogy in the schools was to develop, the crucial first few years of mandatory education were devoted to reading and writing, understood independently of their literary function, and to study the world through the examination and interpretation of common objects. A conscious suppression of literature's role in primary education had occurred, as well as a promotion of *enseignement concret*.

Traditionally, "*leçons de choses*" was a method of acquainting children with everyday items ("*objets usuels*") and natural objects ("*productions naturelles*"), ostensibly as a means of preparing for subsequent instruction in the natural and physical sciences (*Nouveau Petit Robert*). With roots in Ancient Greece, and a large role in the early education of Rabelais's *Gargantua*, "*leçons de choses*" had more than enough historical antecedents to serve as an alternative to, or groundwork for, the study of literary texts. Empirical methods of instruction were especially popular during the Reformation, gave the German *Realschule* its name, and were a tenet of the influential pedagogy of Comenius, the seventeenth-century Czech theorist of pedagogy whose writings were thoroughly and favorably presented in Ferdinand Buisson's *Dictionnaire* discussed in chapter 4 (Palméro 1958: passim). From Plato to Luther and beyond, a single thread unifies the tradition of "concrete instruction": the desire to guard against the potential of words to become autonomous from physical reality. Initiation to the literary did in fact occur in spite of this philosophical precaution, as we will see. However, it first had to be introduced with a dire warning: literature divorced from utilitarian goals and expressing only its own literariness, posed a threat.

Understanding the reasons for literature's danger and the means that the school developed to mitigate it, requires an examination of the practice of literary pedagogy in the republican primary school. After the discussion in chapter 2 of the theoretical groundwork established by the newly credited pedagogy specialists of the Republic, in this section I will examine the surviving evidence from the classroom: the actual materials used by primary teachers for the implementation of the new national mission.

The teleological beliefs implicit in Third Republic policy appear most clearly in the propaganda designed to promote the new school laws, many of which were collected by Henri Marion for a special anthology published for the 1889 *Exposition Universelle* by the *Imprimerie Nationale*. Marion's introduction to his anthology, *Le mouvement des idées pédagogiques en France* (The Evolution of Pedagogical Ideas in France), describes the "end of history" in the advent of the Republic:

> Mais quel bienfait, le jour où, de l'école où elle germe aujourd'hui se sera répandue dans toute la nation cette pensée, aussi féconde que simple, qu'au-dessus des partis il y a la patrie, qu'au-dessus et indépendamment du *credo* religieux, souverainement respectable à coup sûr et même la grande affaire d'un chacun, le premier et commun devoir de tous est d'être d'honnêtes gens dans les relations humaines et des citoyens dans la cité.
>
> [What benefit it will be on the day when, from the school where it is now germinating, this idea as fertile as it is simple will spread throughout the nation: that above political parties there is the fatherland, that above and independent of religious belief which is, to be sure, respectable and even the great concern of each individual, the first and common duty of all is to be honest in human relations and citizens in the metropolis.] (1: 33)

Marion's vision clearly subsumes, and does not replace, the sectarian religious beliefs that are "la grande affaire d'un chacun," but that cannot fulfill the destiny of humans to become citizens in the most elevated sense of the term.

Before the advent of the Third Republic, it looked as if the preservation of the educational role of the Church and the democratization of the schools were compatible aims. During the Second Empire, the conservative strategy was to demonize the *laïcistes* so as to make Catholicism appear to coincide with the general interest. Jules Simon, one of the few Republicans who openly espoused the principle of

Catholicism's role in public affairs, and who was *ministre de l'Instruction publique* during the transition years between Empire and Republic (1870–73), defended this view in *L'école*, a comprehensive history of education since the *ancien régime*. Published in 1865, it remained popular until the end of the century, during which time it stood as the symbol of the gap between Simon's Catholic allegiance and his professed republicanism. One of the fears Simon tried to exploit was that, under the guise of separation of Church and state, the reformers would banish from the classroom, not only the clergy, but any and every reference to God or religion.

> L'histoire des voeux monastiques ne contient rien d'aussi impossible et d'aussi contraire à la nature que ce que vous entreprenez. Ah! Vous ne voulez pas d'un homme qui a fait voeu d'obéir à un autre! Eh bien! regardez à qui vous obéissez, dans quelle entreprise vous vous engagez, à quelle abjection vous descendez. Et les grands écrivains de tous les pays et de tous les temps, nos grands écrivains français des trois grands siècles, qu'en allez-vous faire? On les lira, quand on sera diplômé; mais vous les bannirez de l'école et des bibliothèques scolaires. Voilà une belle éducation et un beau patriotisme!

> [The history of monastic vows contains nothing as impossible and as contrary to nature as what you are undertaking. So! You don't want a man who has made a vow to obey another! Well then! Look whom you are obeying, in what enterprise you are engaging yourself, to what depths you are descending. And the great writers of all countries and all time, our great French writers of the three great centuries, what will you do with them? One will read them when one has a diploma [the *baccalauréat*]; but you will banish them from schools and school libraries. Some education, and some patriotism!] (xxvi–xxvii)

To banish God from the classroom would also be, according to Simon, to banish literature, an act even more contrary to nature than the monastic vows of celibacy and obedience. His alarm at the prospect of a godless, a-literary classroom accompanies a rather shrewd parallel between national education and the priesthood: "on les lira quand on sera diplômé," he says of France's literary texts under the threatened regime of *instruction laïque*. That is the fear that Simon wanted to exploit: that the republican school would resemble the Church in its opposition to direct exposure of young minds to the source of the divine, forbidding the unmediated study (reading) of Scripture (literature) until ordination (certification) has taken place.

Simon betrays the fact that he did not understand or, more likely, that he purposely misrepresented the program of educational reformers, confusing the extreme policy proposals of the First Republic with the much more moderate ones of the majority of the contemporary republican faction. Rather than banishing the authors of the "three great centuries" (sixteenth, seventeenth, and eighteenth), the Republic would depend on them far more than the Church ever had during its monopoly on education. In retrospect, Simon's fears appear unjustified, unless of course one wants to be strict as to what constitutes "reading" French literary "texts": we see in chapters 4 and 5 that French literature took on ever-greater importance at all levels of education, which did not however imply direct access by schoolchildren to the texts themselves.

The Church had its own authority that proceeded *ex cathedra*, and for which the content of school programs it administered was purely accessory. The state, on the other hand, would rely on the content of education to reveal its own sources of legitimate power, and in this process of revelation, institute the same power. "Great" authors of the past regardless of their inspiration would serve that purpose, because it was not the content of literature (religious or other) that mattered, but its form. Simon may well have recognized that the concept of "literariness," manifested by the texts most representative of "literary French," would become the most potent weapons of the new regime, and that it was important to deny them use of this weapon.

Simon shows his acute awareness of the real issue underlying the culture wars, before most people were even aware that a war existed:

> Il s'est produit depuis la révolution un certain nombre de sectes dont le but était de rendre la propriété accessible aux prolétaires, non par l'économie et le travail, mais par une transformation radicale de la propriété. Or, reconstruire à fond la propriété, quand elle est établie sur le droit comme aujourd'hui, et non sur le privilège comme à l'époque de la féodalité, c'est la détruire . . . c'est détruire la société elle-même.

> [Since the revolution, a certain number of sects have arisen the goal of which was to make property accessible to workers, not through thriftiness and work, but by a radical transformation of property. In fact, to redefine property from the ground up, when it is based as it is today on law and not on privilege, as in the feudal period, is to destroy it . . . it is to destroy society itself.] (11–12)

In this attack on the radical Left, Simon compares the principle of redistribution of wealth to the "education without God" being prepared by the leaders of the future Republic. Both are illegitimate; the first, because wealth is no longer a matter of privilege, as it was at the time of the Revolution, but founded in law. It is no more legitimate to rob the bourgeois of his legal rights to property than it is to deny authority to the culture of the past, both abuses of power that the legislators of the First Republic wanted to commit, but not those of the Third.

The link between education and property is that democratization of education implies redistribution of wealth. Not only are culture and property linked causally (free access to culture leads to wider distribution of property), they are linked metaphorically as well: culture *is* property, and its radical redistribution destroys its very nature. This is both an elitist argument and a conservative one: culture can only be accessible to the happy few if it is to avoid desecration (hence destruction), and the institutions of society have the function of preserving, not changing, the means of access to property/culture. The fact that Simon made his arguments in 1865, against a republican pedagogy that did not yet officially exist, helps to explain the apparent error of his aim, which seems directed at the *conventionnels* such as Le Peletier, Masuyer, and Petit rather than to the actual founders of the Third Republic. Of course, it may well be that Ferry and his associates took their cue from Simon when they finally got around to instituting national education, and let God in through the back door of literature. This occurred not only by listing "duties toward God" in the mandatory curriculum of national education (language that Simon himself had fought for passionately), but also by charging literary pedagogy with a spiritual function it had not previously carried.

In spite of his strong stance against *laïcisme*, Jules Simon provides one of the primary justifications of the Third Republic: by distinguishing change in the distribution of wealth under a feudal system of privileges, from change under a system based on legal rights, he shows exactly how the republicans of the 1870s divorced themselves from the violent revolutionary forces that brought about the First and Second Republics. These were republicans *without* a revolution, and their plan did not involve radical redistribution, either of culture or property. Their plan was to take control of French cultural identity and, under the pretense of making it accessible to the masses, actually preserve its inviolability. Extreme cultural conservatism under the guise of progressive reform is the key to understanding the role of literature in the school during the entire history of modern French republicanism.

The philosopher Alain (pseudonym of Emile-Auguste Chartier, 1868–1951) who, like many French intellectuals, had experience teaching in the *lycée* early in his career, took up the mantle of positivist ideology, not to say religion, in the latter part of the Third Republic. In a series of essays gathered under the title *Propos sur l'éducation* (1976, first edition

1932) the notion that the school is a church in which students practice the cult of the Republic attains its greatest development. Alain is able to look back on 40 years of republican education, and especially on the role of literature and language in the construction of national identity, and the salvation of the individual through the assumption of that identity.

> [L]a puissance de la poésie est en ceci, à chaque lecture, que d'abord, avant de nous instruire, elle nous dispose par les sons et le rythme, selon un modèle universel. . . . La grande poésie a prise sur tous. Les plus rudes compagnons veulent la plus grande poésie.

> [The power of poetry resides in the fact that first, upon every reading, before it instructs us, it organizes us through sound and rhythm according to a universal model. . . . Great poetry has a hold on everybody. The most primitive journeymen need the greatest poetry.] (50–1)

The primacy of poetry among the rituals practiced within the schools justifies itself by providing access to a "universal model." "Nos premières idées passent donc à l'état de métaphores, et en même temps le progrès de tout esprit se fait de l'abstrait au concret" [Our first ideas therefore take the form of metaphors, and simultaneously the progress of every mind is a movement from the abstract to the concrete] (82). At first, it would seem that Alain's sanctification of literature as a mode of access to the realm of universal form is diametrically opposed to Ferry's republican desire to base instruction in reality and to proceed empirically and inductively in all subjects, including language and literature. But the importance of abstraction in pedagogy according to Alain contradicts the principle of the *leçon de choses* only superficially; for it is absolutely essential to the universalist aspirations of the school, and to the apotheosis of republican values to which they lead:

> Il s'est fait un grand changement, par l'école laïque, si grand que nous le pouvons juger à peine. Un peuple qu'on ne mène plus par la peur c'est quelque chose de tellement neuf dans l'histoire que les politiques en sont effrayés; mais patience; je vois paraître une génération de politiques qui n'auront pas peur de ne plus faire peur; et on verra une autre métaphysique, sans peur, toute poétique et toute bonne.

> [A great change has occurred due to the secular school, so great that we can barely appreciate. A people no longer ruled by fear is something so new in history that politicians are afraid of it; but let us be patient; I can see a generation of politicians appear that will not be afraid of no longer making people afraid; and one will see a new metaphysics, without fear, entirely poetical and entirely good.] (218–19)

Metaphysics "without fear" is Alain's version of the republican answer to Catholicism and absolutism. Politically, the achievement of republicanism is to replace *la loi du plus fort* by an ostensibly participatory government based on individual rights rather than state power. The need for all previous regimes in French history to base their power on coercion has, for the first time, been eliminated. The millenarian tone of Ferry's definition of the Republic as an end to the chaos of history finds an echo in Alain's anticipation of "une métaphysique . . . toute poétique et toute bonne."

"Poétique" in this context is more than a characterization of the new order as one that is harmonious and pleasing, as all ideal systems should be. As Alain pointed out in another essay in *Propos sur l'éducation*, poetry is literary heritage, which is to become the very means by which the state exercises its unquestionable authority:

> Napoléon . . . a exprimé en deux mots ce que tout homme doit savoir le mieux possible: géométrie et latin. Elargissons; entendons par latin l'étude des grandes oeuvres, et principalement de toute la poésie humaine. Alors, tout est dit.

> [Napoleon . . . expressed in two words what every man must know as well as possible: geometry and Latin. Let us elaborate: understand by Latin the study of great works, and primarily all of human poetry. Then, all is said.] (49)

"Latin," in other words, means "literature," a conflation of terms that is fundamental for understanding the competition between Latin and French that was to play out in the school, especially the *lycée*, in the decades following the republican reforms. Latin for Alain is emphatically not the empty exercises of the Jesuits, for whom the concept of national culture did not apply. Taken together, the two quotes above from *Propos sur l'éducation* summarize the complicated connection between literary texts and the power of the state as it operates within the school. Politics, religion, and education merge perfectly in the vision that Alain, in the 1920s and 1930s, was still able to promote in the wake of Comte, Ferry, Renan, and many others.

In the two chapters that follow, I examine first the texts written by the cadre of specialists entrusted by the Republic with the duty of laying the theoretical groundwork for the teaching of students at the primary and secondary levels; then, I examine a representative group of textbooks or *manuels*, mostly ones created for the teaching of French language and literature, for the purpose of comparing the state monopoly of pedagogy in its practice with the principles on which it is based.

CHAPTER 4

THE FATHERS OF PEDAGOGICAL SCIENCE, GABRIEL COMPAYRÉ AND FERDINAND BUISSON

The History of Education as History of Religion: Gabriel Compayré

In 1869, the *Académie des sciences morales et politiques* announced a contest for the best essay on the history of educational doctrines in France. Because of the dominant role of religious orders and sects in the philosophy of education, and the common vocabulary of religion and education (e.g., canon, seminary, discipline), it was clear that such a history would also be a synthesis of the major doctrines of Christianity throughout the centuries. Attention to the historical and social impact of religion had become one of the central activities of the positivist revolution, and it is important to recall the context in which the call for a history of educational doctrines arose. Ernest Renan had published his *Vie de Jésus* in 1863, calling for a new religion in which science would replace the doctrines of traditional faith, and positivism was to become the basis of Gustave Lanson's literary history. In the wake of Charles Darwin, works such as Claude Bernard's *Introduction à l'étude de la médecine expérimentale* (1865) reinforced the claim that science, unlike Christianity, did not require the agency of "grace" or "faith" (the terms of Luther's return to Christ without the intermediary of the Church) in order to exercise its authority. By reducing religion to the status of a social phenomenon susceptible to scientific methods of inquiry, positivism became an important factor in the trend toward the rule of republican *laïcité*. The contest, held in the waning years of the Second Empire, was to herald the end of religious domination of education by relegating it to the pages of history.

It was not until 1879 that the eventual winner of the contest, Gabriel Compayré, published with Hachette his essay: *Histoire critique des doctrines de l'éducation en France depuis le seizième siècle* (Critical History of Doctrines of Education in France since the Sixteenth Century). By now, both republicanism and positivism had firmly staked out their overlapping positions in the mainstream of French society. Whereas under the Second Empire, Jules Ferry had been a member of one of a range of factions in the republican opposition, he had become, as *ministre de l'Instruction publique*, the leader of the ideological avant-garde of the regime that founded itself on the constitution of 1877. Compayré, along with many others in the growing field of the history and the philosophy of education, participated in this advent of moderate republicanism by fighting for the scientific legitimacy of the republican school. It is an exaggeration to say that Compayré helped more than any other to define the terms of the debate between *laïcité* and Catholicism as it was to unfold during the last quarter of the nineteenth century, but his book was one of the first attempts to place education on a scientific footing.

Compayré's book is an impressive work, all the more so because there were so few histories of the philosophy of education, written in the prepositivist era, which might have served as models. Appropriately and predictably, he puts religion at the center of his study, in particular the Protestant challenge to Catholicism. It is tempting, if overly schematic, to see the conflict between Catholicism and Protestantism in Compayré as a veiled allusion to the contemporary conflict between Catholicism and republicanism; he returns again and again to Protestant spiritual and educational principles as the basis of republican education. In his first chapter, for example, he recounts Rabelais's criticism that the Scholastic pedagogy of Abélard was too abstract, sacrificing reality, life, and even the organic unity of classical texts on the altar of neo-Aristotelian logic (50). Although Calvin failed in his attempt to enlist Rabelais in the cause of the Reformation, Compayré claims that by the sixteenth century the battle lines in the field of education were drawn, and that until the nineteenth century, they followed the pattern set by the wars of religion (66). It may be stretching the facts to make an analogy between the republican fight against Jesuit formalism and the humanist reaction against the medieval university, but that is exactly what Compayré did. Jules Ferry was to repeat the argument that Compayré attributed to Rabelais in an April 1880 speech on the two great shortcomings of rhetorical (Jesuit) literary pedagogy: its dependence on memory, and "l'attachement excessif au maniement des mots au détriment de l'analyse des faits ou de la réflexion" [excessive attention to manipulation of words, at the expense of analysis of facts or of thought] (quoted in Gaillard 1989: 473). The area in which these shortcomings were most apparent according to Ferry was the teaching of French, too often reduced to grammatical rules and spelling: "J'appelle fausses méthodes grammaticales celles qui ne tirent pas la règle de l'exemple . . . celles qui ne procèdent pas du concret à l'abstrait. . . ." [I call false grammatical methods those that do not derive the rule from example . . . those that do not proceed from the concrete to the abstract. . . .] (474). In Compayré as well as in Ferry, one can follow the twists and turns of the Revolution's suspicion of literature: for Compayré, it has its roots in the Renaissance attack on the abstraction of scholastic philosophy, and for Ferry, it manifests itself as an attack on the deductive and formalistic approach to language.

One cannot stress too much the exemplary importance that the religious debates of the Middle Ages, Renaissance, and Reformation had for the founders of the school of the Republic. Compayré was among the first to view this era from the perspective of nineteenth-century political and spiritual conflicts, and in so doing he inaugurated a tradition: Ferdinand Buisson's monumental *Dictionnaire de pédagogie*, to which I turn later in this chapter, also places a heavy emphasis on the excessive abstraction of Abélard's Sorbonne, countered during the Renaissance by Rabelais and Luther, only to reemerge as the formalism of Jesuit pedagogy. This same dialectical plot structure attained the status of dogma in Emile Durkheim's major contribution to the science of pedagogy, *L'Evolution pédagogique en France*, based on a course he taught in 1904 and 1905, and in which he distinguishes two major tendencies in the philosophical origins of modern pedagogy during the Renaissance: the encyclopedic, exemplified by Rabelais, and the formal ("le dire plutôt que la science" [discourse rather than knowledge]), exemplified by Montaigne (264–5). The subsequent Jesuit monopoly over education meant that the formal tendency prevailed, constructing, for better and for worse, the minds of all the great names of the seventeenth and eighteenth centuries (274). Supremely conscious of the shortcomings of Jesuit pedagogy and its many emulators, Durkheim deplored the ahistoricity of "cette affirmation que les vérités cardinales de notre morale ont trouvé leur expression définitive chez les sages de l'antiquité" [this claim that the cardinal truths of our morality found their definitive expression among the wise men of antiquity] (373), and calls for a pedagogy rooted in history and oriented toward science that society had yet to develop (380). The fact that Condorcet, the John the Baptist to Ferry's Jesus Christ, had also called for such a pedagogy, and that it had not been realized more than a century later when Durkheim wrote these words, suggests that the rhetoric of the educational reformers of the Third Republic was very different from what they accomplished.

Compayré was the first not only to write down the plot that Durkheim and others were to adopt unquestioningly in subsequent years, he was also the first to call for a final resolution of the Reformation–Counter Reformation pedagogical debate. He praised Erasmus for having elevated the cult of books to such a high level (127), and the Protestant convert Ramus for having continued the good work of Rabelais and Montaigne by directly challenging the authority of the neo-Aristotelian Sorbonne inherited from Abélard (135). Compayré places great significance on Charles II's appointment of Ramus to the *Collège de France*, the size and influence of which grew at a much faster rate than the Sorbonne during the last half of the sixteenth century, vindicating his anti-scholastic concept of a natural, practical (and hence quasi-positivistic) logic. With Ramus, France came very close to the pedagogical ideal explicitly called for three centuries later by the academics of the Republic, and it is no coincidence, according to Compayré, that he became a Protestant.

Compayré's history recounts major setbacks in the road toward the advent of republican pedagogy as well: in 1587 the Jesuits attacked the Protestant ascendancy in education with the *Ratio Studiorum*, the treatise based on principles set forth by Ignatius of Loyola himself that determined pedagogical practice for those students who continued their studies beyond the First Communion, and was to continue to do so for centuries. While admitting that it usually attracted praise, even from non-Catholics, for its revolutionary emphasis on active rather than passive instruction, Compayré saw the *Ratio* as a huge step backward toward Scholasticism and the worst sort of dogmatic pedagogy. The Jesuit teachers not only reestablished Greek and Latin in the position of unquestioned superiority over French (an issue to which I return in part III), they stressed fluency and rhetorical skills over the reading of literary and philosophical texts, reducing the ancients to "simplement une école de beau langage" [simply a school of beautiful speech [rhetoric]] (192). When he accuses the Jesuits of encouraging "[non] pas de[s] connaissances positives, [mais] des exercices purement formels" [not positive knowledge, [but rather] purely formal exercises] (194), Compayré brings the debate right into the present, subtly reminding the reader that this aberrant pedagogy still held sway in secondary education in general, not just in the Jesuit *collèges*.[1] In particular, Jesuit education served as a means of social distinction, since it became the favorite schooling of the aristocracy and the untitled elite, and still serves as a paradigm for the training of the modern French meritocracy.

Sectarian tension continued to determine the structure of Compayré's historical narrative. As it continues its torturous but ultimately ascending path toward the present, his book recounts how the seventeenth century was the scene of yet more conflicts that anticipated the great battles of the Third Republic. In 1643, the Jansenists founded the *Petites écoles* of Port-Royal, and immediately distinguished themselves from the already all-powerful Jesuit pedagogy by squarely placing French in the center of the curriculum, restoring its rightful position as an appropriate vehicle for literary and philosophical discourse. Furthermore, they favored education for girls as well as boys, and in spite of their "confiance excessive dans le secours divin" [excessive trust in divine providence] (281), they were clearly deserving of the role of precursors that Compayré was anxious to assign to them. Though the Jansenist experiment was short-lived, "les vaincus du passé sont souvent les victorieux de l'avenir" [the losers of the past are often the victors of the future] (246). Clearly, the implication was that the time for the victory of the Jansenists was finally at hand, although it was regrettable that none of them were around to enjoy it. In particular, the conflict over the relative position of French and Latin in the curriculum was an important one for the Republic to resolve. "La question du latin," an intense polemic which pitted conservatives against a radical left-wing, with the republicans in the crossfire, broke out just a few years after the publication of Compayré's essay, and I examine the controversy and its sequels in part III. It is important to read Compayré's characterization (and exaggeration) of earlier conflicts in light of the impending struggle that Jules Ferry and his army of academics knew they had to face, and for which they were bracing themselves. Compayré set the scene by assigning roles in a drama whose final act was about to unfold: the Catholics, with their abstract Aristotelianism combined with Jesuit elitism were the enemy; the Protestants and the Jansenists of Port-Royal, who lost the battle against Church and state, were the precursors whose ideas were ultimately about to prevail.

In their landmark work *Reading and Writing: Literacy in France from Calvin to Jules Ferry* (1977, trans. 1982), François Furet and Jacques Ozouf also see the school as the site of conflict between Catholics and Protestants, long before it became the point of contention between Church and state. In so doing, Furet and Ozouf continued the tradition of Gabriel Compayré and Ferdinand Buisson who placed the wars of religion at the center of pedagogy's historical evolution, especially in the transmission of language and literature. In the seventeenth century, Furet and Ozouf point out that it is the state that resisted the spread of education (believing that an educated populace would be much harder to govern), and it is the Reformation and Counter-Reformation that fought for control over it. For Catholics, at first, all the education necessary for most people centered on the Catechism, while for Protestants, actual reading became an essential component of spiritual devotion: "Luther made necessary what Gutenberg had made possible. . . . [The Bible] replaced the immense body of learned and inaccessible commentaries on the Scriptures by the text of the Word of God itself, now made available to the faithful in their own language" (59). In order to counterbalance Protestant schools, Catholics were forced to increase their commitment to education, as well as to develop a pedagogy that would consciously avoid the danger of competing with the authority of the clergy. One conclusion of Furet and Ozouf is that the history of education in France is, on one level, the survival of Protestantism, or "the posthumous success of defeated protestantism" (62), a conclusion that exactly echoes the one reached by Compayré in 1879. The identification of republican *laïcité* with a modern, hence secularized Protestantism is a recurring motif of the literature on the period.[2] As Furet and Ozouf put it: "Between the initial project of restoring to each child the means of his salvation, and that of merely giving him access to an urban model of socialization, the school probably ceased to be a mystique [or mysticism] to become a policy" (66). The question is whether the passage from the mystical to the political represents as much of a downward shift as Furet and Ozouf suggest, and whether one can limit the secularization of education to a mere "access to an urban model of socialization." Can "salvation," in other words, have meaning in the social and political as well as the spiritual realms?

In the explosion of literature on the history and science of pedagogy under the Third Republic, whether authored by Protestants or not, there was a good deal of sympathy for Protestant educational reforms of the past. Sometimes contemporary pedagogues would see their mission as a variation on a Protestant style of ministry. Félix Pécaut, one of several prominent Third Republic scientists of education who happened to be Protestant, ran the *Ecole Normale Supérieure* for women in Fontenay-aux Roses (cf. the rule of celibacy that I mentioned earlier), and was famous for his practice of addressing homilies to the students at the beginning of each day, making the school into a temple of secular morality (Françoise Mayeur 1981: 547).

One must examine carefully the reason for the continued relevance of Protestantism in the study of Third Republic educational policies, as it is not so much a matter of the religious affiliations of its greatest proponents, as of the fact that the French public perceived them as acting upon Protestant principles. Françoise Mayeur, in her history of education in the nineteenth century, points out that the perception of a Protestant stranglehold on educational reform was so strong that it defined a large part of the terms of the debate: "Quelles que soient les distances prises par Pécaut et Buisson à l'égard du 'berceau religieux où leur âme a grandi tout d'abord,' leur oeuvre et leur pensée sont ressenties comme fidèles à l'inspiration de la Réforme" [Whatever distance Pécaut and Buisson placed between them and "the religious cradle in which their souls first evolved" [quoting the words of contemporary Protestant theologian Auguste Sabatier], their work and thought are perceived as being faithful to the spirit of the Reformation] (547). Mayeur also demonstrates that the relative weakness of Protestantism in France is actually one explanation for its association with educational reform: there were so few Protestant schools in France that they had "nothing to lose" by backing the secular forces of the Republic (232).

Most recent scholarship downplays the Protestant affiliation of people like Pécaut, Buisson, Steeg, and others to assert that the inherently Protestant aspects of Republican education would have emerged in any case. Old-fashioned sectarianism, according to which the school would simply be the new locus for the wars of religion, played no role in the reforms. Instead, Protestantism merely provided a historical precedent for the illusion of a republican challenge to traditional, which is to say Catholic, methods of guarding the sacred. The similarity of republican pedagogy to Protestantism does not arise directly from the religious backgrounds of political leaders, but is quite simply inherent in the nature of any challenge to religious authority. In that sense, both the Reformation and the Revolution provided the Third Republic with examples, and even inspiration, for its own self-representation as a moral as well as political force. But that does not transform Ferry and company into Protestants, and even less into revolutionaries. On the contrary, the thesis I argue in the following chapters is that the school of the Third Republic, in its rivalry with Catholic education, eventually turns into an avatar of Catholicism. French public education is not denominational, so much is certain; but if one wants to see a philosophical parallel between the school of the Republic and the exercise of a particular religion, then I claim that one must look beyond the superficial similarities with Protestantism, similarities that the founders of national education themselves placed in the foreground, and see instead that the Protestant (and positivist) models serve merely as decoys.

Over and over in the nineteenth-century literature on education, the religious conflicts of past centuries prove to be the context for debates over pedagogy. Since the eighteenth century, the wars of religion that had divided the French population for so long gave way to the political tension between Left and Right. The issue of education became the primary link between the political, materialist nineteenth century and the religious past. It was therefore natural that the opposition between Catholic and Protestant, and sectarianism among Catholics, should have been resuscitated during the creation of national education under the Third Republic. This time the conflicts over the definition, transmission, and accessibility of culture could finally emerge from the shadows of the outdated theological structures in which they dwelt previously. Compayré's book concludes with praise for la Louis René de la Chalotais's *Essai d'éducation nationale* (1763), which calls for the establishment of a national religion, so as to end once and for all the foreign monopoly on spiritual authority (a perennial nationalist argument against Catholic education): "Jamais, même aux époques révolutionnaires, on n'a vu affirmer, avec autant de vivacité et de force que dans les écrits de la Chalotais, l'incompatibilité qui existe entre une éducation vraiment civile et nationale et des éducateurs dont le chef est à Rome" [Never, even during revolutionary times, has one seen the incompatibility that exists between a truly civic and national education and educators whose leader is in Rome expressed with as much energy and power as in the writings of la Chalotais] (249). Though no longer ruled by theological considerations, the debates in the nineteenth century were therefore still religious, at least to the degree that national sovereignty and spiritual authority, both seen as emanating from within the geographical confines of the state, overlap. The law of *laïcité*, with all the justification for the separation of Church and state which the term implies, had its own religious overtones, not all of which stem from Enlightenment deism, the "national religion" advocated by la Chalotais. In reality, the school of the Third Republic announced by Compayré was to be different from the national religion la Chalotais had in mind, and that the First Republic briefly instituted; while it was to emanate from the state, as la Chalotais envisioned, it was to be a religion without God.

Creating the Science of Pedagogy: Ferdinand Buisson's *Dictionnaire de pédagogie*

It is difficult to contain one's admiration for the skill of the "opportunists" of the Third Republic in bringing about their vision of national education and culture. It was absolutely necessary, for example, to support their educational reforms with the growing authority of science.

Such was Compayré's purpose, and also the function of the monumental *Dictionnaire de Pédagogie et d'Instruction Primaire*, under the direction of Ferdinand Buisson. According to Eugen Weber, Buisson's dictionary (and its many revised editions extending well into the twentieth century) became "la bible des instituteurs" (1985: 224). It began appearing in 1882, in the middle of the gradual implementation of Jules Ferry's laws. The fact that these complementary events took place so close in time is no coincidence. For years the academic discipline of education, which usually went by the term *science pédagogique*, had been growing in influence as part of the larger revolution of the social sciences within the university. The claim to scientific objectivity underlying the publication of the *Dictionnaire*, following the founding of the journal *La Revue pédagogique* in 1878[3] was no doubt genuine. With their scientific credentials in good order, the republicans were well equipped to take on the opposition. Even among Catholics, *la science pédagogique* was difficult to ignore. The credibility of the new discipline, which had its chair at the Sorbonne (as already mentioned, occupied by Buisson, who was succeeded by Durkheim in 1902), helped make the transition to a new educational philosophy seem inevitable.

Buisson's *Dictionnaire* is a triumph of republican pedagogical ideology, first simply because it exists. Published between 1882 and 1887 and reprinted and revised many times after that, it provided the scientific justification for the subordination of education to the interests of the state. In the guise of disinterested science and historiography, it presented in accessible form all the arguments that Ferry required for the implementation of his policies. Following is a sampling of articles relevant to this discussion.

Inspired by Compayré's historical study, Buisson and his contributors (of whom Compayré was one of the most important) paid considerable attention to the relationship between religion and education, and to the religious nature of education itself, with a strong degree of sympathy for Protestant principles. The article "Allemagne" is essentially a history of Protestant pedagogy and of Luther's own obsession with universal education, and the article "Bible," by Albert Réville, reminds the reader that it is first and foremost a *text*, and not simply a symbol of the relationship between God and His creatures. Liberal Protestantism, according to the *Dictionnaire*, relativizes the Bible, which is a good thing. It is meant to be *read*, and therefore to contain a meaning which every individual discovers separately, rather than to be transmitted dogmatically from the altar. When Réville states: "Ce que la Bible fait dans l'Eglise, pourquoi ne le ferait-elle pas dans l'école?" [What the

Bible does in Church, why would it not also do in school?] (191) a revealing confusion occurs. What he had just described as the textual (one is tempted to say literary) nature of the Bible is actually contrary to the practice of the Catholic Church. Especially when he vehemently criticizes the Catechism as the wrong way to instruct children in religion (or anything else), one senses that Réville should more accurately have written "église" with a lower-case "e," or simply "temple," implying a Protestant place of worship. The revealing aspect of the apparent confusion here between "Eglise" and "temple" is in the fact that there is a gap between the pedagogical ideal represented here by the "relativization" of the Bible as a text, and actual practice in the schools of the Republic in which the study of literary texts, not scripture, retained far more of the characteristics of catechistic learning, and far less of the individual freedom and responsibility that Réville advocated. If Réville's ideal pedagogy is essentially Protestant, regarding the Bible as a text and literature as the secular version of that same text, he does not follow the consequences of his premise; to do so would place the schoolchild in an unmediated relationship to the text, a practice that no pedagogue of Third Republic schools, public or religious, would tolerate.

The Protestant pastor Théodore Gerold wrote the article "Protestantisme," in which he says nothing about the method of instruction in Protestant schools, but simply points out that they are more closely related to the enterprise of national education because, unlike Catholic schools, they had always advocated education as a universal right (2461–70). Gerold's articles on Luther and his disciple, the pedagogue Melanchthon, are much more specific concerning the primacy of language instruction in Protestant education because, as Luther stated in his 1524 letter "An die Rathsherren" (To the Aldermen), the ability to read and write constitute the "vessel" not only for the word of God, but of each individual's potential for reason, the "sword of reason in the sheath of language." Instruction must therefore emphasize reason over memory, a principle that serves as an ideal historical antecedent for the ostensible mission of the republican school to liberate the individual from arbitrary authority by unleashing his (or even her) capacity to draw conclusions from the moral quandaries in life. The application of this principle to national education in the article "Littérature" is that math and science are inadequate to develop reason, and that "*la langue et les lettres*" are the real foundation of critical thinking, an argument defenders of the humanities continue to make (1600).

The task of attacking Jesuit education in the *Dictionnaire* fell, not surprisingly, to Gabriel Compayré, whose article "Jésuites" repeats the refrain that Jesuit pedagogues, unlike the Protestants, were interested only in education as "une convenance imposée par le rang à certaines classes de la nation" [a propriety imposed on certain classes of the nation by their social rank] (1420). Form and decorum are what counted for the aristocracy, not erudition, with the consequence that classical literary texts were taught only in fragments, distorted so that they would not conflict with Church doctrine:

> [C]e n'étaient pas les auteurs anciens dans leur vérité, dans leur intégrité, que les jésuites faisaient connaître aux jeunes gens. . . . [I]ls espéraient, par les travestissements, par les suppressions qu'ils se permettaient, déguiser assez les auteurs pour que l'élève n'y reconnût pas le vieil esprit humain, l'esprit de la nature. Leur rêve était de transformer les auteurs païens en propagateurs de la foi.

> [The Jesuits did not teach young people ancient authors in their truth, in their integrity. . . . They hoped, through the distortions and suppressions that they allowed themselves, to disguise these authors so that the student would no longer recognize in them the old human spirit, the spirit of nature. Their dream was to transform pagan authors into propagators of faith.] (1422)

The question one has to ask after reading Compayré's dismissal of Jesuit pedagogy is: how was the republican pedagogy, the advent of which the *Dictionnaire* announces, going to remedy the problem? If one looks for the answer under the entry "Littérature" written by Emile Marguerin, who also happened to be a successful author of literature textbooks, one sees again an attack on Jesuit manuals of rhetoric that teach oratory over reading. In fact, Marguerin comes very close to advocating a pedagogy based on an individual experience of the text similar to the Protestant principle of a personal relationship to God. Instead of fragments presented primarily for the purpose of illustrating aspects of rhetoric, Marguerin proposes teaching literary works in their integrity so as to justify the use of the term "literature," rather than teaching the art of discourse, the foundation of the Jesuit school: "Il importe donc de considérer de bonne heure des oeuvres réelles . . . pas des conventions arbitraires d'auteurs et d'académies, mais des produits spontanés de l'âme humaine dans des conditions sociales déterminées" [It is therefore important early to consider actual works. . . . not arbitrary conventions (created by) authors and academies, but spontaneous productions of the human soul under specific social conditions] (1601–2).

Given the rejection of Jesuit in favor of Protestant pedagogy by the Third Republic, the appeal for teaching real works of literature in their

integrity must be taken very seriously. It is almost too easy to see where the *practice* of literary pedagogy in national education fell short of this goal. In particular, as we see in the discussion of school textbooks in the following chapters, the idea of respecting the integrity of literary texts quickly fell to the wayside. What is more surprising is that the *Dictionnaire* itself betrays the way in which the lofty ideal spelled out above would not come to pass. The article "Poésie" by Félix Pécaut contradicts Marguerin's "Littérature." First there is the tendentious prescription of what sort of poetry is admissible in the school (a prescription that certainly excludes a very large portion of the literary production of the second half of the nineteenth century, which the republican school fiercely criticized at every opportunity): "[U]ne poésie qui soit esprit et non pas simple musique, c'est-à-dire sensation; qui soit simple, largement humaine, et non pas raffinée, aristocratique, érudite; qui soit virile et non pas efféminée; raison et non caprice . . . qui apporte à notre jeune peuple la santé au lieu des rêves morbides" [Poetry that would be spiritual and not simply musical, which is to say sensory; that would be simple, broadly human, and not refined, aristocratic, erudite; that would be virile and not effeminate; rational and not temperamental . . . that would bring health to our youth instead of morbid dreams] (2389). While poetry is finally to be granted its rightful place as the cornerstone of education, it can be only after a long process of selection and elision has taken place: "[Il faut] discerner . . . les pièces qui conviendraient aux divers âges de l'école, et justifier ce choix . . . [et] les retranchements qu'il faudrait parfois opérer, les strophes à retenir ou à écarter, et pour quelles raisons de morale ou de goût" [[One must] distinguish . . . those pieces that would be suitable for the various school ages and justify one's choice . . . [and] any cutting that might be necessary, the stanzas to be kept or to be removed, and for which reasons of morality or taste] (2390).[4]

The teaching of literature was also recognized as having roots in the teaching of the Bible. Under the heading "Histoire Sainte" (biblical history), a more nuanced approach to the Bible and its history appears than one might expect from such a project rooted in republican positivism. While it is allowed that its teaching has had a beneficial effect on humanity over the years (*histoire sainte* traditionally occupied the place in the curriculum that French history was only then in the process of taking over), the Bible contains numerous "indecent" (*scabreux*) passages, to which Protestant sects foolishly expose their members by requiring them to read the text for themselves. Furthermore, God's favoritism of the Jews is an intolerable example of injustice, of the sort

that must never appear in a text studied in the modern school:

> D'une manière générale, les enseignements que l'école moderne doit
> chercher dans [l'] histoire sont ceux qui tendent à former l'esprit démoc-
> ratique, avec ses caractères distinctifs la liberté de conscience, la liberté
> d'examen, l'égalité devant la loi, la fraternité humaine: c'est précisément
> le contraire de toutes les doctrines qu'on est assuré de trouver dans l'an-
> tiquité, et plus qu'ailleurs peut-être dans l'antiquité juive.

> [In general, the lessons that modern instruction must look for in history
> are those that tend to educate the democratic spirit, with its distinctive
> characteristics: freedom of conscience, freedom of inquiry, equality
> before the law, human fellowship; these are the exact opposite of all the
> doctrines that one is sure to find in antiquity, and most of all perhaps in
> Jewish antiquity.] (1284)

This dismissal of the Bible as a school text is remarkable for the absence
of any attack on its status as a religious document. The fact that it forms
the basis of Judeo-Christian religion is irrelevant, as are its literary qualities. The primary objection to the Bible is political: the arbitrariness of
God's Word (especially in the Old Testament) is incompatible with the
values that school must transmit under a democratic regime. While the
Dictionnaire refers here to the teaching of history, it introduces a principle that will have a determining effect on the teaching of literature: that
all instruction must enhance civic morality. All subsequent debate over
the proper role and method of literary pedagogy during the Third
Republic took place under the assumption that morality and literary
value were connected: "*le vrai, le beau et le bien.*"

Historically speaking, of course, the moral dimension of esthetics is
nothing new, and Buisson's collaborators exploited the classical link
between form and ethics while establishing a strong nonutilitarian focus
in the national curriculum. In the article *Goût* (taste) by Georges
Dumesnil, for example, appears the following passage:

> [Le goût] est au front de la France un des plus beaux fleurons de sa
> couronne, comme c'en fut un jadis pour la Grèce, et qui lui a donné
> l'amour et la vénération de toute l'humanité. Le goût d'un tel peuple ne
> se remarque pas seulement dans ses monuments et dans les chefs-d'oeuvre
> de sa littérature. Il entre avec lui dans ses maisons, . . . et comme le goût
> est en somme l'intelligence retrouvant sa loi d'ordre et d'harmonie dans
> la sensation, on peut dire que le citoyen d'un tel pays a, partout autour
> de lui, de la raison faite beauté.

> [(Taste) is one of the most beautiful ornaments of the crown on France's
> brow, as it once was for Greece, which granted to it the love and adoration

of all humanity. The taste of such a people is not apparent only in its monuments and literary masterpieces. It enters into its very homes, . . . and because taste is after all intelligence finding again its law of order and harmony in the senses, one can say that the citizen of such a country is surrounded by reason made beauty.] (1194)

Here we approach the most significant Third Republic's reinterpretation of the universalist ideals of the Revolution. While the result of the debates in the National Convention, as we have seen, was to banish figurative language, and in some extremes, language itself from the rituals commemorating the Revolution in order to avoid their inherent distortion of the Truth, we now have the beginning of a persistent attempt to define the genius of French culture as "la raison faite beauté," the universal manifest in the individual. The choice of examples (monument, literary masterpiece, house) is significant in its juxtaposition of architecture with literature. Architecture has always been one of the Fine Arts, but unlike the others, it has also been required to satisfy the requirements of *function* as well as beauty. The *criterion of functionality* is more easily understood as a universal than the notoriously relative notion of beauty, and therefore stands for the characteristic of French art (especially literature) that is also universal. Not that literature, of course, is functional in the way that architecture traditionally is: this is a sleight of hand, invoking an example in which universality of function (the hallmark of "good" architecture) is arbitrarily associated with a more hypothetical universality of the French language. The architectural image, if explored farther, suggests additional valuable connotations. As stated at the beginning of this chapter, the role of French language and literature in the teaching of the new discipline of morality (*"l'enseignement moral et civique"* in the words of the statute) was based on the moral value associated with good writing. The better one is taught to use the language, and the better one is taught to appreciate the form (irrespective of the content) of great literary works, the better one is able to make moral decisions. In a somewhat twisted manner, the functionality of good architecture, allowing for the most efficient arrangement of actual space, and the functionality of language, understood primarily as grammar and style, both have moral value. "La raison faite beauté" will become the primary tenet of the conflation of moral and literary instruction.

Let us explore further the moral claim on behalf of French language. If I choose to keep the word *laïcité* in the original French rather than to use the English term "laicism" or any other translation, it is in order to convey the sense that the term has a specifically French meaning, a reference to a historically determined ideological content that is not carried by the English sense of merely opposing or excluding clergy. *Laïcité* has specific connotations in France that are philosophical, sociological, and legal. As such, it frequently is the object of the struggle for political power. Explicitly created for the purpose of assimilating diverse religions or value systems into the transcendent realm of universal human rights, *laïcité* has proven over the years to be a powerful instrument of exclusion, precisely as a result of the universalism contained in its historical justification. In brief, the danger of the universalist character of the French constitutions since the First Republic has been in the justification, inherent in the declaration of universal human rights as the foundation of the French nation, of depriving those individuals who reject full participation in the nation of those same rights.[5] Now that well over two centuries have passed since the adoption of the Declaration of the Rights of Man and of the Citizen, it is time to concentrate on the darker side of the universalist promise, emanating from the dual identity of the individual whose rights are being affirmed: both human being and citizen. The juxtaposition of these two terms, one general and one specific (insofar as one must always be the citizen of some definable subset of humanity, such as the French nation), provides the key to understanding the confusion of absolute and relative values in national education.

The separation of Church and state, which granted *laïcité* even more authority than it already enjoyed when *morale civique* was substituted for religious instruction in the primary school, became a part of French law on December 9, 1905. Its key provision was to forbid the use of public funds for the practice of "cults," which meant the end of the state's role in administering and financing the activities of the Catholic Church in France. This law, one of the strongest statements on the freedom and the privacy of religious worship in the world,[6] has an Old Testament ring to it: by using the word "cult" to designate religious denominations, the law implies that the state itself is not in any way comparable to a religion: the state is the absolute model against which the potentially infinite variety of religions or "cults" are measured. In effect, the Republic had ratified a principle that it had enforced throughout its history: the injunction to the people that "Thou shalt have no other gods before me," God's First Commandment.

It might seem far-fetched to call the principle of *laïcité* as defined by French law and cultural practice a type of religion, just like any other denomination within the Judeo-Christian tradition, but the claim is not new. One of Jules Ferry's avowed intellectual influences, second only to

Condorcet, was Auguste Comte, for whom positivism was not just the philosophical grounding of science, but a religion in its own right. The desire to give the rationalist doctrine of the Republic the status of a secular, state religion is prefigured in Ernest Renan's already mentioned *Vie de Jésus* (1863) in which he attempts to historicize and rationalize the Gospels. Renan's choice of subject—the life of God on earth—clearly indicates the extent of his wager: to meet Catholic theocracy head-on, and transfer to positivism the worldly authority of the Church. This and many other positivist texts contributed to Ferry's increasingly sophisticated grasp of the latently religious aspects of republicanism, an ideology based on a materialist and rationalist philosophy that supports a universal morality structurally resembling the religious authority against which it must compete.[7] The eschatological dimension of the Republic as the regime toward which all of French history had been striving comes from positivism, which sees science as the third (and last) stage of human development after theology and metaphysics. According to Ferry's biographer Jean-Michel Gaillard, the sense that history had come to an end in the messianic advent of the Republic was the foundation of his political activity: "Mettre un terme au cours chaotique de l'Histoire pour stabiliser enfin la France en proie à d'interminables convulsions" [To put an end to History's chaotic course in order finally to stabilize France, prey to unending convulsions] (134).

In the grand messianic rhetoric of positivism and *laïcité*, where do French language and literature come into play? E. Duplan, the *Sous-Directeur de l'enseignement primaire* for the department of the Seine (at the time, the department that included Paris), provided an answer in a report he published in 1891 titled *L'Enseignement primaire public à Paris*. Like other pedagogues of the Republic, he reminds his readers that there was no such thing as literary studies in primary education before 1840. The biggest changes after 1882, according to Duplan, were the replacement of religious instruction by moral instruction, and the increase of *explications de texte* and literary history covering the sixteenth, seventeenth, and eighteenth centuries. What is significant in Duplan's account is his claim that both of these changes, the institution of moral instruction and the increase in literary instruction, were really one and the same. True, the school day still made a distinction between moral instruction and French, which succeeded one another in the schedule, but for him, the two disciplines were more than complementary:

[D]ans nos écoles primaires supérieures, l'enseignement de la langue française, comme tous les autres enseignements, doit avoir, avant tout, un caractère pratique. On veut surtout apprendre aux élèves à parler et à écrire correctement leur langue; mais on ne néglige pas de faire contribuer cette étude à la culture intellectuelle de l'élève; on s'attache à former et à élever son jugement et son goût et on fait ainsi de l'enseignement de la langue maternelle un des principaux éléments d'éducation morale.

[In our advanced primary schools, the teaching of the French language, like all other forms of teaching, must have above all a practical aspect. One wants most of all to teach students to speak and write their language correctly; but one must not forget to make this study contribute to the student's intellectual culture; one is careful to educate and raise his judgment and taste, and thus one makes instruction in the native language into one of the primary elements of moral education.] (144)

Over and over, the claim that apprenticeship in the French language is also an initiation into morality, more effective than any religious injunction, occurs in the Third Republic's discourse on the school. Léon Bénard, a professor of French literature in Châteauroux, wrote in 1878 a typical formulation of the new morality based on familiarity with the formal aspects of great literature: "[la lecture] éclaire l'esprit en . . . conduisant au vrai; elle forme le coeur en nous portant au bien; elle épure le goût par le spectacle du beau" [[reading] enlightens the mind by . . . leading to truth; it trains the heart by lifting us to goodness; it refines [one's] taste with the spectacle of beauty] (137). Such characterization of moral instruction based on linguistic forms rather than content, style rather than precepts, will, as we shall see, attain a more sophisticated degree of expression in the philosophical debates over the teaching of French and Latin by figures such as Henri Bergson and Alfred Fouillée.

CHAPTER 5

THE SUPPRESSION AND EXPRESSION OF LITERATURE IN PRIMARY EDUCATION: EVOLUTION OF THE *MANUEL DE FRANÇAIS*

The following quote is from a letter Honoré de Balzac wrote to Countess Hanska, dated October 10, 1844:

> [J]'ai trouvé une affaire admirable . . . il s'agit de la publication d'*un livre encyclopédique pour l'instruction primaire*. Rien qu'à le bien rédiger, il y a la renommée d'un Parmentier à récolter; car c'est un livre qui est comme la pomme de terre de l'instruction, une nécessité, un bon marché fabuleux . . . etc.

> [[I] thought of a wonderful business . . . it is the publication of *an encyclopedic book for primary education*. Just by writing it well, one could reap the fame of a Parmentier; for this is a book that is like the potato of education, a staple, a fabulous bargain . . . etc.] (Quoted in Dupuy 1953: 128)

One can only regret that Balzac never wrote his primary school textbook. Probably, as in a number of his moneymaking schemes, he was simply too far ahead of his time: the genre to which he alludes, an "encyclopedic book for primary instruction," simply did not exist. There were *manuels* (literally "handbooks") in great number, but they were true to the literal meaning of the word: small, convenient books containing distillations of grammar, spelling, arithmetic, and so on; reference works, in other words, that emphasized skills over knowledge. The Third Republic was to see the unprecedented flourishing of an industry and a market that Balzac only divined, and that did in fact produce a "Parmentier": G. Bruno, whose encyclopedic textbooks became to primary education as the potato is to French cuisine. But first, let us examine the history leading up to the triumph of a new kind of pedagogical text.

The teaching of literacy skills cannot succeed without content, that is to say, texts. A fact so obvious is only worth mentioning because of its incompatibility with one of the perduring concerns of primary education: to limit and control students' capacity to make use of the freedom (of choice, of interpretation) that literacy inevitably creates. There were differences, though often subtle ones, between the Third Republic and its immediate precursors in the way that authorities managed the tension between literacy and literature, between controlled and uncontrolled reading.

The *Ecole Normale* of Saint Cloud in 1973 published a compilation of every public decree from the ministry of Public instruction in the nineteenth century concerning the proper teaching of French in primary education, and much can be learned from this succession of answers to the dilemma. The lack of any important decrees during the First Empire and Restoration shows the relative neglect in which elementary pedagogy languished. During the July Monarchy, however, the ministry was once again very active in this area, no doubt because of the impetus given to general education by the *Loi Guizot* of 1833, one of the precursors to the Third Republic's educational reforms. In the summer of 1835, a series of *procès-verbaux* stipulated which books needed to be included in the collections of the libraries of all primary schools, primarily religious texts and French grammars, but also the works of Fénelon, La Fontaine, Boileau, La Bruyère, Massillon, Buffon, Racine, and Corneille (5–6). These names continued to stand for the core curriculum of literary pedagogy throughout the century, and this document is evidence of one of the first official attempts to create a national canon through the institution of public education at the primary school level.[1]

A decree emanating from the ministry in the waning months of the Second Republic went much further, establishing an exclusive list of texts which were to serve in elementary schools for the exercise of *lecture raisonnée*, the practice of reading aloud and understanding. The word "understanding" in this context meant nothing more than knowing the words well enough to be able to paraphrase—the ministry was concerned that too many schoolchildren, in regions where French was not the native language, were simply mouthing the texts they were being taught without a clue as to the meaning, such as in the classroom scene in Rétif de la Bretonne's memoirs mentioned in the Introduction. The texts consisted of: Fénelon's *Fables*; selected fables of La Fontaine; Claude Fleury's *Mœurs des Israëlites et des Chrétiens*; the *Doctrine Chrétienne* and *Histoire de la religion et de l'église* by Charles François Lhomond (an eighteenth-century priest whose *Eléments de grammaire française,* closely modeled on his equally famous *Eléments de grammaire latine,* was the primary textbook for learning French in primary schools during the first half of the nineteenth century); parts of Bossuet's *Discours sur l'histoire universelle,* and authorized "*recueils de morceaux choisis dans les bons auteurs*" [collections of pieces selected from good authors] (12).

The first statement on the teaching of French emanating from Ferry's ministry, a *circulaire* dated August 10, 1880, at first seems to directly oppose the ever-increasing centralization of authority displayed by his predecessors in the establishment of "authorized" literary texts: "Les instituteurs et les institutrices titulaires de chaque canton dressent la liste des livres dont ils désirent se servir" [[Male and female] teachers in charge of each canton draw up the list of books that they want to use] (75). However, this delegation of authority to the teacher is effectively repealed by the following sentence: "Toutes ces listes cantonales sont centralisées au chef-lieu du département, où une commission présidée par l'Inspecteur d'Académie les examine et les révise" [All these cantonal lists are gathered in the capital of the *département* where a committee, chaired by the *Inspecteur d'Académie,* shall examine and revise them] (75). The revised lists are then forwarded to the *Recteur* of each *Académie* (the position to which the *Inspecteurs* must answer), who has the final say on their approval. Ferry's *circulaire* continues:

> La loi ne vous confère pas, elle ne reconnaît pas même au Ministre le droit d'interdire un livre, mais elle ne vous défend pas d'inculquer à vos subordonnés une telle connaissance et un tel amour des méthodes intel-ligentes, de les rendre si exigeants pour eux-mêmes, si sévères dans leurs choix, si jaloux enfin des progrès de leurs élèves, qu'ils se refusent désor-mais à prendre pour leurs classes d'autres instruments de travail que le meilleur et le plus parfait en chaque genre.

> [The law does not grant you (*speaking to the* Recteurs), nor even to the minister the right to ban a book, but it does not forbid you from incul-cating in your subordinates such knowledge of and love for intelligent methods, to make them ask so much of themselves, so rigorous in their choices, and finally so proud of their students' progress, that they will hereafter refuse to adopt for their classrooms other tools than the best and most perfect in every category.] (76)

It does not seem likely that Ferry's statement would have seriously dimin-ished the power of the state to determine the content of the literary curriculum in each class. As it turned out, the establishment of a list of canonical authors and texts became the responsibility of a partnership between the state, operating through the oversight of the primary and secondary curricula through the ministry and the University, and the textbook publishing industry, which Hachette and Belin soon dominated.

In the article on literary *manuels* of the Third Republic in Pierre Nora's *Les Lieux de mémoire* (1984), Daniel Milo describes the "official" literary canon as a pyramid: textbooks on French literary history encompassed hundreds of authors; anthologies of *morceaux choisis*, both for primary and secondary education, usually did not exceed a hundred authors; official curricula issued by the state usually did not exceed 30, while the program for the *baccalauréat* constituted a kind of "promised land," with at most 13 authors (535). Milo is careful to state that the school was not, properly speaking, the creator of a national canon: it simply disseminated a hierarchy of reputations that had already been established (519). At most, one might argue that the school perpetuated certain anomalies that did not exist outside of the "official" canon: Bourdaloue, Massillon, Fléchier ont bénéficié très longtemps, d'une survie purement scolaire. . . . Balzac, mort en 1850, a dû attendre presque un siècle pour être cité, pour la première fois, dans les programmes officiels de français" [Bourdaloue, Massillon, Fléchier survived for a very long time only in the school. . . . Balzac, dead in 1850, had to wait almost a century before being included for the first time in official French literature curricula] (518).

While it would be wrong to place responsibility on the state for the canonization process itself, here again I would suggest that a partnership is at work between public and private forces: when the open market of literary reputation favored the cultural agenda of the state, such as the dominance of the seventeenth century, the two worked in harmony; when the market did not coincide with the state's agenda, as in the case of Balzac or, just as dramatically, the "decadent" authors of the late nineteenth century, the state must somehow manage that tension, forbidding or at least postponing access to the "promised land" of the schoolbook. The question of canonization that Milo raises is crucial. To a large extent, the French literary canon was a matter of state only in the sense that the school ratified judgments that had already been made in the literary field; however, the school's role became far less passive as the curriculum moved beyond the seventeenth century, as we will see. Furthermore, the state did not choose texts so much as determine the means by which they were taught: its role was to establish a methodology more than to define a corpus.

The process that made the school so dependent upon literature for the execution of its socializing function is the same one I alluded to at the beginning of this book: the transition from the Enlightenment "conse-cration of the writer" as supreme authority to the Republican consecration of the *text* as supreme authority. The centrality of French language and literature in the school curriculum, which is in so many ways a part of the arguments I present, therefore did not fully come about until well into the second half of the nineteenth century. Tristan Hordé points out that French texts were absent for so long from the curriculum because their meaning was considered self-evident, and only Latin texts required *explication* (50). Ironically, it is precisely the attribute of self-evidence ascribed to French literary texts that eventually made them so valuable to the school. Literary concerns, which inevitably lead one away from the "self-evident" and toward the discovery that, for example, La Fontaine's *Fables* are not nearly as moral and unambiguous as they appear at first glance, have absolutely no place in the school. The value of literature for primary education (and, I would argue, beyond the strictly educational realm) depends on a perpetual deferral of specifically literary concerns. What, therefore, does literary pedagogy consist of? An examination of some concrete examples is in order.

As mentioned above, Hordé asserts that Victor Cousin, during his stint as *ministre de l'Instruction publique* in the Thiers cabinet in 1840, was the first public official to challenge the assumption of transparency of French literature and to recognize the challenge it offers by introduc-ing it into the curriculum (50–1). Even then, very little progress occurred until the reforms of the 1880s (Fayolle 1979: 8), and the defi-nition of *"Belles Lettres"* as consisting of the imitation of Latin (and some Greek) texts with an emphasis on grammar and rhetoric—the hallmark, in other words, of Jesuit education—continued to stand for the "real" discipline of literary studies long after initial challenges to its monopoly.

When the study of French literature finally established itself in primary and secondary schools, it did so not only slowly and gradually, but also indirectly. The study of the history of French literary pedagogy is a burgeoning field, but one that has already reached important conclusions. One of the most significant is that the school of the Third Republic, while marking the "triumph" of French literature as academic discipline, nevertheless did not practice literary studies in any current sense of the term. Part of the reason for the suppression of literature at the very moment that its position in the primary curriculum was confirmed rises out of the fear that we saw among legislators during the First Republic of the dangers of substituting words for things. The quid-dity, if one will, of literature—that which makes it distinct from other phenomena, and leads to the analysis of literature on its own terms—was precisely the characteristic that literary pedagogy could not afford to recognize.

The *Manuels* of the Republic and Literature in the Classroom

One of the founders of the modern discipline of the history of literary pedagogy is Emmanuel Fraisse, who in 1985 published a study of 62 literature *manuels* used in advanced primary education printed between 1872 and 1923, or a little less than 10 percent of the entire production during that period. Fraisse repeatedly makes the point that what these books teach is not literature, but various substitutes thereof. Often, literary *manuels* simply follow the pattern of other elementary school textbooks that focus on skills, knowledge, and morality that the student can use in his or her everyday life: "[L]es auteurs de manuels se sentent constraints—ou en droit—de faire appel à des écrivains consacrés pour communiquer ces 'connaissances usuelles' indispensables à la vie ultérieure de l'élève" [Authors of textbooks felt obligated—or entitled—to call upon consecrated writers in order to convey the "common knowledge" necessary for the student's later life] (103). The term "connaissances usuelles" was clearly associated with the *leçons de choses*, and the role of literature was paradoxically subordinated to the apparently unrelated pedagogical goal of "concrete instruction."

Nor is this subordination of literature to the status of illustration for "*connaissances usuelles*" limited to the seven-odd years of mandatory education. At the secondary level, the tradition of teaching literature for the sake of teaching something *other* than literature was already well established. Before Gustave Lanson, René Doumic, and others created their famous literature textbooks in the wake of the educational reforms, the most popular *manuel* for the secondary schools was Désiré Nisard's *Histoire de la littérature française*, first published in 1844, and revised and reprinted continuously almost until Nisard's death in 1888. In the preface to the first edition (reprinted in all subsequent editions), Nisard wrote:

> Ce que j'ai osé faire, . . . ç'a été de mettre en relief, dans l'examen historique de nos chefs d'oeuvre, le côté par lequel ils intéressent la conduite de l'esprit et donnent la règle des moeurs. . . . [J]'ai cherché . . . moins l'habileté de l'artiste que l'autorité du juge des actions et des pensées. . . . Peut-être même sera-ce le principal défaut de ce travail, que ma foi y paraîtra superstitieuse, et que j'aurai abaissé mes dieux en les supposant si occupés de moi.
>
> [What I dared to do . . . was to bring out, in the historical examination of our masterpieces, those aspects by which they speak to the conduct of the

mind and regulate mores. . . . I sought . . . less the skill of the artist than
the authority of the judge of acts and thoughts. . . . It will even perhaps
be the greatest flaw of this work, that my faith will appear as superstition,
and that I will have lowered my idols by assuming that they are so
concerned with me.] (vi–vii)

Whatever criteria determine the list of works belonging to the national
canon, one would assume that they derive from some definition, explicit
or not, of literariness. Impossible as "literariness" is to define, *habileté de
l'artiste* is nevertheless a legitimate starting point for the critic who
understands his duty as one of identifying and explaining the greatness
of a text. Nisard confesses that this concern was subordinate to the value
of the texts as guides for human thought and action, which are no doubt
worthy functions, but have much less immediate relevance to the notion
of literariness. True, Nisard dodges the issue of literariness from the
outset by stating that he selected texts of edifying value out of the corpus
of "*nos chefs d'oeuvre*," so the status of the texts as great literature is not
in doubt. However, it is important to identify his strategy as a secular
application of religious proselytism: the works in his anthology are to be
considered *chefs d'oeuvre* not because they have practical value for everyday life, nor do they have practical value because they are *chefs d'oeuvre*.
The characteristic of greatness, which here stands for literariness, is
simply a given. The use of such texts for the purpose of concrete instruction is a way of diverting attention away from the fundamental question: why are these texts great? The nonanswer to that question is simply
that they emanate from the pens of writers who have taken over from
God the ability to write words of absolute value. Nisard's comment that
his *modus operandi* as an anthologizer of great texts runs the risk of
appearing to the world as superstition rather than faith is significant. He
astutely draws the parallel between the selection of literary texts for their
edifying value, and what was understood at the time to be the origin of
the practice of religion in primitive society: a means simply to guide
one's decisions in life (one thinks of oracles and talismans), rather than
the sublime worship that it can and should be. If one takes words such
as "faith" and "consecration" applied to literary texts at face value, then
Nisard's successors in the Third Republic were, like him, caught in the
dilemma of appearing to misuse and even desecrate the holy objects in
their safekeeping, for such is the charge one levies against those who,
like the money changers in the Temple, would practice worldly endeav-
ors where only the solemn activity of worship is permitted. One can,
however, look at this apparent *détournement* of the literary in a different
light: by drawing the student's attention away from the study of texts for

themselves, the school perpetuates an aura of mystery around the term "*chef d'oeuvre.*" In other words, to study literature as if it were nothing more than a guide to wisdom handed down through the centuries is to foreclose any attempt to come to grips with the characteristics that distinguish it from other kinds of discourse. This is a practice that, far from desecrating the object of veneration, actually enhances its aura as a pure, hermetic vessel for the unattainable Godhead.

Whenever they purport to seek an explanation for the elevated status of literature, the anthologists abandon the role of critic for which most of them were trained and take on the role of priest. Daniel Bonnefon, for example, a Protestant minister and teacher who wrote a popular *manuel* in the latter part of the nineteenth century, provides a justification for the supremacy of the authors of the seventeenth century, who commandeer over a third of the 567 pages of the 1872 edition of his anthology (which was still being published at least as late as 1927). Those authors, Bonnefon states, do not owe their glory to the fact that they were alive during the reign of Louis XIV; on the contrary, Louis XIV owes his glory to them (116),[2] a fact that adds meaning to the famous epithet "*le grand Corneille.*" That is an almost perfect, and very likely inadvertent, supplanting of God by literary authors in the doctrine of the divine right of kings.

Fraisse points out that in all the *manuels* he studied, the characteristics that make these literary fragments appropriate for teaching practical knowledge are never clear. Greatness is obviously the criterion for inclusion, but no basis for greatness other than the guarantee of the author's famous signature is apparent: "[C]'est parce qu'il est classique qu'un morceau est choisi; inversement, il est classique parce qu'on l'a choisi" [A piece is chosen because it is classic/classical; inversely, it is classic because it has been chosen] (104). Most important, the texts themselves are invariably transformed, "tronqués, découpés, remodelés même" [truncated, cut up, even remodeled] (104), in a manner that tends to erase their individuality.

Félix Hémon's 1889 essay on the history of French literature in the manuels (cited in part I) addresses the problem of "mutilation" of texts used in the primary school, stating that "Il ne s'agit pas . . . de mutiler arbitrairement une oeuvre compacte et indivisible, mais d'observer et de marquer certaines divisions naturelles" [It is not a question . . . of arbitrarily mutilating a compact and indivisible work, but of noticing and indicating certain natural divisions] (3: 434). My purpose is not to examine what criteria Hémon and other pedagogues used to discern "natural" divisions in texts (criteria that undoubtedly are open to question), but rather to show that the issue of the organic integrity of the literary text was very much a question of concern. Pedagogues of the time knew very well that they had to "mutilate" texts, not only to adapt them to the anthology format, but also in order to predetermine the interpretive activity of the class. Their approach to French literature was based on the founding notion that a specific, desired outcome should emerge from the exercise of reading. Literature in the classroom had to support the enterprise of teaching *laïcité*, regardless of what other lessons it might contain.

Fraisse emphasizes the resulting uniformity of style and meaning, regardless of the texts' origins, almost as if they all had one and the same author, constituting "un noyau dur, une sorte de vulgate classique à l'usage des enfants du peuple" [a hard core, a kind of classical vulgate intended for the children of the masses] (104). The notion of an ideal single author for all of French literature is, in a sense, the ultimate goal of the literature handbooks, and irresistibly evokes the comparison with Scripture, a text traditionally acknowledged as having had many human amanuenses, but only one Author. Although such a notion appears to contradict the profoundly individual status of each author that Bénichou's literary Pantheon glorifies, in reality it does not. The authors of the Pantheon belong there because of what they have in common, not what they offer individually. The nature of the commonality among them cannot adequately be expressed. Since the basis for their common consecration escapes definition, the literary pedagogue has only one course of action: to proclaim a divinity that exists beyond proof; to present individual works as expressions of one and the same underlying Godhead; and to point students away from the actual texts, and toward the practical moral wisdom that certain great texts incidentally (one might even say accidentally) provide. The medium for such wisdom was an almost undifferentiated mass of text whose common value lay in their qualities of formal clarity and moral edification.

It is important to remember that Nisard's anthology (1844) served the needs of secondary school students of French literature, and was to be gradually replaced during the Third Republic by the literary histories of Lanson, Doumic, and others. In the younger classes, in which there was no need to concern oneself at all with literary questions, the dominance of practical concerns over literary concerns was even more solidly established. The statistics Fraisse compiled provide valuable insights. When he analyzed his data, he found that while La Fontaine appeared the most often, with an aggregate 6.2 percent of all texts in the corpus, nineteenth-century authors, beginning with Hugo (5 percent of texts), accounted for 79 percent of the authors and 66 percent of the texts in the primary school anthologies (105). The dominance of La Fontaine is easy to explain. His *Fables* lend themselves to memorization and recitation, thereby continuing the tradition of placing reading ahead of writing in the pedagogical hierarchy (it would take the republican schools a very long time to impose one of its most fundamental, though least-recognized reforms: the simultaneous teaching of both reading and writing); La Fontaine already placed his poems in a pedagogical context with his preface addressed to the *Dauphin*, the original and exemplary schoolchild for whom they were ostensibly written, and the Jesuits began using them in the eighteenth century as a starting point for the rhetorical exercise of *amplificatio* (Albanese 1999: 825); and, finally, because of the long tradition of seeing them as a moral compendium that could displace the Gospels. According to Ralph Albanese, it was Désiré Nisard himself who declared the *Fables* to be none other then the *catéchisme laïque*, the Holy Grail announced by d'Alembert's proposal to the *Académie* (824). Nor did the challenge, emanating most famously from Rousseau and Lamartine, that La Fontaine's *Fables* are actually immoral, cause any concern. The *Fables* are perhaps intellectually immoral, with such Machiavellian precepts as "la loi du plus fort est toujours la meilleure" [the law of the strongest is always the best (might makes right)], but they are *sentimentally* moral, an interesting inversion of Félix Hémon's claim that it is transparency and reason, not sentiment and inspiration, that are the qualities that best distinguish the French national canon. The irrational intuition of true morality in La Fontaine, more important than the rational under-standing of his superficial amorality, is what makes his work so perfectly appropriate for the schoolchildren of France. In fact, the critics of La Fontaine show their inability to grasp that essential aspect, and therefore reveal a fundamental betrayal of the French spirit that La Fontaine successfully defines and exploits (Albanese 1999: 836n). Of course, blaming the Genevan Rousseau's misunderstanding of La Fontaine on his status as a foreigner backfires as soon as one tries to include him in the French literary tradition as well. François Enne's work of propa-ganda, *Le Panthéon Républicain*, mentioned earlier, makes an awkward attempt to forgive him his occasional lapses into a foreigner's obtuseness toward the French literary heritage: " . . . Rousseau toutefois est bien français. C'est en français qu'il a composé presque tous ses écrits, et il descendait de parents français" [Rousseau is nevertheless truly French. He wrote almost all his works in French, and he was born of French parents] (105).

It would seem that the creators of the *manuels*, in striving for uniformity, wanted to present texts that would be above all intelligible; hence the preponderance of recent, and even contemporary authors and texts, and the need for extensive bowdlerization. "Pour en faire des textes scolaires, il a fallu réduire des textes littéraires à ce qu'ils ne sont pas: des textes informatifs" [In order to make them into school texts, one had to reduce them to what they are not: texts conveying information] (Fraisse 1985: 107). The textbooks of Claude Augé, discussed in the following chapter, provide a good example of the phenomenon that Fraisse describes.

The dominance of La Fontaine, followed immediately by Hugo, and the overall predominance of texts by more recent and even contemporary authors are the hallmarks, once again, of primary education. The goals of literary pedagogy at more advanced, secondary stage of education are sufficiently different that they required, for example, an almost complete suppression of contemporary and even nineteenth-century authors. As an example of the first transition into the next phase of education beyond the mandatory seven years, there is the *Premières leçons d'histoire littéraire* by Croisset, Lallier, and Petit de Julleville (1889), which devotes only a small appendix to the most recent period (1848–83) in which not a single author is actually mentioned, never mind quoted.

Philibert-Soupé's *Analyse des ouvrages français indiqués aux programmes* (1888) conveniently explains the major characteristics of each text on the various *programmes* of every single secondary school examination, including the *baccalauréat (lettres* and *sciences)*, the *certificat d'études secondaires* (for students in *enseignement spécial*), the *diplôme* (for graduates of *écoles de jeunes filles*), the *brevet supérieur*, and others. In stark contrast to primary school anthologies, not a single living author appears in Philibert-Soupé's *manuel;* furthermore, the nineteenth century is represented by very few authors other than Hugo, and is completely absent from the *programme* of the *baccalauréat ès lettres*, the most important of the exams listed here. In fact, the only texts in the official curricula (out of a list of almost 50) *not* written in the seventeenth century are excerpts from: *La Chanson de Roland*, Joinville, Montaigne, Massillon's *Petit Carême*, Montesquieu's *Considérations sur les causes de la grandeur et de la décadence des Romains*, Voltaire's *Correspondance*, *Histoire de Charles II*, and (no surprise here) *Le Siècle de Louis XIV* (7–13). In the mid-1880s, one can justifiably speak of a virtual monopoly of the seventeenth century in secondary schools, the effects of which have never stopped being felt.

In spite of his conclusion that the primary school literature handbooks of the Republic could in no way be construed as a means to study literature *per se*, Fraisse acknowledges two countervailing factors: first, the 1882 reforms did officially require for the first time in primary education the exercise of "*lecture expliquée*," which is to say a degree of literary interpretation, as opposed to mere illustration of moral and practical knowledge (106), though the actual implementation of this directive at the primary school level was extremely limited; second, the literary quality of the texts, in spite of the completely a-literary criteria of selection and high degree of distortion present in the anthologized text fragments, nevertheless came through. He compares them to "*des 'paternoster' laïques*" (107) through which the population gained some access, however limited, to the "literariness" inherent in the texts. The actual evidence that such materials succeeded in teaching "literature" in spite of themselves is scant; one must assume that Fraisse, in affirming the effectiveness of this pedagogy in the face of such obvious efforts to turn the student away from literature itself, is also speaking from faith.

Of course, literature was one of several subjects that constituted the raw material of primary and secondary public education. Furthermore, most of the political arguments put forward to promote education, such as the claim that Prussia defeated France because of the higher degree of education of its troops, certainly did not appear to imply that literature should be a privileged subject ahead of, let us say, math and geography. In fact, a large portion of public opinion, members of the radical leftist opposition as well as free-market advocates, adopted in the 1880s the utilitarian argument that the state should put purely strategic economic concerns above all others when supporting education, and require only applied sciences, modern languages, and any other subject which had a direct impact on France's competitiveness in the world. In part III, I analyze the polemic that arose when Raoul Frary, a left-wing journalist, published this very thesis in a book called *La Question du latin* in 1885, the title of which became a catch phrase for the debate, not only over Latin's status as an obligatory component of the *baccalauréat*, but over the broader question of whether the disinterested study of literature, either classical or modern, was still sufficiently relevant after the *défaite* to deserve its position as one of the pillars of national education.

Until now, I have discussed the institution of primary education in the Third Republic as being hostile to literature, presenting at best an adulterated and diluted version of the French canon instead of the real thing. The reasons for this initially reduced status were many, but usually fall into one of several categories: suspicion of the polysemous potential inherent in literature; a Jacobin-inspired attempt to place nature and physical reality ahead of the artistic works of humanity; and economic and military competitiveness with France's great rivals in Europe and America. At this point, I would like to change course, and present the primary school of the Republic as a place in which the cult of literature was very much alive. The *manuel* was, in the context of this discussion, a supremely ambivalent genre. Though it did not, for the most part, represent the literary tradition with any accuracy, it nevertheless claimed to do so; and in so doing, it necessarily put the *idea* of literature, if not literature itself, at the very center of the pedagogical enterprise. One possible formulation of this ambivalence is that the *manuel* and the primary school establishment of which it is the product teach literature while avoiding the literary at all costs. By doing so, they paradoxically affirm the absolute value of literature, and hence of the literary. In part III, we will see how the "literary" as absolute value was simultaneously placed on an altar and occluded through the teaching of classical languages at the secondary level. The defense of Latin and of its direct offspring, the study of literature, gradually came to distinguish staunch supporters of the Republic from their political adversaries, including the radical inheritors of 1848 and of the *Commune*. Why did the school adopt such a fundamentally anti-utilitarian, anti-empirical stance? The obvious answer, that literature is an important constituent of national identity, is insufficient: something other than a modern *Défense et illustration de la langue française* is at work.

CHAPTER 6

THE THEME OF ASSIMILATION IN PRIMARY SCHOOL TEXTBOOKS

The suppression of "literature in itself" that I described in chapter 5, most evident in Emmanuel Fraisse's description of a homogenized canon abstracted from the diverse mass of texts in the French literary corpus, allowed nonliterary concerns to dominate the teaching of French literature. One such concern was the urgent need to process the trauma of the defeat and mutilation of France in the Franco-Prussian War, requiring the school to seek reasons for national pride in areas other than military and political might. It was only natural that the school would fall back on the notion of cultural superiority in the wake of military defeat. What is more surprising is that the fact of defeat itself could be turned into a source of national pride. The example of this paradox that follows comes from the teaching of history, but it becomes apparent later that primary linguistic and literary pedagogy depended on similar paradoxes. Charles Bigot showed how one is able to derive national strength from defeat in his popular textbook on civic morality[1] for advanced primary school children, *Le Petit Français* (The Little Frenchman), first published in 1883:

> La France a de graves et insupportables défauts, dont aucune leçon ne l'a bien corrigée. Elle est légère, vaniteuse, téméraire dans la bonne fortune, prompte à s'abandonner dans la mauvaise. Elle a été querelleuse souvent, arrogante plus d'une fois, injuste à l'occasion. Elle a aussi abusé de la force contre des faibles, accablé et opprimé, fait sentir au vaincu le poids de son talon. Elle t'a fait sa confession sans réticence quand tes maîtres te racontaient son histoire.

> [France has serious and intolerable faults that no lesson has ever fully taught her to correct. She is whimsical, vain and foolhardy in good times, prone to despair in bad. She has often been quarrelsome, arrogant more than once, at times unjust. She has abused of her strength against the weak, she has burdened and oppressed, has made the conquered feel the

weight of her foot. She made her confession to you without reservation when your teachers told you her history.] (79)

The structure of the confession, curiously inverted in this passage in which the classroom is the place where the nation seeks absolution from its future citizens, and the act of faith demanded in order to interpret France's history as glorious, even, and perhaps especially, in its moments of physical and even moral weakness, are essential elements of the *culte laïque*. But these are matters of doctrine: they speak to the content of republican secular ideology, and not so much to its practice. And yet it is in the practice, I would argue, that the power of such ideology manifests itself. My approach to the study of the school system assumes that the practice within which the initiation into, or conversion to the cult of the nation takes place is primarily the teaching of literature.

The spiritual authority of religion seems most closely related, in the pedagogical sphere, to the "literariness" of literature, one aspect of the school curriculum that escapes rational analysis. It often seems that there was no real difference, for republican pedagogues, between the social functions, and therefore justifications, of religion and of art. When attempting to define "literariness," the pedagogues of the Republic could only fall back on moral terminology, such as in Louis Liard's (1882) claim in his anthology *Lectures morales et littéraires* (Moral and Literary Readings) that has a dual table of contents, a historical one that lists works of literature according to time period, and a thematic one that lists them according to moral categories—*courage, patriotisme, fidélité*, and so on: "Les grands écrivains sont aussi les meilleurs maîtres de morale et de patriotisme, ceux dont la leçon saisit le mieux les âmes" [Great writers are also the best teachers of morality and patriotism, those whose lesson best takes hold of the soul] (I).[2] While it is important to recognize that Liard does not state that all great literature is inherently moral, but merely that literature, when it happens also to be moral and patriotic, is best suited to transmit those values to the student, he nevertheless makes the case that literature that conveys moral lessons is superior to literature that does not. He solves the contradiction between teaching "French genius" and "human morality" by positing an essential identity between the two: "ce petit cours de morale, professé par les grands écrivains, est en même temps une histoire abrégée de la littérature de notre race" [this small course in morality taught by great writers is at the same time an abbreviated history of our race] (II). Liard implies here that the great writers assume a professorial function in the same way that Matthew and Luke inscribed their gospel with an instructional value, and it is on this purported ability of French literature to be the best vehicle for moral instruction that I now want to concentrate.

In order to fill in the picture of literary pedagogy at the primary school level, I now turn to an analysis of two monumental (in terms of numbers of copies printed) textbooks from the first half of the Third Republic. The first of these, Claude Augé's series of *Grammaires* (1881–89), though not a literary anthology, teaches the French language with the purpose of introducing the student to the world of literature. The second, G. Bruno's *Le Tour de la France par deux enfants* (The Tour of France by Two Children) is the primary school encyclopedia, the "potato" of primary education that Balzac envisioned in his letter to Madame Hanska quoted in chapter 5. It also does not teach literature *per se* (nor does it intend to), yet it prepares the student for a certain understanding of the function of the literary. In between Augé and Bruno, I examine one of the few literary texts used at the advanced primary level as the clearest example of literary pedagogy outside of the *lycée*: *La Chanson de Roland* presented by Edouard Roehrich (1885).

Claude Augé's Series on French Language and Literature

Claude Augé was famous for running the department at Larousse that produced the famous *Dictionnaire Encyclopédique*. The status of the *Petit Larousse* as by far the most popular French dictionary was partly the result of his stewardship. Before working on the dictionary, however, Augé's biggest success at Larousse was his series of textbooks for French language and literature. The popularity of the series was due in part to Augé's decision not to write just one or two books covering only a part of the years of mandatory schooling, but rather a series of texts that covered the entire range, from ages six to thirteen. School administrators appreciated the continuity of simply moving from one *Augé* to the next. He shrewdly outwitted his competition by responding in a single coordinated fashion to the entire demand created by the new laws on mandatory schooling, rather than the scattershot approach of most editors who published books by different authors, for different levels, using different pedagogical methods.

Augé's series begins with the *Grammaire enfantine* for schoolchildren just beginning to learn how to read. It would normally be used in the second year of school, after the child has learned the rudiments of writing using only a slate and chalk. This would have been the student's very first book, at least outside of the home. It contains a number of commonplaces of French pedagogy that every French person would recognize, mainly because they still occur in more modern textbooks. There is the obligatory reference to *la Gaule et les Gaulois* as the *Urvolk* from which stems the modern French spirit, if not its actual ethnic heritage. Lessons begin with simple anecdotes, such as the story of the surrender of Vercingétorix to Julius Caesar.[3] The rhetorical exercises of composition and oration exist in the forms of questions on the texts or pictures, to be answered orally, and *rédactions d'après l'image*, in which the student must compose a text based on a picture or series of pictures. But the greater emphasis is on the basic elements of literary appreciation: memorizing and reciting poems, writing dictations, reading and copying down moral stories, and even a primitive form of *explication*: giving an oral or written "*réflexion*" on the moral of the anecdote that starts off the lesson.

One of the most striking things about Augé's textbook is the choice of authors of the poems that the children must learn by heart. In stark contrast to the literary anthologies in use at the late stages of mandatory education (discussed in the chapter 5), or in the still-emergent field of French literary studies at the secondary school level, the authors in Augé's most elementary books are mostly contemporary, with a preference for members of the Parnasse and their disciples such as Théodore de Banville, François Coppée, and Marceline Desbordes-Valmore. These texts were not part of the pedagogical literary canon, in which anything after Romanticism was of far too recent vintage, but it was literature nonetheless. Of course, at this stage in their education, it was important that the children have texts that were accessible, hence consistent with contemporary usage. The poems in *Grammaire enfantine* in fact are not Banville or Coppée's "serious" works but were expressly written for children, and quite possibly for this book in particular.[4]

The slightly more advanced *Premier livre de grammaire* is a good deal thicker, and presents itself as "*une petite encyclopédie.*" Consequently, it contains much more raw information on history and the physical world. From the literary standpoint, the biggest difference between this and the more elementary textbook is the introduction of a new and important element: style. Whereas before, the poems were supplemented by prose anecdotes that had a purely moral value, now the emphasis is on the *manner* in which a character speaks. Several stories tell of famous instances in history when individuals were saved from certain disaster by their sense of *repartie*. Ironically, one of these is taken from Rousseau's *Confessions*, a text that generally speaks of the author's inability to shine in conversation, the "*esprit de l'escalier*" that is the opposite of *esprit de repartie*. Augé recounts Rousseau's childhood memory of having been sent to his room without dinner for some infraction that he does not remember. Contrite and terribly unhappy (for the family was having roast beef that night), he obediently goes to each member of the household to say *Adieu*. Just before climbing the stairs to his room, on a sudden inspiration, he looks at the roast turning on its spit and says: "Adieu, rôti!" (*Livre du Maître* 1890: 145). Everybody laughs so much that his father forgives him and lets him stay downstairs for dinner. Other anecdotes in Augé's text put a similar emphasis on the ability of the main character, usually the weak member of a power relationship, to avoid punishment or some other ill fate by his use of language: the Grenadier and the Maréchal de Saxe (51), Buffon's servant (56), and many more.

In the Rousseau story, and in the other accounts of famous reparties, there is no "moral" in the traditional sense of the word. This is in contrast to the *Grammaire enfantine* in which morality was directly, sometimes violently portrayed, such as the classic story of the "*vase de Soissons*," about the Frankish soldier who broke the vase he had taken at Soissons so as not to be forced to surrender it as tribute to the bishop, and whose head Clovis crushed (117).[5] The purpose in the *Premier livre de grammaire* is not so much to instill civic or personal morality (though it contains many stories that function as such), but to develop a desire to use language in social situations quickly, effectively, and *à propos*. In fact, it is rather surprising how amoral, if not immoral, these scenes are, since the protagonists are tricksters who outwit the other characters by their mastery of language, rather than persons who deserve to win on moral grounds. We are clearly far removed from the revolutionary ideal of a national language based on transparency and truth, back to the more "aristocratic" literary tradition of language as a medium to be manipulated.[6]

Much has been said already in this book about the need of the school to produce a lay catechism that would take the place of the teaching of the Church. What seems equally important, based on Augé's book, is to instill a respect for the power of language for its own sake, regardless of purely conventional moral concerns. Not only does Augé's pedagogy fly in the face of the revolutionary distrust of rhetoric, being in fact a full-scale rehabilitation of aristocratic wit at the earliest level of public instruction, it appears to subvert the principles of contemporary republican pedagogy as theorized by Compayré, Buisson, and their ilk, and codified by Hémon. Nobody, of course, would expect the pedagogy of late-nineteenth-century France, even when it emanates from the same public–private complex created by the alliance of the ministry, the Sorbonne, and the publishing industry, to be coherent. Contradictions are bound to exist at every level in the elaboration of both a theory and a practice of republican pedagogy. Some contradictions, however, manifest a deeper coherence. In the case of Augé, I argue that the throwback to rhetoric and *ancien régime* principles is the symptom of a phenomenon that scholars have too often ignored: the gradual replacement of religion by nationalism, Latin by French, and Scripture by literature through a process of *imitation* rather than opposition. In simplistic terms: the school of the Republic gradually became the school that it had tried to replace.

The manner in which Augé's books illustrate this mimetic aspect of republican pedagogy becomes even clearer when one studies the techniques and examples of the more advanced volumes in the series, including such staples of the French classroom as: creating a prose version of a verse poem; giving an oral account of a text that the student has read; reading a subject that the teacher has written on the blackboard, developing each sentence orally, then writing down one's development in the form of a composition. Each exercise promotes the active, individual development of expressive means within a rigidly circumscribed context. Furthermore, the style taught by Augé in his elementary textbooks is closer in spirit to the seventeenth-century ideal than to contemporary authors, in spite of the large number of contemporary poets that provide his examples. In the *Deuxième livre de grammaire*, a more advanced version of the *Premier livre*, he gives some "conseils préliminaires" to the student on how to approach the written *Exercice de style*:

> Quand on est bien pénétré de son sujet, les mots viennent sans peine, tout naturellement, sous la plume. Ces mots, il faut les accepter tels qu'ils viennent et se demander simplement s'ils rendent l'idée à énoncer. . . . On doit écrire comme on parle: le style est d'autant meilleur qu'il est naturel.
>
> [When one has fully absorbed the subject, words come out of the pen without effort, completely naturally. One must accept these words as they come and simply ask if they render the idea to be expressed. . . . One must write as one speaks: style is better the more it is natural.] (*Deuxième livre de grammaire* 1900: 169)

Augé advises the schoolchild not to encumber his or her composition with extraneous literary effects. The result of such a mistake would be a lapse in taste. The goal of the *Exercice de style* is not to rid the student's writing of all literary effects, but to cultivate one *particular* literary effect: the spare, adequate, harmonious, and objective style that is the nineteenth-century interpretation of the seventeenth-century ideal.

The first impression one gets from Augé's textbooks is that of an outright prejudice against literariness, one which very much supports the Althusserian critic Renée Balibar's distinction between primary and secondary French: the former is an ideal of transparency that enables immediate transmission of power from the center to the periphery, the second (coinciding with literary study) presents the French language as a secret code that only an elite is privileged, through secondary education, to master. Balibar discusses this important tension between transparency and mystification, already dominant in the educational debates during the French Revolution, in *Les Français fictifs: le rapport des styles littéraires au français national* (Fictitious French: The Relationship Between Literary Styles and National French; 1974). True to the primary school's ideal of transparency, Augé is extremely reticent in his references to literature itself. La Fontaine's *Fables*, a staple of French primary education that Augé includes in the *Deuxième livre*, are for him more important as models of form rather than moral content. While certain pedagogues of the nineteenth century, as Ralph Albanese points out in an article quoted earlier, refuted Rousseau and Lamartine's accusation that his fables are actually immoral, teaching one to be selfish, cynical, and otherwise emphasizing the qualities of the trickster rather than *l'honnête homme*, many others, like Augé, presented a more nuanced view, acknowledging the validity of the accusation, but calling it irrelevant: it is the perfection of La Fontaine's style, and not the content of his stories that makes him a positive influence on children. One might add that La Fontaine's trickster animals are not much different from the characters in the *Premier livre* like young Rousseau, who know what to say and when to speak.

Honesty and morality are therefore matters of style rather than content. When one learns to write clearly and directly, that is more important than whether one identifies with the cynical *renard* or the gullible *corbeau*. At the end of the *Deuxième livre*, Augé presents for the first time in his series of textbooks a short section on rhetoric defined as the different types of figures of speech. In his description of the techniques of periphrase, and the difference between proper meaning and figurative meaning, Augé makes it very clear that the student is supposed to recognize these phenomena, but not use them (166–7). The aspects of literariness that exceed the boundaries of "natural style" exist, and one must acknowledge them. They are, however, like dynamite for the student, who must always handle them from a distance. The antirhetorical legacy of the First Republic was therefore still alive in Augé, though in greatly modified form. It was no longer a question of distrusting literature as a whole, but of distinguishing between those who were entitled to write it from those who were taught to read it. Respect for the aristocratic exploitation of language without regard to truth had officially returned.

The description of language and literature in Augé reaches its greatest degree of complexity in the *Troisième livre de grammaire*, which is the final stage in the student's education before he or she reaches the *lycée*; it therefore represents the highest level of mass instruction created by the laws of 1882. The book begins with an introduction to linguistics, which summarizes the Republican ideal of the French language, carefully bridging the gap between local and universal speech by comparing *dialecte* and *patois*: "il y a entre le dialecte et le patois cette différence essentielle que le patois ne donne pas naissance à des oeuvres vraiment littéraires, tandis que le dialecte n'exclut ni la délicatesse des pensées, ni l'élégance du langage" [between dialect and patois there is an essential difference: patois does not give rise to truly literary works, whereas dialect is not incompatible with delicacy of thought, nor with elegance of expression] (*Le Troisième livre de grammaire* 1892: 4). Augé performs a gesture that is both exclusive and inclusive. One cannot expect all people to speak ideal French. Nor can we, in a democracy, deny the majority the right to "*délicatesse*" and "*élégance*" in their style, in other words: the right to literary expression. As a result it is necessary to grant some status to regional diversity by allowing "*dialecte*" the status of a language, but controlling the linguistic anarchy that might ensue by denying "patois" that same status. The distinction is arbitrary—the two words are virtually synonymous[7]—but it is necessary to make it in order for the linguistic policies of the Republic, which rest on the justification of universalism, to succeed.

Following a more developed series of readings and exercises, in which far more excerpts from literary works of the past are quoted than in the more elementary textbooks, *Le Troisième livre* introduces a new section: "Etude du style—Notions élémentaires de littérature" (Study of Style—Elementary Notions of Literature). It contains a very classical summary of rhetorical devices, using the Aristotelian/Jesuit categories of *inventio*, *dispositio*, and *elocutio* in order to make the transition between theory (types of tropes) and practice (composition and oration), between passive and active modes of learning. There are for the first time no warnings to the student that these tools are simply to be recognized, but not used. Finally, it seems, the teacher can trust the students to experiment with the full range of literary devices, having presumably learned the appropriate reflexes against bad taste during years of training in the classical/primary mode. Following is a list of subjects of compositions that prepare the student for the genre of the *dissertation* that some of them will soon encounter in the *lycée*. Finally, there is a section on the relatively new field of *histoire littéraire* that gives a brief overview of French since the Middle Ages, mentioning a handful of representative authors from each period. In the *livre du maître* or teacher's manual, the section on literary history is 40 pages long; in the student edition, it is 4 pages long. Does Augé believe that the student is not ready yet at this stage for full immersion into this subject, just as in the *Deuxième livre* he is not yet ready for rhetoric? There is no indication for the teacher of how to transmit to the student the information on literary history in the textbook, and its position in the *Troisième livre* indicates that it does not belong in the curriculum in any real sense. Nowhere in the exercises is there a need to refer to the historical information at the end, and it appears to be a simple reference section, giving the vaguest historical context to the readings and exercises that make up the bulk of the textbook. The teacher simply needs to have a much larger and more detailed reference section, so that his or her expertise will always exceed that of the student. The literary history in Augé's textbook, therefore, suggests its lack of importance in the curriculum before the secondary level, and reflects its status as an advanced discipline in the University. The implicit morality contained within grammar, the link between literacy and literature, is much more important: "C'est dans les ouvrages des bons écrivains que l'on trouve l'application des règles de grammaire" [It is in the works of good writers that one finds the application of the rules of grammar] (8n), an argument that will reappear in the debates over secondary education.

The pattern of slow, gradual revelation of literature set by Augé is reproduced in other textbooks. The primary school student evidently had to absorb a potentially large number of isolated or fragmentary texts before being granted the opportunity to learn what any of them might actually mean, independently of their value as an illustration of practical knowledge and morality. Poet and dramatist Ernest Legouvé, for example, enjoyed huge success with his *Art de la lecture* that had approximately 40 different editions between 1877 and 1911. Legouvé proselytized in this and other books for the reading aloud and recitation of literary texts. For him, "*lecture*" meant reading in the literal sense, reproducing the sounds encoded on the page, and limiting the process of interpretation to the expressiveness of the oral delivery. Legouvé was arguing against both the growing vogue for literary history, which substituted literature with facts, and *explication*, which placed too much emphasis on the students' version of the text, rather than the words of the author. Reading, for him, was a return to the source of literary authenticity. Legouvé was not alone in believing this. Again and again, one sees warnings in the instructor's editions of literature textbooks against allowing the student to exercise his or her own capacity for understanding, and not just at the primary level. For example, in 1873 A. Sorieul, a professor at the *lycée* of Alençon, published for the benefit of his colleagues a *Mémoire sur la manière d'expliquer les auteurs français dans les classes de grammaire* (Report on the Method for Analyzing French Authors in Grammar Class; 1873). For him, going beyond reading for sound and for literal meaning is a privilege reserved for a happy few: "Cultivons la mémoire, mais surtout, n'oublions pas le jugement. Je parle bien entendu des élèves qui ont reçu de la nature cette précieuse faculté: les autres ne comptent pas" [Let us cultivate memory, and above all let us not forget judgment. I speak of course of those students who have received this precious faculty from nature: the others do not count] (5). The message is clear: memorization and reading are the common lot; only those with the innate potential to approach literature more deeply should be allowed to do so, and they are a small minority indeed. Gustave Merlet, who taught French at *Louis-le-Grand* and wrote a very popular *manuel* for secondary education: *Etudes littéraires sur les classiques français des classes supérieures* [Literary Studies on French Classical Works for Advanced Classes; 1883] warned that, even in the rarefied atmosphere of the prestigious *classe de rhétorique*, one must exercise extreme care lest the students, be they the very best in the class, be tempted to use their own judgment:

> En supposant même que [les élèves] approchent directement ces textes, il faut bien reconnaître que le sens critique s'éveille très tardivement à un âge où opèrent surtout les facultés passives. Aussi le zèle des mieux doués a-t-il besoin d'être secondé par un guide exercé qui signale les bons endroits, indique les points de vue, habitue l'oeil à regarder, en un mot apprenne à des intelligences novices l'art si rare et si difficile de lire avec cette réflexion clairvoyante qui transforme en idées nettes des instincts vagues ou confus.

> [Even supposing that [students] approach these texts directly, one must recognize that the critical faculty awakens very late at an age when mostly passive faculties dominate. Therefore the zeal of the most gifted students must be supported by an experienced guide who points out the good parts, shows the points of view, trains the eye to watch, in a word: who teaches these novice intellects the rare and difficult art of reading with this lucidly penetrating thought that transforms vague and indistinct impulses into clear ideas.] (ii)

The emphasis on passive, highly mediated reception of the literary text, even at the level at which literature is finally revealed as more than sounds to memorize or illustrations of practical knowledge, appears as a leitmotiv in theories of literary pedagogy. I discern two principal reasons for this practice. For one, as Désiré Nisard explicitly stated in the introduction to his *Histoire de la littérature française*, the effect of such a practice is to deny literature its autonomy. Pedagogically speaking, no text is an end in itself, but simply a means to a nonliterary end, usually presented as some sort of moral edification, but arguably more political: the reinforcement of the values and interdictions supporting the social order. But there is a converse aspect of this apparent relegation of the literary to a secondary role: by constantly hiding from the student any aspect of the text which might give a clue as to the nature of its status as literature, in other words, by teaching literary texts nonliterarily, the school creates an aura of mystification. As Fraisse pointed out in his study, there is an absolute lack of explanation for the inclusion of anthologized texts into the corpus of national literature. The student has no choice but to assume that these texts are great literature, because if they were not, they would not be learning them. Inside this tautology that, to some degree, plagues the discipline of literary studies in every place and time where it is practiced (why do we read and teach the books that we read and teach?), there lies a profound truth. The role literature plays is that of an idol: literary culture becomes the object of a cult. One must not question what makes the sacred different from the rest or reality, one must only worship it. In this way, the marginalization of the literary, to the extent that the texts themselves are not even made available to students, or at least not made available in their actual form, paradoxically plays into the status of literature as a secular religion. The less is known about the text, the more the words of the teacher come to replace the words of the author, and the stronger the cult of literature will be. We now examine a rare example of actual introduction to a literary text at the primary level.

Edouard Roehrich, *La Chanson de Roland* à l'usage des écoles

Edouard Roehrich's translation of *La Chanson de Roland* for school-children was part of a surge in publication of medieval texts, many for the first time, during the Third Republic. The birth of medieval literary studies during this period, as well as its relationship to the school, has itself been a subject of research, such as Howard Bloch's (1989) contribution to a colloquium on the origins of *L'Identité française* in which he points out that texts considered canonical today did not even exist in print until the Third Republic, such as the *Fabliaux* (published in their entirety in 1876) or the *Roman de Renart* (in 1887). Roehrich was part of the growing tendency to bring at least some medieval texts into the school curriculum, although *Roland* was for a very long time the only one to make it. In his introduction, he justifies the use of a medieval text by students who have not yet attained the *lycée* level. His text was therefore intended for a wide audience, encompassing future *lycéens*, as well as future students of *enseignement spécial* and even individuals who would not continue their education longer than was required by law:

> [Les enfants] vivent parmi nous comme des étrangers. Nous autres adultes, parents et professeurs, hommes d'action et savants de cabinet, nous n'avons guère de prise sur eux parce que nous pensons autrement qu'eux. Notre culture met une trop grande distance entre nous et nos enfants. Mais ceux-ci pensent et sentent exactement comme pensaient et sentaient nos ancêtres à l'époque où la culture moderne n'existait pas.

> [[Children] live among us like foreigners. We adults, parents and teachers, both men of action and scholars, have little hold on them because we think differently from them. Our culture places too great a distance between us and our children. These children, however, think and feel exactly as our ancestors thought and felt at the time when modern culture did not exist.] (6)

The implication of Roehrich's statement is quite clear. Children are, figuratively speaking, foreigners, as well as primitives. Lanson made almost the same point (minus the allusion to their "foreignness") in the preface to his *Histoire de la littérature française* (1894 edition): "Cette enfance de notre littérature, comment nos pédagogues n'ont-ils pas encore vu que c'était vraiment la littérature de l'enfance?" [How can our educators not have seen that this childhood of our literature is in reality the literature of childhood?] (xii). The claim that medieval literature is more accessible to children because they are so much more like people in the middle ages than modern adults, supports an enterprise in which the child, in the process of acquiring a chronological knowledge of literature, gradually loses his alien status. If children are part of a "foreign" culture that is premodern, then an entirely new significance of Augé and Bigot's emphasis on "nos ancêtres, les Gaulois" emerges. Not only does the placing of the Gauls at the origin of the French race make the assimilation of the physically and culturally alien the *sine qua non* of citizenship, it also creates an even more direct link between schoolchildren and their putative ancestors: children are much closer to our ancestors than adults, for the simple reason that our ancestors lived and thought like children. Roehrich makes the very bold claim that children are inherently better equipped to understand the *Chanson de Roland* than are adults (and if the Gauls had left a written literature, children would presumably have even better insight into it than they do with *Roland*).

What we have in the use of a medieval text in the setting of primary education is a process of initiation that resembles at times a related, but far more radical process: spiritual conversion—but here it is conversion of a secular kind, therefore one that defies precise definition. To begin to describe it, one could say that secular conversion, like religious conversion, refuses to acknowledge faiths that compete for the child's allegiance. Roehrich admits as much when he states outright in his teacher's manual that the only verse of the *Chanson de Roland* that he omitted from his translation was the one most expressive of Christian fanaticism, the one describing the revenge of Charlemagne's army on the city of Cordoba and that deals, not coincidentally, with conversion: "En la cité, il n'est pas un païen qui ne soit tué ou devenu chrétien" [In the city, there is not one pagan who was neither killed nor become a Christian] (40).

The mention of *Roland*'s role in the curriculum raises an important question relative to the construction of national identity in the classroom from a republican perspective. As a subject of study, is not history the most appropriate means of creating a sense of national destiny, and of reinforcing the legitimacy of republicanism as the *telos* of the narrative that begins: "nos ancêtres, les Gaulois?" The history class in the Third Republic school repeatedly asks the student outright to make a leap of faith, a suppression of the rational process, that is akin to religious initiation as represented by Catholic traditions such as Catechism, First Communion, Confirmation. The school required its students to believe that the value of French history is other than the values of strength and virtue, a belief that was especially important given the recent history of an illegitimate regime in place for almost 20 years, followed by the humiliation of the Franco-Prussian War. Nowhere is the process more evident than in the most popular textbook for primary education during the Third Republic, *Le Tour de la France par deux enfants* by G. Bruno.

G. Bruno, the Parmentier of National Education

G. Bruno was the name under which Mme Alfred Fouillée (née Augustine Tuillerie), who was the wife of one of the Sorbonne's most prominent professors of philosophy (whom I discuss in part III), wrote a number of elementary school textbooks. She selected as her pen name G(iordano) Bruno in homage to an earlier professor of the Sorbonne who sought to reconcile the worldly and the spiritual, an enterprise to which she saw both herself and her husband contributing: as we have seen, the pedagogical philosophy of the Republic is defined by an opposition between spiritual and material, between the transcendent and/or vacuous, signified by literature, and the real, signified by science and "*leçons de choses*." Augustine Fouillée (to whom I will hereafter refer by her pen name) evidently saw her mission as nothing less than the reconciliation of the two. Her most famous and popular book was *Le Tour de la France par deux enfants*, first published in 1877 and reprinted, with many revisions, well into the twentieth century.

Her career as the most successful author for the French republican school began quietly in 1869 with the precursor to *Le Tour de la France*, an elementary school textbook entitled *Francinet: Livre de lecture courante* (Francinet: A Daily Reader; like all her books, published by Belin). Francinet is an orphan (like the two heroes of *Le Tour de la France*), a fact that allows the suppression of competition from paternal authority, so often at loggerheads with the authority of the teacher, and echoes revolutionary-era proposals to remove children from their families in order to educate them effectively. Though far less rich in content than its successor, *Francinet* presents a number of interesting characteristics. One is struck, at first, by its extreme degree of concreteness. Francinet, instead of going to school himself, where he might learn reading and the abstract skills associated with it, becomes an apprentice at a mill. His budding class-consciousness makes him rage against "*les riches*" and he throws a stone at the mill owner's granddaughter. The girl, named Aimée, tells the foreman not to punish Francinet, thereby nipping the boy's feelings of proletarian solidarity in the bud. The two children become friends, effecting on a small scale the class reconciliation for which the Republic stood. Francinet joins in Aimée's private lessons, thereby receiving the ideal education of which G. Bruno's book is supposed to be the record. Each chapter relates a *leçon de choses*, or examination of some ordinary yet important object or activity affecting everyday life such as food, tools, modern industries, or world events, followed by a *leçon de morale*. Already, one can discern one of G. Bruno's major contributions to the pedagogy of her time: until then the *leçon de choses* had been an autonomous exercise, an alternative (and antidote) to the "book learning" that initiation into literacy required and enabled. By inserting such lessons into her narrative, she in effect erased their status as a counterbalance to other forms of instruction, and relegated the age-old tradition of "concrete instruction" to a mere subcategory of reading. The link between the concrete example and the moral lesson, recreated in each chapter, is also a sign of Bruno's originality.

Etymologically, *leçon* is related to *lecture*, and originates from the practice of reading or singing passages of Scripture during nocturnal services, especially matins (*Nouveau Petit Robert* 1993). The structure of G. Bruno's first textbook therefore consists initially in displacing the object of reading from a (sacred) text to a physical object or activity, and then drawing a moral lesson from that "reading," which has the same relationship to the initial object as the sermon has to a biblical passage in the structure of the Catholic Mass. The focus on contemporary reality to the exclusion of history and literature lends *Francinet* a utilitarian aspect, suggesting both the fear of the literary potential of language manifested during the educational debates of the First Republic, and the push toward a more practical, technological national education that was to challenge the dominant position of language and literature in the curriculum (and to which I return in the discussion of *La question du latin* in part III). It is important, however, that although the "*leçon de choses*" was to remain a significant part of elementary instruction (serving in particular as initiation into the natural sciences), G. Bruno's incorporation of it into a text as part of a larger narrative, rather than keeping it as a separate classroom exercise in its own right, represented a substantial shift.

The narrativization of concrete education describes the basic structure of *Francinet*. Two historical figures appear in the few parts of the book that do not deal with immediate, everyday issues, and neither of them is a man of letters, nor even French: one is George Stephenson, the English inventor of the locomotive, and the other is Abraham Lincoln, whose climb out of poverty and emancipation of the slaves are exemplary traits of "true" nobility; the destinies of both illustrate the meritocratic self-image of the Republic, and resonate generally with a more ancient ideology of bourgeois revolt against privilege. They are, in effect, part of the institution of new forms of privilege by the social order that had replaced the feudal system. They also echo the similar role played by George Washington in Enne's *Panthéon Républicain* mentioned earlier. Both Enne and Bruno were motivated by similar concerns: the choice of foreigners as exemplars of the republican ideal in order to avoid accusations of political partisanship, emphasis on the universal aspects of republican ideology, and the conquest of actual space and time (the American continent, the railway) over less easily measured accomplishments in the realms of letters or abstract sciences. A hint that G. Bruno would later become one of the creators of a republican pedagogy that restored language to its central place is the statement that, of all the inventions in the history of humankind, the most important is the printing press: for all her glorification of the real, G. Bruno's pedagogy laid the groundwork for the limited initiation into national literature that would later serve as the capstone of mandatory education, as well as the stepping-stone to higher education.

Le Tour de la France is an entirely different work. The two have in common the orphaned status of their heroes, a predilection for presenting practical skills over abstract knowledge, and a characteristic which Robert Good astutely identified in a recent article as G. Bruno's contribution to republican philosophy, traces of which exist in the work of her husband Alfred Fouillée: the rare female characters in each book invariably exercise a gratuitously altruistic function, a "good will" identified as a specifically female trait that society requires in order to survive (51–2). Unlike the *Augé*, the *Bruno* does not present a series of unrelated texts, or short moral tales, but rather the coherent narrative of two boys, André and his little brother Julien, who escape from their hometown of Phalsbourg in Lorraine after the Prussian annexation, and embark on a trip through several regions of France. Everywhere they go they meet friends, people whom they recognize as French in spite of their regional differences, and learn some aspect of history, science, or technology in the process.

Between 1877 and 1947, *Le Tour de la France* sold approximately eight million copies (Dupuy 1953: 133). Since many had passed from hand to hand, it is safe to say that a very large majority of schoolchildren in the late nineteenth and early twentieth centuries grew up using it during their school careers, whether in Catholic and other denominational schools or in the *école laïque*; it is to G. Bruno's credit that it was just as likely to be attacked by the radical Left as by the religious Right (Jacques and Mona Ozouf 1984: 292). Beginning in 1905, its use declined, especially in the public schools that gradually replaced the Bruno with textbooks based on the model of the *Morceaux choisis*, consisting of excerpts of literary texts rather than an encyclopedic narrative (Dupuy 1953: 133). The reason for the change in the choice of textbooks can be attributed at least partly to French literature's increasing importance as the new secular Scripture, a process that accelerated in 1902, with the creation of a *baccalauréat* in which French literature took the place of Latin, and again in 1905 with the official separation of Church and state, providing literature with a new spiritual authority, and removing once and for all any reference to religion in the curriculum. Further evidence of the impact of the 1905 law is the fact that beginning in 1906, all references to God, even interjections such as *mon Dieu!*, were completely removed from Bruno's text (Jacques and Mona Ozouf 1984: 300), a textual variation on the gradual and systematic removal of crucifixes from public buildings begun under Jules Ferry.

Le Tour de la France consists of over one hundred chapters corresponding to stages in a journey, each one preceded by a moral precept that will be illustrated by some part of the story. Bruno reproduces the didactic thrust of La Fontaine's *Fables*, valorizing an existential situation on the basis of a particular ethical precept. The purpose here is to fulfill as many pedagogic goals as possible: a *leçon de morale* as well as a *leçon de choses* and, both in its content and through Bruno's concise style that makes use of the entire range of grammatical structures belonging to the new, national standard French, a linguistic and even a literary exercise.

One of G. Bruno's inspired decisions was to give her textbook the form of a narrative with which schoolchildren could readily identify. The initiatory tale of André and Julien is all the more potent because they are orphans. The boys are compelled to leave Lorraine because their father's last word to them on his deathbed was "France!" They manage to cross the border into French territory,[8] and are "adopted" by surrogate parents in every region they visit on their centripetal journey to Paris, the figurative "center," and finally to their new home on a farm in the Orléanais, the spiritual and geographical center of France and endpoint of their journey. Instead of a circular "Tour" beginning and ending at the same point, the boys' trajectory is an alternating journey toward the center and back toward the periphery; they end up in Phalsbourg, where they started, then head back toward the center (Paris). The forays toward the center occur whenever the boys travel by land: at the start (Phalsbourg to Clermont-Ferrand), middle (Montpellier to Bordeaux), and end (Lille back to Phalsbourg, and then to Paris and finally the Orléanais countryside); they head toward the periphery when they travel by sea, around rather than inside the country (Marseille to Cette, now spelled Sète, Bordeaux to Nantes, Brest, and Lille). It is as if the boys were being alternately drawn toward the center and away from it: whenever it is possible to travel by sea and avoid the French territory altogether, they do so. As a result, they miss seeing for themselves huge portions of the French territory (Brittany, Normandy, Anjou, Touraine, etc.), about which they only hear from other characters or read in books. In Bruno's narrative, direct and indirect experience, seeing and reading, are both essential elements of education: information is absorbed through direct observation or through listening or reading, just as the journey itself alternately turns toward and away from its destination, toward land (and direct observation) and toward sea (while on ship, they only read or hear about the regions they pass).

Sometimes by attending school, sometimes by speaking to people in their homes, fields, and workshops, the two boys learn about their homeland's past and present. Early on, there is a direct reference to the educational enterprise of the state that underscores the reliance on books more than on things, indicating a continuation of the evolution Bruno started in *Francinet* by inserting the "*leçon de choses*" within a text:

[L]es écoles, les cours d'adultes, les bibliothèques scolaires sont les bienfaits de votre patrie. La France veut que tous ses enfants soient dignes d'elle, et chaque jour elle augmente le nombre de ses écoles et des cours, elle fonde de nouvelles bibliothèques, et elle prépare des maîtres savants pour diriger la jeunesse.

[Schools, adult classes, school libraries are the gifts of your fatherland. France wants all her children to be worthy of her, and each day she increases the number of schools and lessons, she founds new libraries, and trains knowledgeable teachers to guide young people.] (Bruno 1889: 45)

Unlike *Francinet*, therefore, *Le Tour de la France* balances practical and intellectual skills, and supplements science and technology with history and culture.

Bruno's strategy was still very different from that of Augé, who placed literature and history at the center of his primary school textbooks to the exclusion of other topics. When *Le Tour de la France* does overlap with Augé, significant differences emerge. For example, Bruno does not place the reference to the Gauls as the origin of the French race at the beginning of her narrative, but only in the section that shows the boys' stay in Auvergne (where Vercingétorix surrendered), a considerable distance from Lorraine, and therefore starting only on page 132 of the 1930 edition. Augé's presentation is chronological, Bruno's geographical. These contrasting manners of presenting the point of origin of national history (and of the French language, the moment when Latin first invaded the territory that was to become France) are meaningful. Bruno subordinates the temporal to the spatial, the abstract to the concrete. In the nation understood as space, the history of the Gauls is simply another fact to be juxtaposed with the rest of the facts that mark the territory as French. In Augé's temporal presentation of the nation, the point of origin is ambiguous: does the moment when history begins itself belong to history? In Bruno's geographical presentation it most certainly does, and therefore must be thoroughly integrated within the narrative representation of the nation.

Because we know that André and Julien are from Lorraine, the story of the surrender of Vercingétorix to Caesar is even more poignant. After recounting the story, their teacher tells them: "Enfants . . . demandez-vous lequel de ces deux hommes, dans cette lutte, fut le plus grand" [Children . . . in this battle, ask yourselves which of these two men was the greatest] (138). Obviously, the surrender of Vercingétorix is greater than the victory of Caesar (or Kaiser). This presents a contradiction that the post-1870 spirit, that reappeared in 1940, helps to explain, but does not resolve. To say that Vercingétorix is greater than Caesar is an act of repression that, like all such acts, serves to circumvent an intolerable situation or memory. Since one generally has more sympathy for the weaker participant in a conflict, and the Gauls had at least the virtue of having fought hard against the larger and better-equipped Roman army (no French technological superiority here), it is not illogical to look upon the Gauls as somehow more glorious in defeat than the Romans in victory; the same argument, after all, justified the claim that the *Fables* of La Fontaine are truly moral. The wolf might win according to the rules of war, but the lamb is morally (sentimentally) victorious: he wins the debate and loses his life. Those who, such as Gustave Lanson, defended La Fontaine's morality against the critiques of Rousseau and Lamartine, said after all that he presented the world as it is, not as it should be.

Bruno's reference to the Gauls has another function besides the moral and historical ones: it has to do with ethnicity, and the reconciliation of the homogeneous concept of race and the heterogeneous concept of assimilation as foundations of national identity. Few people are aware that the classic phrase "*nos ancêtres, les Gaulois*," forever symbolic of French public education, was associated for years primarily with G. Bruno, even though the phrase appears in many other nineteenth-century elementary school texts.[9] Clearly, it was necessary to place the Gauls at the center in the modern construction of French racial identity. However, Bruno's complete quote introduced by those famous words describes these Gauls physically in a way that clearly shows their ethnic and cultural *difference* from, and not similarity to, the contemporary French population: "Nos ancêtres, les Gaulois, étaient grands et robustes, avec une peau blanche comme le lait, des yeux bleus et de longs cheveux blonds ou roux qu'ils laissaient flotter sur leurs épaules" [Our ancestors the Gauls were tall and strong, with skin as white as milk, blue eyes, and long red or blond hair that they let grow below their shoulders] (135). Most schoolchildren of the Third Republic, even the ones from Brittany, would have had almost as much difficulty recognizing themselves in this physical description as the schoolchildren in French colonies, who are commonly assumed to have read the same text (though recent research has challenged that assumption[10]). The description of the Gauls, therefore, presents a paradox nearly as stark as the surrender of Vercingétorix; for how can the race that is presented as the origin, and therefore the essence, of the nation's population, be so different from today's French in aspect, not to mention language and culture (neither of which Bruno mentions)?

I believe there is an explanation for such a paradox that not only accounts for the physical differences between the ancient Gauls and the modern French; it even requires that these differences be emphasized. At the heart of the pedagogical enterprise in which Bruno participated was the attempted reconciliation between national identity and otherness. The overcoming of otherness, manifest as foreignness, strangeness (of appearance, of behavior), and even, in the case of literature, as exaggeration or eccentricity of style understood as deviation from the seventeenth-century classical norm, was to be a dominant characteristic of republican pedagogy. In *Le Tour de la France*, the function of overcoming otherness is placed squarely at the point of origin of the French race: "*nos ancêtres, les Gaulois.*" The book's plot is nothing other than an exercise in overcoming difference, which is another way to describe the acquisition of citizenship. Because they are from Lorraine, André and Julien are both foreigners from a legal standpoint; in addition, because they are children, they cannot yet be considered French *citizens* either from a legal or moral standpoint. Their epic journey through France belongs to the genre of *Bildungsroman* and leads them to Paris, where they ceremoniously obtain the status of French citizens and shed their childhood innocence. The particular quest structure of their story is of a laborious reconquest of their true national identity: turned into foreigners by the Prussian conquest, they gradually purge themselves of their otherness, and after obtaining French citizenship, return not to Lorraine, but to a farm in the Orléanais, destroyed during the war, and which they must rebuild. Of course, this destiny is none other than that of all French people, beginning with their collective, mythic origin in the racially "different" tribes of Gaul (whom one might connect visually to the stereotype of the absolute "foreigner" of the period: the blond or red-haired and blue-eyed Germans[11]).

The physical description of the Gauls is one of only two passages in Bruno that are explicitly ethnographic. The other is on the four races of

humankind (white, yellow, red, and black) that not surprisingly, desig-
nates the white as "la plus parfaite des races" [the most perfect race],
with physical characteristics that Bruno describes negatively as a lack of
any salient trait ("bouche *peu* fendue, lèvres *peu* épaisses" [*not very* wide
mouth, *not very* thick lips]; emphasis added), in contrast to the immod-
erate characteristics of all other races, described in a manner that directly
mirrors the "negative" portrait of the white race: Asians ("pommettes
saillantes, nez applati" [prominent cheekbones, flat nose]), Amerindians
("yeux enfoncés, nez long et arqué, . . . front *très* fuyant" [sunken eyes,
long hooked nose, . . . *very* low brow]) and Africans ("nez écrasé . . .
lèvres épaisses . . . bras *très* longs" [flattened nose . . . thick lips . . . *very*
long arms]; 188, emphasis added). The description of the Gauls, even
though they belonged undoubtedly to the white race (and are even
super-white: "la peau blanche comme le lait" [skin white as milk]), is
similar to these different typologies of the "other" in its enumeration of
physical features that deviate from the "neutral" white norm, even in
something as vague and trivial as their large builds and long hair. Jacques
and Mona Ozouf point out that the *Livre du maître*, or teacher's edition,
"ne pense jamais la division française à travers l'ethnographie mais à
travers la politique" [never conceives of French division as ethnographic,
but rather as political] (1984: 297). Indeed, Bruno's idyllic, mythic
construction of national identity is never presented as ethnically or even
culturally diverse (everybody everywhere looks the same and speaks
perfect French, with one notable exception that the Ozoufs over-
looked[12]), political divisions are signs of outdated allegiances, and
Bruno prophesies the disappearance of political parties (Jacques and
Mona Ozouf 1984: 298). In summary: in order to build national unity,
Le Tour de la France had to present such unity as *already acquired*. To
place the visibly alien Gauls at the root of the ethnic tree is to foreclose
any attempt to exercise the "right to difference" within the boundaries
of the nation. Any attempt to affirm regional identity or, for that matter,
ethnic, class, or individual identity is swallowed up by the fact that the
nation itself is founded upon the "other" (albeit a preternaturally white
"other"), and that the journey from the margins to the center, as illustrated by André and Julien, is not a matter of choice: the margins are,
already, at the center. Their trip affirms that the symbolic nature of
French citizenship resides in the fact that it is a form of cultural conversion, substituting cultural and even ethnic strangeness with civil, political, and cultural homogeneity. When the boys arrive in Paris for the first
time, André is inspired to exclaim: "Ce Paris est un Gargantua, comme
on dit" [This Paris is a Gargantua, as they say] (276). He could not have

chosen a more apt metaphor for assimilation as constituent of national identity.

The assimilation by France of the genetic otherness of the Gauls has a linguistic equivalent. As Dominique Maingueneau points out in his book *Les Livres d'école de la République* (The Schoolbooks of the Republic 1979), the Latin language had, for the Gauls, the same function as French had for the French (259), which is perhaps the real historical parallel between the two peoples, less tenuous than the genetic heredity claimed by Bruno and so many others. But Mainguenau falls into the easy tendency to see those languages as pure vectors of power that substitute ideal Latin or Latinate French clarity for the "natural" and therefore contingent and chaotic native language and culture. When pointing out that, rather incongruously, every person in every region that André and Julien visit speaks French (with one exception, as I noted above), he adds:

> [U]ne même transparence uniforme, celle du français national, baigne toutes les provinces de France. . . . [E]lle s'enracine dans le fonctionnement même de l'école, qui enseigne l'arithmétique, la morale et la grammaire française d'un même mouvement.

> [A unified and uniform transparency, that of the national French language, covers all the provinces of France. . . . It is rooted in the very operation of the school, which teaches arithmetic, morality and French grammar in the same motion.] (249)

Given the existence of an institution of national education, one cannot exactly fault those responsible for the curriculum for having placed French alongside arithmetic, moral instruction, and other subjects that claim a hold on truth. The logic of linking the three dominant subjects of elementary education is that math is demonstrably universal, morality arguably so, and so is French grammar, by association with the first two. But the greater problem with Maingueneau's analysis is his exclusive insistence on French as a vector of power, the purpose of which is everywhere to substitute one authority (the state) for others (the parish, the hearth). The strategy of the state in its national educational policies is more subtle. Latin may well have functioned as a means of destroying Gallic culture, a perfect example of colonization in its raw form. Under the republican regime, however, French was the instrument, not so much for merely overcoming, which is to say annihilating the "other" in his or her regional, cultural, or religious differences, but for founding the national identity *upon* the other, a process for which a method for constituting and transmitting a cultural, and especially a literary heritage was necessary. Unlike a constitution or other legal texts that manifest a desire for "transparency" and therefore universality (contracts, after all, are designed to mean exactly the same thing to more than one person), literary texts display and even emphasize diversity. And the school of the Republic, as I try to show in subsequent chapters, while it parades the seventeenth century as an era of classical balance and even "transparency" in literature, projecting an image of harmony onto a period marked by political disunity, nevertheless proved itself perfectly capable of dealing with avant-garde literature as well. If the strange-looking Gauls are at the very origin of the French race, then there is no person or artifact, no matter how strange, that the school cannot assimilate.

But let us return to the Vercingétorix paradox and examine it further. If we are to take literally the proposition that the Gauls were greater than the Romans, or that Vercingétorix was greater than Caesar, we must ask how this can be the case. Being a courageous underdog is not quite enough. If we look at the parallel between the battlefields of Alésia and Sedan, other factors begin to emerge. When the Third Republic was in its infancy, immediately following the surrender to the Prussians and the repression of the *Commune*, the question of finding out who was responsible for the defeat was urgent. The obvious suspects, beginning with Napoleon III himself, did not come under nearly as much criticism as the school system. Surprisingly, the defeat of 1871 was blamed on the teachers (see Claude Digeon, *La Crise allemande de la pensée française* 1959, for a thorough account of this phenomenon). Why?

There had always been a suspicion that school reform in Prussia had played a major role in its rise to the rank of world power. People pointed to Fichte's 1807 call for a national education in Prussia (so often praised by post-1871 propagandists, as shown in part II), and the *Ligue de l'enseignement* was founded with the express purpose of encouraging the imitation of Prussian pedagogical methods (Dupuy 1975). An obsession with an "education gap" persisted, and rumors circulated after the war that French soldiers had outdated maps of enemy territory that they did not know how to read properly. The answer to this was to make education less concerned with Latin and rhetoric, and more concerned with practical matters such as geography, science, and modern languages: in other words, to bring about the utilitarian education that polemicist Raoul Frary would call for in the 1880s.

But that is not the education that Ferry and his army of academics had in mind. To follow the Prussian example in education not only would be a second defeat, it would go against the philosophy that they were putting into practice: the idea of a secular religion, based not only on the real and the transparent, but on an idealized French literature as well. It is true that teaching a set of linguistic and cultural practices derived from seventeenth-century values does not win wars, at least not in the short run. But it was also not in Ferry's and the Third Republic's intentions to wage wars, at least not against adversaries that were powerful enough to win.[13] Instead, they needed to wrest control of the schools away from the *revanchistes* and the leftist utilitarians, both of whom wanted a modern, technological curriculum, and the cultural conservatives, who wanted to maintain a Latin-based curriculum. In this light, the idea that France is more glorious in her defeat than other countries are in their victory takes on a whole other meaning: it promotes the superiority of the cultural values upon which the Republic wanted to found its own political legitimacy, while sidestepping the issue of military and economic competition with France's rivals.

G. Bruno's textbook is therefore faithful to the Republic's project of taking control of the cultural identity of the nation, even if literature itself plays a scant role in the boys' adventures, as it did in primary education generally. Literature is only one subject among the many that they have to learn about. They only read or hear about a few authors, mostly when they happen to be in the region where they were born. The authors mentioned (but never quoted) are: Bossuet, Buffon, Montesquieu, Fénelon, Descartes, Corneille, La Fontaine, Racine, and Boileau. All, with the exception of Montesquieu and Buffon, are from the seventeenth century, and all form the nucleus of the classical French canon which pedagogues of the Republic had enlisted in their fight to make French the rightful heir of Latin. *Le Tour de la France par deux enfants* proves, however, that it is not necessary to introduce the canon itself at this stage of the educational process; indeed, as Augé suggested in his teacher's manuals, it is dangerous to do so. It suffices at this early (and, for most schoolchildren, final) stage of the educational process to create a sense of respect for the canon as the ultimate fulfillment of the universalist aspects of national identity. That is a goal that Bruno's book attains easily. The cultural values that she promotes are, from a practical standpoint, disinterested: there is no concrete advantage to considering defeat, for example, morally superior to victory. There is a significant advantage, however, in making a disinterested education—one that does not put practical knowledge ahead of the value of culture for its own sake—appear more desirable. Practical knowledge is truly universal: it belongs to the world, and the world belongs to those who can master it.

But French culture is "universal" in a special sense. The characteristics that make it universal, its capacity to serve as the most adequate vehicle for truth according to the paradigms of the seventeenth century, are also what make it French. Vercingétorix and Boileau coexist in the pages of elementary school manuals for the same reason: they help resolve the contradiction of basing a republican regime within a particular national framework and on principles that are universal in scope. It lets France, as defined by the Third Republic, be the fatherland for the entire world while still remaining itself. That is something that Prussia, with as many victories as it can manage, will never achieve. It is almost superfluous to point out that Bruno produced a program for France's messianic civilizing mission by placing the process of assimilation at the very heart of her book. In light of the passages analyzed above, Eugen Weber's characterization of Bruno's book, in which he comments on the void left by the prohibition against *histoire sainte*, a former staple of elementary education, takes on additional meaning: "Biblical history, proscribed in secular schools, was replaced by the sainted history of France" (1976: 336).

PART III

LITERATURE IN SECONDARY EDUCATION: THE QUESTION OF LATIN, THE CRISIS OF FRENCH

CHAPTER 7

LATIN AS SYMBOL FOR THE MYSTERIES OF FRENCH

When Montaigne's father had him learn Latin before learning French, he was combining two standard pedagogical principles that had been widely accredited: the use of Latin in order to teach reading in primary education, and then to teach elocution in secondary education. As Françoise Waquet shows in her study of the history of Latin in modern times (*Latin or the Empire of a Sign: From the Sixteenth to the Twentieth Centuries* 1998, trans. 2001), during the *ancien régime* students learned to read by learning to read Latin. Although its grammar is far more complex than the French one, the fact that Latin had a more rational system of spelling and pronunciation was an argument for using it as a basis for the subsequent assimilation of French texts. As mentioned in the Introduction, it is also relevant that the Latin texts in the *syllabaires* with which children practiced their skills were not classical but Catholic: prayers, psalms, parts of the liturgy, and so on. The pedagogy of French that I discussed in chapter 6 was therefore the product of a relatively recent occurrence: the gradual substitution of French for Latin as the means to acquire literacy. Except for a few experiments in the direct acquisition of French literacy without recourse to Latin in some Protestant schools and in the *petites écoles* of Port-Royal, the use of Latin as a preliminary stage in the apprenticeship of written French was eliminated only well after the Revolution (Waquet 2001: 12–19). Even as late as the latter part of the nineteenth century, Latin was considered necessary for a full understanding and appreciation of French: "a pedagogic practice . . . under which French as a written language was not taught directly but through translations from Latin and imitation of classical authors" (186). In other words, French was taught as if it were a foreign language.

The practice, in both Catholic and Protestant schools, of teaching students to read French through the screen of Latin, and the use of familiar sacred utterances such as the *paternoster* in the process, placed traditional primary education squarely under the aegis of religion: school and church were mutually supportive institutions. According to Waquet, there was indeed a difference between Catholics and Protestants concerning the status of Latin both in religious practice and in the school, but not as great a difference as one might suspect. The Council of Trent in 1546, which considered allowing the use of the vernacular in services on the model of Protestantism, finally affirmed the monopoly of Latin in Catholic rituals; but this did not occur because of any greater belief among Catholic clergy in the inherent sacred or magical property of Latin: on the point of the separation between the Latin language and the revelation it contains, there was basic agreement with Protestants (47). The two theological points of divergence on the subject of Latin between the Church and the Reformation resulting from the Council of Trent were, first of all, that the ceremony of mass for Catholics "*contains* a precious doctrinal treasure [the mystery of transubstantiation]" while for the Protestants, mass "*is* just a teaching" (49); second, that maintaining respect for the sacred mysteries of the mass required that the faithful be kept in the dark, and that Latin was therefore an instrument of religious mystification. The value of Latin for Catholicism was therefore its opacity, which in turn perpetuated the inviolable, hierarchical distinction between the "holders of knowledge" (the clergy) and the "passive recipients of instruction" (the faithful) (50). The impression that the Church undermined this distinction by also teaching Latin in its schools, thereby making transparent (at least to part of the population) that which needed to remain opaque, is in reality false. Quite simply, the apprenticeship in Latin that the relatively privileged classes underwent was far from effective. At every period in its history, including the centuries during which it was both the corner- and capstone of formal education, the teaching of Latin failed to provide more than a tiny minority with anything but the most rudimentary proficiency. A moderately well-educated man in the seventeenth century may well have gained enough skill finally to understand the words of the mass, and more, yet his proficiency would not have allowed him to cease thinking of Latin as a basically mysterious and formidable entity. Françoise Waquet demonstrates that while the number of European writers until 1700 who were able to read and even produce original texts in Latin was impressive, the notion that Latin proficiency was sufficiently widespread to allow for ease of communication among the broader membership in the educated classes is seriously mistaken (124–71: passim).

The school, which should have promoted the use of Latin as an instrument of cross-cultural communication and scientific research, did exactly the opposite. Throughout the fifteenth, sixteenth, and seventeenth centuries, according to Philippe Ariès in *La France et les Français* (Encyclopédie de la Pléiade), "[l']étude . . . du latin classique a tué le latin vivant" [the study of classical Latin killed Latin as a living language] (904). Whatever practical advantages Europe enjoyed from having a *lingua franca* inherited from the classical age and enforced by Christianity were few. The sacralization of Latin, both as the medium for Catholic rituals as well as the holy *Ursprache* of the humanistic philosophical tradition, placed it out of reach. The desire to teach Latin faced the much stronger injunction against its demystification. We face here a dilemma that apparently runs counter to the principle, which we have seen, that the teaching of French and the reinvention of French literature advocated during the Revolution were an attempt to restore to French its nonliterary transparency, that is to say, the direct correspondence of signifier and signified. The dilemma is that Latin's ideological value (which according to Ariès caused its decline as a mode of communication) was precisely that, unlike vernaculars, Latin represented a type of uncorrupted language in which the dangers of confusing words with the things they represent simply did not exist. Such is the point made by Benedict Anderson in *Imagined Communities* (1983) when he compares nations to religious communities that share a sacred language and script (or Scripture): dead languages such as Latin, or Classical Arabic and Chinese, hold an enormous advantage over their modern equivalents because it is presumed that the arbitrariness of the sign does not apply to them (20). In fact, the attempt by the Revolution to assign these same sacred values to the contemporary French vernacular is not contradictory at all. First of all, one has to remember that the Revolution did in fact bring about a "classical revival" precisely because of the aura of Latin and Greek as languages uncorrupted by the vagaries of the sign that French-writing poets had so egregiously abused. Second, it is perfectly appropriate to see the French Revolution as a time during which the sacred value of Latin that had been monopolized by the Church was simply transferred to French, the revitalized (one might say redeemed) language of the new secular religion. In their elevation of French to the status of sacred language, capable of carrying the burden of revelation, but *only on the condition* that its sacred form be clearly distinguished from popular speech, the First and the Third Republics are closely related. The relationship between Latin and French is no longer simply one between pure language and vernacular, but an antagonistic one between the vehicle of sacred truths and the pretender to that status: a linguistic Death of the Father.

The shared identity of, rather than difference between French and Latin in the educational system has already emerged in the course of scholarly debates on the subject. Anne-Marie Thiesse and Hélène Mathieu (1991) expressed it very well in a recent article that applies the term "classical" to both Latin and French: "This double effect of teaching letters (the mastery of a *classical* language, namely of a class dialect, and the acquisition of a cultural capital redoubling in the symbolic order the power given by economic capital) was the real stake in the struggle for academic reform that occupied the first years of the Third Republic" (75). The merging of "classical language" (Latin) and "class dialect" (literary French) determined the evolution of the curriculum and of pedagogical practice in secondary (and higher) education, the means changing, the end remaining constant.

Latin in European history was therefore considered essential not for what it was, but for what it did. Furthermore, what it did was not to enable better communication, or better access to ideas and values than modern languages; on the contrary, it was a useful tool for imposing *limits* on communication, for guarding against the danger that modern languages, under the dual influence of Protestantism and scientific progress, were becoming too transparent and efficient. Latin was not only a barrier against the rational debunking of religious beliefs, it also stood for the capacity of language to preserve the mystery and inviolability of any text. Whereas Holy Scripture, for example, is a type of text for which impenetrability (hence inviolability) can be a positive value, and scientific and philosophical texts are examples for which they are, by and large, negative values, there is one other category of text that is arguably closer to the religious paradigm: literature. In this sense, Latin came to represent the "literariness" of literature, defined as its capacity to frustrate attempts to apply rational analysis to the act of communication.[1]

Latin's capacity to mystify the masses, because of the difficulty of learning it and the near impossibility of using it for normal communication, created the erroneous impression of a "magical language" that progressively took root throughout Europe. Like the magician's incantation, which only diverts attention away from the sleight of hand that is the true source of the "magic" she performs, Latin became confused in people's minds with the true nature of the ceremony of which it is in reality a nonessential part. This confusion became solidified in a set of beliefs that were widely held in the late nineteenth century, and continue to be held by many people even today: that Latin is necessary for the full assimilation of French; that its acquisition constitutes an intellectual exercise that facilitates the acquisition of other, subordinate subjects including the sciences; that it builds character; that it contains a spiritual dimension; and finally, that its absolute esthetic value imposes a standard of good taste against which all utterances in any language can be measured (Waquet 2001: 185–200). Each of the preceding beliefs lacks a scientific basis: they were, and in some circles continue to be, articles of faith.

When Benedict Anderson made the comparison between nations and religious communities based on a dead, "pure" language, he intended it as a figure of speech. In the case of Latin, for example, Anderson claims that "[its] religious authority never had a true political analogue" (44), meaning that Latin, although it facilitated the administration and hegemony of the Church, never served as the vehicle for the creation of a modern nation-state. Strictly speaking, that is true. Indirectly, however, I believe that France provides a counter example to that statement. The founding of the French state in the French literary heritage, undertaken by the school of the Third Republic was, in a sense, the emergence in the modern world of the political authority of Latin. The following chapters show how French language and literature did not, as is often argued, violently supplant Latin in the school system the way one political regime replaces another. On the contrary, French merely became what Latin was. To use the imagery of evangelism: the advent of French as something more than the vernacular of a nation had been prophesied by the modern practitioners of Latin, and while there are those even today who remain irrationally attached to seeing Latin instead of French in that role, the role itself has not changed.

Latin was the first and most important area of overlap between Church and school. It is also the link upon which any argument for continuity between Catholic ritual and Republican education, such as the one in this book, depends. The sequence is roughly as follows: the mysteries of the Church were both revealed and concealed by the use of Latin in the liturgy, in front of congregations of speakers of vernacular languages, from the third or fourth century onward (Waquet 2001: 41–2); Latin was the means to acquire literacy, including literacy in French, up until the Revolution, despite the existence of a literary, written vernacular tradition at least since the eighth or ninth century; Latin language and literature continued to be symbols of culture, because of the impression that there was something inherently sacred or magical about them, as compared to the relative simplicity and transparency of living languages, including French; finally, under the pressure of seeking political legitimacy, the government of the Third Republic undertook to transfer the weight of tradition, and the illusion of sacredness that Latin had acquired over the centuries, to French language and literature. The final stage in the sequence, which is also in some ways the most improbable, is what I would like to discuss in this chapter and in chapter 8.

In the primary schools of the Third Republic, as we have seen, the French language had only recently taken over the pedagogical function of Latin. The dimension of French that defied analysis and description, its spirit or soul, and that which also constituted its potential for literariness, had a symbol: Latin.[2] The evolution of primary education in the nineteenth century is the acquisition by French of its ability to stand alone as a language without relying on the authority of its progenitor. Since primary schools are mostly concerned with literacy, and only secondarily with the knowledge and understanding of literature, the substitution of French for Latin was not difficult. But what about secondary education, especially defined as schooling beyond the age of 13, the minimum age for the fulfillment of mandatory education under the new laws? It proved far more difficult to dislodge Latin from secondary schools, in part no doubt because of the relatively small number who went on to study at such a level.

While French could stand on its own as a means of acquiring literacy, it had a much harder time imposing itself as an adequate, much less a privileged means for acquiring culture. The vast amount of cultural capital symbolized by the omnipresence of Latin in the secondary school curriculum had placed it in a strategically dominant position: the fortress of Latin had withstood countless attacks over the years. Françoise Waquet suggests that it was not until 1968, when Education Minister Edgar Faure eliminated Latin from the *sixième* (a grade level roughly equivalent to Junior High School) in the wake of the May revolts, that one could speak of a definitive relegation of Latin to the status of a specialized discipline among many, rather than a cornerstone of general education (17–18).

The defense of Latin in the school was so successful because its liturgical roots contributed to the illusion of magical potential, but also in part because of the ease with which it could be separated from those same origins. It was possible to defend Latin without making any appeal to the traditional religious monopoly on education. Latin had become an autonomous sacred institution, as French was to become. Its capacity to hide and to exclude, which the Church hierarchy had exploited to its own benefit, could just as easily be applied to the secular realm.

The importance of mystification in education is illustrated by one of the most conservative leaders in the history of the Third Republic, Albert de Broglie, who began his public career at the age of 20 under the reign of Louis-Philippe. He gave an impassioned speech at the 1841 *Conférence d'Orsay* on the future of public education in which he made two professions of faith that stand, in a way, for the entire debate in the nineteenth and twentieth centuries over the respective roles of Latin and French in the secondary school curriculum. The first of these concerns the primacy of *lettres humaines* over all other academic disciplines:

> [I]l n'est point de découvertes heureuses, dont les sciences exactes et physiques aient doté notre pays, point d'institutions salutaires dont la politique ait fait hommage à la liberté des peuples, point de trésors dont l'industrie nous ait enrichis, qui ne soient dus, à le bien prendre, aux travaux philosophiques de nos plus grands écrivains.

> [There are no great discoveries with which the physical and exact sciences have endowed our country, no beneficial institutions with which politics have paid homage to the freedom of peoples, no treasures with which industry has enriched us, that are not owed, all things considered, to the philosophical works of our greatest writers.] (8–9)

Having argued the supremacy of the author over all other contributors to society (in a manner consistent with Bénichou's description of the spiritual power of the writer[3]), de Broglie spoke of the humanities in a way that undermines their status as a universal component of education, even of secondary education. While it is true, he said, that "l'éducation classique doit rester parmi nous la première éducation, et la seule qui ouvre les portes des positions supérieures de la société" [classical education [i.e., Greek and Latin] must remain among us the dominant one, and the only one that opens the doors to the highest ranks of society] (10), its role is not to spread the benefit of classical literature to the greatest number of people, so much as to restrict access to the highest echelons of society to those very few most deserving of it. His speech was not a call for free access by all to the soul of classical (and hence French) culture; it was for the universal application of classical education as a means to identify *vocations*, that is to say students who could demonstrate, by their mastery of Latin, their suitability for acceding to (or, in most cases, remaining in) the highest ranks of society:

> Le gouvernement qui aura ainsi suscité, par ses efforts, la sollicitude du public, aura beaucoup fait pour répandre les bienfaits des lettres classiques dans toutes les régions que le pouvoir, la considération, la fortune peuvent aujourd'hui visiter: il aura beaucoup fait aussi pour assurer aux efforts de l'ambition paternelle une récompense légitime et pour éclaircir, à chacune des portes de la vie, les rangs de la multitude qui l'assiège.

[The government that will thus have called forth by its efforts the public's solicitude will have done much to spread the benefits of classical culture in every region where power, status, and fortune can exist: it will have done much as well to guarantee a legitimate reward for fatherly ambition and to thin out, at each of the doors of life, the ranks of the multitude that lay siege to it.] (18)

De Broglie made the apparently paradoxical argument that classical education must be available in every region that power, status (*considération*), and wealth may exist—which is to say, everywhere. The universal access to Latin and Greek implied by his argument has a strictly elitist function, however: to thin the ranks of aspirants to social status at each "door" through which such access is granted. Classical education, the key to the supremacy of the author over all other professions, is to be used strictly as a method of initiation into the world of the *notables*. De Broglie comes very close to admitting that such initiation, which is the "legitimate reward" of ambitious fathers, is to be limited to those individuals who, by virtue of power, status, and wealth, already have a claim to society's highest positions.

The struggle of the Third Republic with the role of Latin in the secondary curriculum was to take place under the paradox expressed by de Broglie in 1841. The alternate attacks on and defenses of classical education by the Republic, and the long, slow process of granting French the same power previously belonging to Latin, occurred within the opposition between the mystification and demystification of culture. Antoine Prost, in his authoritative and comprehensive *Histoire de l'enseignement en France—1800–1967* (1968), identifies three major tendencies during the 1880s: the all-out attack on Latin from partisans of modern education as the new standard, according to which students needed instruction in areas relevant to the success of the nation in the world; the moderate reformers, who wanted to save Latin and Greek, but reduce the number of hours devoted to them in the curriculum, and change the methods used to teach them; and the reactionary, mostly Catholic faction that wanted to maintain and strengthen the *status quo*. As often happened during the Third Republic, the moderates won the battle. It is significant, however, that in so doing they preserved the role of Latin as sine qua non of secondary education, and established French only as a back-up hieratic language for the day, far in the future, when the anti-Latin forces would prevail (250). In other words the Republic, most closely aligned with the "moderate" pro-Latin camp, gave in to many of the demands of the reactionaries. The final result, while appearing to be a compromise, in fact often ends up being an implementation of a conservative agenda under the guise of reform. The final stage in the process, as we will see, was the "latinization" of French that quietly took place while the battles surrounding the role of Latin in the curriculum raged. The elitist goals that de Broglie in 1841 had presented as the benefits of classical education were, by the beginning of the twentieth century, attainable through recourse to French. When the Third Republic began, that was not yet possible. Following is the account of how French became the vehicle of the sacred, and the symbol of impenetrability, that Latin had been exclusively.

Latin to French: The Transition

From its origins in the Jesuit *collèges* in the sixteenth century until 1880, *l'enseignement classique* did not undergo any substantial changes. Such is the bold claim of André Chervel, author of *Les Auteurs français, latins et grecs au programme de l'enseignement secondaire de 1800 à nos jours* (French, Greek, and Latin Authors in the Secondary Education Curriculum from 1800 to the Present, published in 1986 by the Institut National de Recherche Pédagogique). The point Chervel makes is that until 1880, both classical languages and French were taught rhetorically, and after 1880, French in particular was taught literarily, which meant a change not only in pedagogy, but in content as well:

> La sélection des auteurs français du programme, qui s'était opérée jusque-là plus ou moins comme la doublure de la liste des auteurs latins ou grecs, fait appel désormais à des critères de choix d'une toute autre nature: si l'oeuvre doit rester une source d'imitation, elle doit également être lue et expliquée pour elle-même. Avec l'explication des textes, c'est l'histoire littéraire et la culture générale qui pénètrent dans les lycées et les collèges. . . . De tout côté, la littérature française déborde ce champ étroit où revenaient sans cesse Massillon, Télémaque, Boileau et *Le siècle de Louis XIV*. . . . C'est le seizième siècle, bientôt le moyen-âge, qui vont s'ouvrir devant l'élève. Et malgré les résistances qu'on devine, il faudra bien faire également leur place aux écrivains de la première moitié du [dix-neuvième] siècle.

> [The selection of French authors for the curriculum, which until then had been modeled on the lists of Greek and Latin authors, henceforth based itself on entirely different criteria: while the work still must serve as a model for imitation, it must also be read and analyzed for itself. With the analysis of texts, literary history and general culture make their appearance in *lycées* and secondary schools. . . . On every side, French literature spills out beyond the narrow field in which Massillon, [Fénelon's] *Télémaque*, Boileau and [Voltaire's] *Century of Louis XIV* constantly reappeared. The sixteenth century, and soon after the Middle

Ages, opened up to the student. In spite of the resistance one can imagine, it became necessary to grant their space to the writers of the first half of the [nineteenth] century.] (15)

For the first time in history, according to Chervel, secondary education in France was predicated on the ability of students to understand, rather than imitate, the literary qualities of texts. Although one might quibble with Chervel's emphasis on 1880 as the separation between two radically different pedagogies (in part II, we saw evidence that the literary study of texts, especially French texts, appeared as early as the eighteenth century), it is clear that a new paradigm in secondary education had arrived. In the official programs for the classes of *seconde* and *première*, for example, in which the most intensive exposure to literature occurs, a comparison between 1874 and 1885 is instructive. The Greek and Latin lists barely change at all, while the French lists become far richer and more diverse.

Programmes for the year of *seconde* (adapted from Chervel 1986: 170–1)

1874	1885
French: Bossuet; La Bruyère; Massillon; Théâtre classique; Boileau	*French*: Selected poetry and prose, 17th, 18th, and 19th centuries; Pascal; Bossuet; La Bruyère; Fénelon; Voltaire (*Siècle de Louis XIV*); Buffon; Corneille; Molière; Racine; La Fontaine; Boileau
Latin: Cicero; Tacitus; Virgil; Horace	*Latin*: Cicero; Titus Livius; Tacitus; Terence; Lucretius; Virgil; Horace
Greek: Homer; Plato; Demosthenes; Euripides	*Greek*: Homer; Plato; Demosthenes; Sophocles; Aristophanes

Programmes for the year of *première* (adapted from Chervel 1986: 200–1)

1874	1885
French: *Morceaux choisis*, 16th century; Pascal; Bossuet; La Bruyère, Fénelon; Voltaire (*Siècle de Louis XIV*); Buffon; Théâtre classique; La Fontaine; Boileau	*French*: *La Chanson de Roland*; Joinville; selected poetry and prose, 16th, 17th, 18th, and 19th centuries; Montaigne; Bossuet; La Bruyère; Voltaire (*Letters*); Corneille; Molière; Racine; La Fontaine
Latin: Cicero; Tacitus; Plautus; Lucretius; Virgil; Horace	*Latin*: Cicero, Titus Livius; Tacitus; Virgil; Horace
Greek: Homer; Plato; Demosthenes; Aristotle; Sophocles; Aristophanes	*Greek*: Homer, Xenophon; Plato; Plutarch; Euripides

Chervel's research shows even more additions to the French literature program in the years following: the above comparison is part of a trend that extends to the turn of the century and beyond, and includes epic struggles over the number of class hours devoted to each subject.[4]

Various stages in the evolution of the school system from Latin to French took place. As one might expect, the period around 1880 saw the beginning of a gradual, yet dramatic decline in the number of Latin and Greek textbooks published, even though the overall number of students in secondary schools increased.[5] It does not follow, however, that the actual importance of Latin in the curriculum declined. The teaching of Latin changed from an emphasis on listening, speaking, and writing to an emphasis on reading, which, as any language teacher will attest, is by far the easiest of the four skills to impart. The "dumbing down" of Latin during the Third Republic can be summed up as follows: the emphasis before 1870 on Latin composition and oration, of which *le thème*, or the translation of a French text into Latin is an example, gave way to *la version*, the translation or paraphrase of Latin texts into French (Mayeur 1981: 562). But it was not simply the *baccalauréat* that changed during the Third Republic. As we have noted, the attempt to institute national identity through the medium of French literature took place at every level. In primary education, the process was relatively simple. French literature had little or no competition, and the only problem (though a significant one) was the laborious development of a lay morality powerful enough to supplant the religious instruction previously mandated and now superseded. Literature, as we saw, was the solution to the problem. A fairly effective institution of a cult of French language and literature finally proved feasible at the educational level through which every citizen must pass.

The secondary level, whether the prestigious national *lycées* and private *collèges*, or any institution for education beyond the mandatory period, presented a different challenge. Although the percentage of the population passing through such institutions was much smaller than in the primary schools, the symbolic effect of the education they disseminated was enormous. One of the biggest obstacles the Third Republic faced in its drive to make French the language of a new, national cult was the elevated status of Latin, which seemed to prevent any attempt to make French language and literature the appropriate vessels for sacred beliefs. Both in the Church and among the educated elite, Latin was far preferable to French as a vehicle for truth, a code for initiates, and a hallmark of culture and class. To criticize the privileged status of Latin therefore was also to attack a wide range of entrenched institutions.

To be for or against Latin, in the late nineteenth century, was to reveal one's social and political sympathies.[6] In following this debate, it is important to remember that it concerns primarily the role of *secondary* education, and specifically the function in society of the *baccalauréat*, a certificate that represented a relatively rare degree of academic achievement. The previous discussion of *manuels*, by contrast, concerned education until the age of 13, the cutoff point for mandatory schooling. The *manuels* are therefore primarily about education of the masses, and Latin about the education of the upper classes. The line between the two discussions often blurred, however, and whether the topic was primary or secondary education, debates over the role of language and literature in education were very much about the very soul of the nation itself. So what did Latin really signify in the debates of the Third Republic? More precisely, what possible importance could the practice of a dead language with strong ties to Catholic liturgy have in the new definition of the national culture? Was it necessary, or even possible, to propose French language and literature as a viable substitute for classics in the development of a curriculum based on *laïcité*?

In a recent article, Philippe Cibois provides a valuable history of the role of Latin in the school curriculum since the eighteenth century, and its "revival" during the debates surrounding national education at the end of the nineteenth. In order to understand the depth of feelings aroused by plans to replace Latin with French, one must keep in mind a few simple facts. The legacy of the *querelle des anciens et des modernes* was a culture that continued to think of Latin as a "living" language, to the extent that d'Alembert felt that he was being very radical when, in his Encyclopedia article on *collège*, he argued that one must learn Latin only in order to read the classics, not in order to write in imitation of them (Cibois 2000: 8). The fact that such an argument was deemed controversial also confirms the dominance at the time of Jesuit pedagogy, with its emphasis on rhetoric over erudition. The expulsion of the Jesuits in 1762, resulting in the takeover of their *collèges* by the *parlement*, allowed for some implementation of d'Alembert's suggestion: in addition to requiring more French texts in the schools, the president of the Paris *parlement*, Rolland d'Erceville, specifically requested that all inscriptions on public monuments be in French rather than the customary Latin (9). Clearly, the call for public monuments consisting of inscriptions rather than statues was already well established before the Revolution. From there, it was only a short step to the extreme suspicion of eloquence, figurative speech, and literary language (never mind Latin) that characterized the policies of the First Republic, and which were echoed in more temperate form by Condorcet's appeal for the teaching of science over the humanities.

Cibois points out that the Revolution's attack on Latin (which nevertheless fell well short of eliminating it as a mandatory subject of study in secondary education) led to a nineteenth-century backlash, which he calls Latin's "revival," and which the founders of the Third Republic could not afford to ignore. Among the statistics Cibois mentions is the fact that the number of hours devoted in the *lycée* to the study of science, which approached 50 percent of class time during the First Republic, dropped to 10 percent during the Restoration, managed to go up to 20 percent during the implementation of the reforms of the Third Republic, before dropping back to 10 percent in 1902 (15). Humanities in general, and especially the competing fields of Latin *version* (emphasizing reading ability), *thème* (emphasizing writing ability), and French language and literature, were the beneficiaries of this conservative trend.[7] Another statistic in Cibois's article, borrowed from research by Etienne Brunet, shows that the number of Latin words contained in French *literary* texts increased throughout the sixteenth and nineteenth centuries, and decreased in the seventeenth, eighteenth, and twentieth (15), suggesting a possible causal link, and not simply a correlation, between the status of Latin in the schools and degree of "latinity" in contemporaneous literary production.

Pierre Kuentz analyzed the role of Latin in the school of the Republic, and gave it a different status from the one claimed by its supporters and detractors. Latin, in brief, is a convenient way to allude to an entire complex of cultural practices; the word closest to a precise designation of the role of Latin in these debates is "literariness." "'Le latin' désigne un objet *réel*, pas une manipulation idéologique. Cet objet n'est pas une *langue*, mais des 'pratiques canoniques' et 'rhétoriques' et 'sociales'" [The word "Latin" designated a *real* object, not an ideological manipulation [/illusion]. [However] that object is not a *language*, but rather a set of "canonical" and "rhetorical" and "social" practices] (111). Indeed, the defenders of Latin generally take for granted that it has a sacred quality that is important to protect through specific rhetorical and social applications. This "sacredness" is also the basis for the power of French. The debate is really over whether sacredness inheres in the French language by itself (as represented by the French literary canon), or whether it derives from Latin. Instead of a theological debate between Catholic and Protestant (a common theme in Third Republic historiography, as we have seen), we have a situation more aptly represented by the difference between Christianity and Judaism, where Latin is the God of the Old Testament, and French is the Christ. Nobody denies God His divinity. But what about the claim made on behalf of His Son—the French language—that He/it is in and of Himself/itself divine? Kuentz says that "[l]e latin fonctionne comme un leurre" [Latin functions as a decoy] (112). It does, if we accept that Latin is the crystallization, in the first half of the Third Republic (and much of the second half as well), of people's concerns with the sacred as a source for authority, as a legitimating power. Kuentz borrows Voltaire's *mot* concerning God and man: "Le latin a fait le français à son image, mais le français le lui a bien rendu" [Latin made French in its own image, but French returned the favor] (114).

In 1925, Edmond Goblot wrote a very influential critique of the elitist aspects of Latin and education in general, laying some of the groundwork for Pierre Bourdieu's later theories on the acquisition and transmission of cultural capital: *La Barrière et le niveau: étude sociologique sur la bourgeoisie française moderne* (The Barrier and the Level: A Sociological Study of the Modern French Bourgeoisie) examines the relationship between language, literature, and class. The "barrier and the level" refer to the separate functions of exclusion and conformity that a cultural marker, such as knowledge of Latin, can serve. In the nineteenth century and beyond, there was a widespread assumption: "la principale différence entre un bourgeois et un homme du peuple fut . . . que le bourgeois savait, et même savait assez bien le latin" [the main difference between a bourgeois and a man of the people . . . was that the bourgeois knew Latin, and even knew it rather well] (79). There may never have been a golden age of the French bourgeoisie when knowledge of Latin was a given, as Françoise Waquet suggests; but what is certain is that by the end of the nineteenth century, though Latin was still the marker of education and of class, an ever-shrinking minority could actually read or write it with any ease. As a result, the *baccalauréat* and its social significance became even more important: "Il faut [au bourgeois] qu'un diplôme d'Etat, un parchemin signé du ministre, constatant officiellement qu'il a appris le latin, lui confère le droit de ne pas le savoir" [[The bourgeois requires] a state-issued diploma, a piece of parchment signed by the minister that, by officially recognizing that he has learned Latin, confers upon him the right not to know it] (84). In conclusion, Goblot says that the primacy of education as a political issue in the early days of the Third Republic is entirely due to the need to use the institution of the school to perpetuate a distinction which had begun to dissolve: "Pour qu'une société se scinde en classes, il faut que quelque chose d'artificiel et de factice remplace les rampes continues par des marches d'escalier . . . c'est-à-dire crée un ou des obstacles difficiles à franchir et mette sur le même plan ceux qui les ont franchis. Telle est la fonction— l'unique fonction—du baccalauréat" [In order for a society to divide itself into classes, something arbitrary and artificial must replace the continuous ramps [of social mobility] with steps . . . that is to say, one or more obstacles that place those who have overcome them on the same level. Such is the one and only function of the *baccalauréat*] (87).

The fiction that mastery of Latin expression (as distinct from Latin culture) was necessary for social success owed its power largely to the legacy of the Jesuit monopoly over secondary education. After the symbolic banning of Jesuits from the schools by Ferry in 1880, a back-lash took place during which conservatives, Catholics and non-Catholics alike, rallied around the Jesuits and their curricular emphasis on Latin, Greek, philosophy, and seventeenth-century French literature. By 1890, 25 Jesuit *collèges* out of a total of 27 were back at full strength after the purge of 1880 (Bush 1975: 126). It was extremely difficult (in other words: politically costly) for the government to make any radical changes in the content of the *baccalauréat*. Secondary education without Classics (or *enseignement moderne* rather than *enseignement classique*) suffered from the stigma of being associated with the *enseignement spécial* created by education minister Victor Duruy in 1866. Duruy had created a second track that had a professional and technical rather than humanist emphasis, and helped create the fear which there might be more than one road to salvation: a utilitarian and genuinely democratic one, as well as a classical and elitist one. In the 1880s and beyond, when it became a question of replacing Latin with French as the royal road to cultural capital, one must understand the formidable obstacles that the Republic encountered in the context of the need to preserve Latin's exclusive power as a legitimating force.

CHAPTER 8

AGAINST LITERATURE: THE "QUESTION OF LATIN"

In 1885, three years after the official founding of the national school system, and five years after Ferry's reforms of the secondary school curriculum began to undermine the centrality of Latin, a controversy erupted which illustrated the issues at hand. Raoul Frary, a former *normalien* and *lycée* professor turned journalist, published *La Question du latin*, a book in which he argued that the teaching of Latin, and of Classics in general, should be reserved only for students in the school system who were to become specialists in the field of classical studies, rather than imposed upon each and every postulant to the *baccalauréat*. Frary's book gave rise to a polemic that lasted years, and which produced, aside from numerous articles and letters in the press, several books and pamphlets, mainly hostile, written by members of the clergy and university establishment.[1]

At the root of the polemic lay a simple question: to what extent, if any, is the teaching of Latin (and Ancient Greek) an essential part of the education of a French citizen? In the background of Frary's book, there is the desire of part of the left wing in France to use the schools as a means for social engineering by making the criteria of "citizenship" as inclusive as possible, and making "high" culture irrelevant to general education. As it turned out, whatever promise for social change the institution of national education held quickly vanished, and the inherent conservatism of Jules Ferry's "second revolution" held sway.[2] As Bourdieu remarks in *La Distinction* (1979), nobilities are by nature essentialist; and nothing structurally distinguishes the republican nobility of culture, identified by the diploma, from the traditional nobilities, identified by titles. The Republic wanted nothing less than the realization of ". . . [le] rêve platonicien de la division des fonctions fondée dans une hiérarchie des êtres. . . ." [the platonic dream of the division of functions founded upon a hierarchy of beings] (Bourdien 1979: 23). What is most interesting, therefore, is the reaction that Frary's so-called "utilitarianism"[3] called forth, not only among traditional conservatives, but among the very supporters of the fledgling Republic itself: *La question du latin* was attacked by both Right and Left.

Until 1882, the role of the school in social and national identification was less of an issue, since access to education was still very much a matter of class origin and social ambition. In the absence of obligatory education for every citizen, education itself was a prominent sign of class distinction. The *programme* of the *baccalauréat* mattered in so far as it defined the space separating the educated elite from the masses. This role was challenged as soon as education became a right instead of a privilege, and the functional, utilitarian goals of education could replace the ethos of learning for the sake of learning.

Raoul Frary severed the alliance of education and social standing. Speaking of the contemporary tyranny of classical education, he writes:

L'essentiel est toujours, à ce qu'il semble, de mettre les modernes à l'école des anciens, et d'élever tous les Français comme s'ils devaient être gens de lettres ou gens de loi.

[The essential purpose is always, it seems to me, to make the moderns conform to the ancients, and to raise all French people as if they were going to become academics or members of the legal profession.] (40)

Frary wastes no time in defining what is at stake: education in its current form treats all students as potential "men of letters" or lawyers, the only professions for which Latin has any practical value. Clearly an entire nation cannot be fed on a diet of Latin and Greek, since those subjects serve only to perpetuate an outmoded elitism: first, by imposing a strenuous rite of passage on those who aspire to be *lycéens*, and second by making life miserable for the *lycéens* even after they get in. By implying that the current system subordinates the *modernes* to the *anciens*, Frary introduces another element as well: the revolutionary idea that culture takes place in the present. Without actually reviving the *Querelle des anciens et des modernes*, he nevertheless insinuates a cultural argument into the debate, according to which the nation would gain by the liberation of literature from the classical model.

Like many polemics, the "Latin question" was symbolic of much wider concerns: "*la question*," as it came to be known, drew the line between ideologies that dealt variously with religion, politics, and national culture. Right-wing Catholics angrily defended the status quo, for reasons that have to do with more than the need for a social structure based on the existence of cultural markers separating the governing elite from the masses. The Left by and large supported the accelerated marginalization of Greek and Latin, though not as strongly or unequivocally as Frary. Complicating the issue beyond the clear dichotomies of Right and Left, Catholic and anticlerical, was the comparatively recent attempt finally to put into practice the revolutionary debate concerning a French national culture, a debate in which all parties claimed an interest.

Frary's most controversial move was to dismiss the relationship between education and national culture by calling the debate irrelevant. In arguing against the classics, he does much more than take a populist position against the cultural elite: he argues far more radically in favor of the relegation of culture itself to the private sphere, thereby putting himself at odds with the republican establishment which sought to promote more, not less, involvement by the state in cultural matters. "La démocratie n'admet point de caste et ne connaît pas de nobles, mais elle a ses bacheliers" [Democracy admits of no castes and recognizes no aristocracy, but it does have its *bacheliers*] (73), and: ". . . l'aristocratie des arts libéraux n'est pas de notre siècle" [The aristocracy of the liberal arts does not belong to our century] (96). The "cultural aristocracy" to which Frary alludes continued to grow in power, as the real aristocracy declined. The bourgeoisie had merely replaced *naissance* with *culture* (i.e., Classics) as the first prerequisite for social status. The issue arose, as soon as the primacy of Greek and Latin was threatened, as to whether "culture" could function separately from its corollaries of elitism and class privilege.

In Frary's utilitarian utopia, culture ultimately lives outside the confines of public education. The illusion that social advancement can only be achieved by submitting to the arbitrary dictates of classical education perverts the goals of learning. About the unreasonable difficulty faced by one who tries to master Greek and/or Latin, Frary states:

> Aussi [l'élève] se lance-t-il dans cette voie douloureuse par un acte d'obéissance et de foi [. . .] ce n'est plus l'instruction qu'il cherche, c'est le succès.
>
> [[The pupil] throws himself upon this *via dolorosa* by an act of obeisance and faith . . . it is no longer education he seeks, but success.] (121)

Mastery becomes gratuitous, an end in itself; as it can serve no legitimate purpose (being outside of *l'instruction*), it can only serve the clearly illegitimate purpose of arbitrary class distinction. The allusion to Christ's sacrifice and to an "act of faith" is certainly intended to remind one of the deceptive link between education and religion, both literally (most schools having been founded by religious groups) and metaphorically (cultural value as a matter of faith rather than empirical fact).

Frary's pragmatism does not lead automatically to Bourdieu's contemporary model of a constructed French culture, however; nor does it ultimately challenge the status of Classics as a "privilege." On the contrary, by affirming the incompatibility of national education and classics, he simply preserves elitism within the private sphere, ultimately denying the state any cultural role. Nothing is more elitist than his opinion, no doubt expressed partly for the strategic purpose of winning over the bourgeois lovers of classical culture, of thousands of *lycéens* poring over the same relics of antiquity:

> Peut-être aussi est-ce rendre aux muses un hommage plus délicat que de ne point pousser dans leur temple une foule trop nombreuse pour n'être pas un peu profane.

> [Perhaps as well it would be paying a more delicate homage to the muses if we were not to shove into their temple a crowd far too numerous not to be slightly profane.] (15)

What remains radical in Frary's statement that the masses cannot be expected to appreciate the initiation into classical languages, is his proposal that such study be henceforth the result of genuine choice rather than social rank or aspiration. He argues that if Greek and Latin no longer constituted the hallmark of a complete education, then they would no longer signify social status (a naïve argument, since it must not have been hard for him to imagine that other disciplines—such as French literature—would simply take their place; or that Latin, instead of being a marker for the bourgeoisie, would, thanks to its rarer dissemination among the population, become an even more valuable cultural commodity and source of *snobisme*). According to Frary, only classicists who have practical reasons to undergo such an initiation, would do so: literary culture becomes a specialized field of learning, like engineering or biology, but is also imbued with a sacred status which prohibits access by any but the "happy few" who now would constitute a private sect rather than the clergy of a national religion.

The sympathetic reaction of many academics provides insight into the popularity of Frary's position. In 1890, while the polemic was still in force, J. Wogue, a professor at the lycée of Reims, published an article in the prestigious *Revue de l'enseignement secondaire et de l'enseignement supérieur* supporting the expansion of *l'enseignement spécial* in opposition to the stubborn belief among pedagogy specialists that classical, and even modern literary education is somehow an essential foundation for all other studies. He critiques, first of all, the "Monsieur Jourdain" mentality that had taken over secondary education, the materiality of business corrupting the nobility of culture:

> [T]oute une population d'écoliers qui encombrent l'enseignement classique, et que leurs familles, par un sentiment de vanité étroite, aimaient mieux voir devenir de mauvais latinistes que de bons commerçants.
>
> [An entire population of schoolchildren who clutter up classical education and whose families, for reasons of narrow vanity, would rather see become poor latinists than good shopkeepers.] (400)

The blame for this situation rests squarely on the shoulders of the academic elite that managed—anachronistically, in Wogue's opinion—to skew national education with its cult of literature, both classical and modern:

> Notre Université, pourtant si libérale, renferme encore quelques esprits, qui croient à la vertu immanente des vieilles humanités. . . . [E]levés dans le culte et l'admiration des chefs d'oeuvre, ils repoussent l'érudition sous toutes ses formes, comme attentatoire à la religion dont ils sont les pontifes. . . .
>
> [Our university, usually so liberal, still contains a few minds that believe in the immanent value of the old humanities. . . . Raised in the cult and adoration of masterpieces, they reject erudition in all its forms as an attack on the religion of which they are the high priests.] (403)

As Wogue shows by his positive use of the term "*érudition*," he stands firmly behind the proponents of literary history, against not only the classicists, but any who would try to place the study of literature itself, as distinct from literary history, at the root of all learning. As Wogue sees it, "l'histoire littéraire à la base et la critique littéraire au sommet" [literary history at the base and literary criticism at the top] (409). The questions raised by this slightly more nuanced contribution to the polemic are several: are we speaking here, as we did in the case of the literary *manuels* intended for the primary schools, of a simple attempt to replace the teaching of literature itself with something else that can easily stand for literature? In other words, is the attack against Latin, and the attack against literary studies in general which it contains, simply an attempt to teach an ersatz morality or literary history that nonetheless depends on the existence of a sacred national corpus? Do Frary and his associates perhaps help the cause of literature by placing it on the same altar as did the primary school pedagogues?

In true republican tradition, Frary does not directly challenge the sacred, but simply purges it from the public sphere, exactly as the Church itself had been removed from the schools. The religious point of view, simply expressed, was that Latin and Catholicism were mutually dependent: when one was attacked, the other suffered. A conservative Catholic resistance to the entire process of nationalization (and popularization) of education, for which Latin was sacred, attacked Frary. L'Abbé Leroy, during the 1887 *distribution des prix* ceremony at the *gymnase catholique du Haut-Rhin*, when the *question du latin* was still raging, echoed the argument according to which it is the cornerstone of the religious state by claiming that Latin was not imported into France by Caesar's armies, but by "les prêtres romains, qui vinrent prêcher l'Evangile en Gaule" [Roman priests who came to preach the Gospel in Gaul] (8), thereby throwing a new light on the legitimacy of the Latin *Ursprache*. Where Frary argues that Latin culture is indeed a temple, which needs to be preserved from the desecration of too many worshippers, l'Abbé Leroy defined the sacredness of Latin through its role in the founding of the Catholic state. The fact that Latin at the secondary level is literary and not liturgical made no difference: "les poésies de Virgile et d'Horace firent oublier les fiers accents des Bardes" [the poetry of Virgil and Horace made them forget the proud tones of the bards] (8). The pagan poetry of the classics was so much preferable to the equally pagan but less literary poetry of the Celtic bards that they actually helped achieve the goal of evangelization.

But it is still for control of the French soul that Church and state are locked in struggle, as l'Abbé Jail, in another speech inspired by Frary, given at yet another *distribution des prix* ceremony, reminds his audience:

Non seulement il nous est défendu de circuler dans nos classes les livres que l'Etat a condamnés—car l'Etat, depuis quelques années, a lui aussi son Index;—mais, par un raffinement de coquetterie, on nous oblige, nous prêtres, à commenter des ouvrages que tout père respectueux de l'âme de son fils ne laisserait pas tomber entre ses mains . . . à l'unique fin de raviver de vieilles haines contre une congrégation à laquelle on ne peut pardonner sa science et sa vertu.

[Not only are we forbidden to circulate in our classrooms the books which the state has condemned—for the state has had its own Index for some years—but, by a further refinement of coyness, they force us priests to comment on works that any father who respects the soul of his son would never let fall into his hands . . . with the sole purpose of reviving ancient hostilities against a congregation whose knowledge and virtue one cannot forgive.] (7)

More interesting than the reaction of the teacher-clerics is the powerful response to Frary's polemic among members of the public educational establishment, not always easy to distinguish from the Catholic response. For them also Latin possessed a sacred status. H. Pigeonneau, a teacher and the general secretary of an ad hoc organization called *Société pour l'étude des questions d'Enseignement secondaire*, warned of what would happen if Latin was removed as the cornerstone of all education (Pigeonneau's book came out of the same publishing house as Frary's, serving as a type of "*droit de réponse*"):

> Ce qu'on est convenu d'appeler aujourd'hui le français ne tardera pas à passer au rang des langues mortes et à tomber par conséquent sous le coup de la proscription. La végétation du nouvel idiome anglo-germano-slavo-arabo-sino-française pourra s'épanouir en toute liberté et la France verra encore de beaux jours, à moins qu'il n'y ait plus de France, ce qui est probable, et ce qui simplifierait la question.
>
> [What we conventionally designate today by the word "French" will soon join the ranks of dead languages, and will therefore be forbidden. The vegetation of the new Anglo-Germano-Slavo-Arabo-Sino-French dialect will be able to flourish in complete freedom and France will still see glorious days, unless there is no longer a France, which is likely and would simplify matters.] (26)

Pigeonneau's humorously apocalyptic warning, based on the logic that a *langue morte* will always become a *langue interdite* under the republican regime, needs to be placed in historical context: in 1885, German and English were perhaps an even greater perceived threat than they are today. The vitality of French and of France, therefore, easily appeared to depend on the continued study of Latin at all levels of the educational process. Pigeonneau expressed two of the greatest reservations about educational reform: that eliminating Latin is simply the first step towards eliminating culture, specifically French national culture, from the curriculum; and that French itself is in danger of becoming irrelevant, once the first step away from Latin is made (significantly, Frary advocated a modern language curriculum, with emphasis on English).

Both arguments—cultural identity and linguistic darwinism—exceed in importance the one concerning language and social status that de Broglie expressed so memorably, and that Pigeonneau reiterates: "quel sera le criterium pour distinguer le charabia le plus invraisemblable du plus pur parisien?" [what criterium will distinguish the most outrageous gibberish from the purest Parisian French?] (26). The answer to his question is Latin, of course, although its ability to help in distinguishing *charabia* from *parisien* (the latter a term usually designating *argot*, but used here to refer to its exact opposite) is a beneficial product, and not a justification, for its continued dominance in the secondary schools. Pigeonneau practices what he preaches, preferring the Greco-Latin word *criterium* to either *critère* (criterion) or even *critérium* (with an accent), to distinguish his own speech from nonsense or *charabia*, a word borrowed from the Arabic that literally means "Arabic language": ultimately, Latin (a foreign language no matter what the pro-Latinists say) is the means not only to distinguish between good and bad French, but between French and non-French (of which Arabic—*charabia*—is as good an example as any).

One of Frary's most vocal academic (as distinct from Catholic) opponents was Albert Duruy (no relation to the republican reformer of education Victor Duruy, with whom he had nothing in common ideologically), who published two conservative defenses of traditional education, *L'Instruction publique et la Révolution* (1882) and *L'Instruction publique et la démocratie* (1886). The latter contains a diatribe against *éducation moderne* inspired by *la question du latin*. The sectarian argument (Catholic against secular) is present in Duruy's pamphlets, such as his outrage at the marginalization of clerics: "De l'expulsion des jésuites à la réforme des études classiques, il n'y avait qu'un pas" [From the expulsion of the Jesuits to the reform of classical education, there was only one step] (1886: 317); but his main arguments for the preservation of Latin are political. The replacement of Latin by French in the secondary curriculum would constitute "le plus détestable système de compression intellectuelle qui ait jamais pesé sur la jeunesse d'un pays" [the most despicable system of intellectual compression ever imposed on the youth of a country] (v), and represent "[une] pédagogie d'importation étrangère et souverainement antipathique à l'esprit français" [a pedagogy imported from abroad and royally antithetical to the French spirit] (vi). The value of Latin is therefore primarily its power to distinguish the elite from the masses (whereas French would "compress," i.e., make distinctions less apparent), and to reveal the "French spirit."

It is typical of the arguments in favor of Latin that the spirit, soul, or whatever term is used to designate the true identity of French be considered inaccessible from within the French language itself, and must be revealed through a recourse to Latin which, despite being the ancestor of French, is nevertheless foreign to it. The solution to this paradox— the recourse to Latin in order to know French—has several parts. First, there is the fact that "modern" education was a feature of predominantly Protestant societies, such as Britain and Germany, where the study of the national language and literature did not (at least according to Duruy and others of his camp) rely on the prior study of the classics. While it is true that only romance languages such as French have the privileged relationship to Latin that comes from their origins as a vernacular, from which comes the belief that French shares with it some common essence, in practical terms, the grammatical and lexical advantages of studying Latin are probably just as great, and just as limited, for native speakers of French, German, or English. The dominant argument, however, is that the tradition of placing Latin at the center of literacy acquisition and secondary education is stronger in France, which is enough to justify its perpetuation.

Ferdinand Réal, an ally of former *ministre de l'Instruction publique* Jules Simon who had by now established his staunch opposition to the educational reforms of the Republic that he had once enthusiastically supported, joined the fray with a pamphlet on *La Réforme de l'enseignement secondaire* (The Reform of Secondary Education) published in 1890. He used the occasion to champion the academic reaction against Frary and his sympathizers within the government, by arguing for the restitution of Latin to its rightful place, not in secondary education (where it was still relatively secure), but in primary education:

> [Les professeurs] vous diront que les enfants leur arrivent aujourd'hui plus faibles, *même en français*, qu'à l'époque où les premiers éléments du latin leur donnaient l'étymologie et l'orthographe de la plupart des mots de notre langue.
>
> [[Secondary school teachers] will tell you that children come to them today weaker, *even in French*, than in the days when the basic elements of Latin gave them the etymology and spelling of most of the words in our language.] (19)

Based on the consequences of the loss of Latin on students of primary education, Réal shudders to think of the consequences of a similar sacrifice of Latin in secondary education: "la suppression des études classiques serait la décapitation intellectuelle de la France" [the suppression of classical education would be the intellectual decapitation of France] (25). He distinguishes therefore Latin as a necessary component of general education from Latin as an advanced, autonomous discipline in its own right:

> [L]es études classiques proprement dites ne doivent être le lot que d'une sorte d'élite intellectuelle. . . . Des spécialisations s'imposent.
>
> Mais je crois d'autre part qu'il n'appartient ni à un père, ni à un chef d'institution, ni à personne d'opérer trop tôt et au hasard ces spécialisations.

[Classical education proper must not be the fate of only one sort of intellectual elite . . . Specializations are necessary.

But I also believe that no father, no school administrator, nobody at all has the right to impose such specializations too early and at random.] (25)

Réal was far from being a conservative on all fronts. His ideas on education were strikingly original, going so far as to propose eliminating the *baccalauréat* entirely in favor of a system of *"casiers scolaires"* (which we know as academic transcripts[4]) that students would use to apply for admission to universities, or simply on the job market. Furthermore, as the above passages prove, he did not believe that all secondary school students needed to follow an intensive program in Latin unless they chose. Such a choice required that the student already have been exposed to Latin, however, meaning that it had to be mandatory up until the moment at which the student opted for a specialization. By supporting the maintenance of Latin's position as a prerequisite for all advanced instruction, Réal situated himself in the mainstream of the educational establishment of his day, from which one could hear a secularized echo of the outraged reaction to Frary's arguments by the priests.

It is easy to understand why the Church would be heavily invested in the belief that the study of Latin is basic to its own survival in society; but why should academics feel the same way? The academic attachment to Latin is one of the most revealing characteristics of the cultural institutions of the late nineteenth century. It illustrates in a concentrated manner how the sacred permeates culture, continuing to be the marker of educational sophistication and of national identity. First of all, Latin is valuable precisely *because* it does not serve the material prosperity of the nation—therefore, it can only be understood as belonging to the spiritual domain, as expressed by a journalist, Hignard, in 1886:

M. Frary est fidèle à son principe que tous les citoyens soient des *producteurs de richesses matérielles.* Mais il y a, et il doit y avoir . . . autre chose dans la société, d'autres professions non moins utiles, n'en déplaise à M. Frary.

[Mr. Frary remains true to his principle that all citizens are *producers of material wealth.* But there is, and must be . . . something other in society, other professions that are no less useful, whatever Mr. Frary may think.] (17)

The gratuitousness of the sacred, defined here literally as its existence outside of the realm of economic production, is a defining characteristic, a *sine qua non*, if national identity is to continue to function as a sacred entity: Latin's uselessness is its connection to the doctrine of *l'art pour l'art*, itself an offshoot of the grounding of aristocratic identity in the rejection of economic activity (*otium vs negotium*).

Another example of the sacred applied to culture is the appeal made by G.-A. Heinrich (*Doyen* of the *Faculté des Lettres* of Lyon) to the category of timelessness:

> [Les langues modernes n'offrent] à l'intelligence aucune place de sûreté où l'on puisse, abstraction faite des querelles du moment, se recueillir en face des idées, et sonder l'âme humaine, sans en faire jaillir inopinément les récriminations de nos polémiques contemporaines.

> [[Modern languages offer] no secure place to one's intelligence where one can, removed from the quarrels of the moment, collect oneself in the company of ideas, and plumb the depths of the human soul, without having it suddenly burst forth with the recriminations of our contemporary polemics.] (71)

Latin offers a means of escape from the contingencies of history, such as the diatribes that arise precisely from controversies like this one. Another kind of timelessness is characterized by the *Inspecteur* for the Academy of Paris, A. Vessiot, a member of the growing caste of civil servants who stood at the intersection of School and state:

> Dans les littératures étrangères, ou plutôt dans les littératures modernes, c'est l'imagination qui règne en souveraine; dans les lettres anciennes, c'est le bon sens et la raison.

> [In foreign literatures, or rather in modern literatures, imagination reigns supreme; in classical literature, it is common sense and reason.] (68)

Both foreign and modern literatures are ruled by the imagination: ancient literatures (and French literature inasmuch as it derives from them), by implication, are not. Timelessness instead of transience, *le bon sens et la raison* instead of imagination, are the qualities of a French national culture that provide it with the inviolable status of an altar, relic, or piece of scripture.

With those principles firmly established, the educational establishment continued to resist the utilitarian onslaught led, in greater and greater solitude, by Frary. Speaking of the authority of ancient texts, Frary said: "[A]ujourd'hui, la théorie du progrès a diminué ce prestige" [Today, the theory of progress has diminished this prestige] (133), and later: "Quels maîtres irons-nous chercher à Rome que nous ne puissions trouver plus près de nous?" [What masters will we find in Rome that we cannot find closer to home?] (148). The privileged position of Classics in the French school system did not sustain itself indefinitely; it did not, after all, survive unscathed the transition from a primarily Jesuit pedagogy to the new, republican one.

In spite of the real decline in Latin, however, there is an important sense in which the legacy of classical education was transferred intact from the "pre-1882" educational landscape to its "post-1882" counterpart. The legacy in question can best be defined as the explicitly noncatholic and nonreligious concept of the sacred embodied by literary texts, for which the classical corpus is simultaneously both illustration and paradigm.

Two quotes by Frary, in conclusion, appear to deny the educational system any canonizing authority: "Non, nous ne sommes pas des Latins: nous sommes Français et rien de plus" [No, we are not Latins: we are French, and nothing more] (161), and "Faut-il conserver une liste sacrosainte des livres classiques éternellement imposés à l'admiration des élèves?" [Must one conserve a sacrosanct list of classical books that students will forever be forced to admire?] (226). The first statement is consistent with the ideological goals of the Third Republic's educational project. The second asks a question that the subsequent development of the national school system thoroughly suppressed.

Indeed, the legacy of a cultural ideal represented by a "sacrosanct" corpus of texts, explicitly Latin texts, and a pedagogical method was of paramount importance to Frary's academic adversaries. *Inspecteur d'Académie* Vessiot (quoted earlier) used Frary's book as proof of how a certain kind of education benefits even those who attack it:

> [La jeunesse lycéenne] lira donc [le livre de Frary] . . . elle y apprendra comment l'on rabaisse ce qu'il y a de plus haut placé dans l'estime et l'admiration des hommes; comment l'on tourne au ridicule ce qui a droit au respect; et cette leçon piquante et cruelle d'irrévérence et de dénigrement, elle le recevra d'un de ses anciens maîtres, qui retourne contre les écrivains classiques tout le talent qu'il a puisé dans leur commerce.

> [[The students of the *lycée*] will therefore read [Frary's book] . . . they will learn how one lowers what is most high in the estimation and admiration of humanity; how one ridicules that which deserves respect; and they will learn that cruel and caustic lesson in irreverence and denigration from one of their former teachers, who uses against classical authors all the talent that he drew from their acquaintance.] (70–1)

This is a variation on the old argument that certain institutions provide the practical means for their own critique, thereby rendering the critique itself invalid. The parallel argument in the political sphere that bourgeois democracy is the only type of regime that tolerates radical protest; therefore, the purpose of radical protest, which is to call for an end to bourgeois democracy, is self-defeating.

French language and literature gradually became the substitutes for Latin, fulfilling the same function of providing both a "timeless" and a "rational" counterpart to the diversity and unpredictability of political and social realities. The *Querelle* did not lead to Frary's utopia. Latin, as Frary accurately stated, functioned as the private reserve of a cultural elite; what he did not foresee, was that French could take over every aspect of that function. When elevated to the same status that Latin had previously enjoyed, the French language was even able to accomplish what Latin could not: to serve as the absolute measure of the degree of one's initiation into the sacred dimension of culture by taking on the qualities of timelessness and rationality formerly reserved exclusively for the Classics, without alienating those members of society outside the *lycée*: in that sense, inclusiveness joined the pantheon of republican values. Under the guise of democracy and free universal access to the highest realms of culture (and society), the elevation of French to the same status as its Latin ancestor permitted the institutions of the Third Republic to maintain a cultural hierarchy, by virtue of which the social stratification of society was reflected in, and sustained by, the transmission of French literary heritage.

Frary's arguments and the reaction they caused reverberated in French society for generations. As we will see, the battle lines became increasingly difficult to discern, and the academic and journalistic debate over the value of Latin for general education metamorphosed into a much more complex debate over the value of, and the best vehicle for literariness. The shift from Latin to literariness created complexity for the simple reason that it was no longer clear exactly what was at stake. As long as Latin and French were seen as opposites, it was easy to take a stand, especially since Latin had strong associations with the Catholic Right, and French with the secular and utilitarian Left. Frary not only wanted to free up time in the schools for the study of more practical subjects, he wanted to free society from the continued use of Latin as a sign of social distinction. He did not anticipate, however, that French would become such a sign.

In fact, the earliest attempts to institute the teaching of French literature were also attempts to promote literature *per se*. It is ironic that one of the institutions traditionally associated with the teaching of French literature, and the centrality of literature in the curriculum, was a Catholic secondary school. Ever since its founding as a military school by Benedictine monks in 1776, the *collège de Sorèze* had been known for its progressive curriculum, and in fact was considered to be the first educational institution that practiced a pedagogy based on the *Encyclopédie* (Cibois 2000: 11). One of its most audacious policies was to reduce the amount of time spent on Latin by teaching it for reading, rather than for oral and written expression. The monks of Sorèze did not, however, believe that they were relegating Latin to secondary status in the process. On the contrary: by improving the ability to read Latin, they were able to introduce literary texts in their integrity, instead of mere fragments (11). Reading entire works with the goal of understanding and appreciating those works on their own terms was nothing short of revolutionary. Sorèze, in a way, was one of the birthplaces of the academic discipline of literary studies as distinct from rhetoric.

In 1873, almost a century after its founding, yet well before the educational reforms of the Third Republic and the polemic surrounding Latin, Sorèze was still at the vanguard, rejuvenated by the recent directorship of the reform-minded priest, Père Lacordaire. In his Easter speech of that year, one of the Dominican monks who taught at the school, Frère Godefroy, made a daring statement: "Je l'affirme hautement, ni dans l'antiquité, ni dans les temps modernes, aucune nation n'a produit une littérature comparable à la littérature française" [I claim loudly and clearly, that neither in antiquity, nor at the present time, has any nation produced a literature comparable to the French one] (6). To affirm the superiority of French literature over all others, including the classics, is not new; in the context of secondary education, however, it is quite new. It inaugurates, quite separately from the attack on Latin from the utilitarian perspective, an entirely new trend: the replacement of both Latin and rhetoric as prestige subjects in the secondary school curriculum by French literature. The progressive pedagogues that were the Dominican Fathers of Sorèze were ahead of their time, and it is ironic that they had to leave their school after the adoption of the laws of 1882 because of Ferry's infamous "article 7," the same decree that shut down the Jesuit *collèges* (according to the Ecole de Sorèze website, www.soreze.com).

The replay of the *querelle*, carried on this time not by the producers of literature but by the teachers of literature, did not fully come into its own until the the very end of the nineteenth century even if, as the quote from Godefroy's speech suggests, the positions had already been staked out long before then. The delay was probably due to the fact that the reforms of the 1880s focused attention on primary education. Even though the Republic eventually gained control over the secondary school curriculum as well, the relative number of students at that level was much smaller, especially after the legal establishment of *obligation* greatly increased the size of primary school enrollments, and the issue of "moral and civic" replacing "religious" instruction did not pertain to the same degree. Furthermore, Frary's attack on Latin was fundamentally an attack on the importance not only of classical education, but on any attempt to place the humanities at the center of general education. It was not, strictly speaking, an attack on the definition of what constituted the Humanities, especially literary studies.

The situation changed not long thereafter. The Humanities and their literary component survived the attack from the utilitarians; but if their dominant status in the secondary curriculum was preserved, it came at the expense of an entirely new, internal conflict. For if the transcendent value of literature met with universal approval, the question of *what* constituted literature remained very much open. The redefinition of literary value in such a way that French would receive at least the same recognition as Greek and Latin occurred first as an attempt to escape from the strict duality of the classical-utilitarian polemic. In a pamphlet prefaced by Jules Simon, the Catholic republican who grew increasingly hostile to Jules Ferry's policies, Edmond Petit wrote the following defense of French as a viable cornerstone of general education at the secondary level:

> [I]l n'est pas prouvé que, par une méthode simplifiée, par une étude spéciale des textes français, on n'arriverait pas à donner, tout aussi vite, tout aussi bien [que par l'ensignement classique], le goût de la langue française aux petits Français. . . . Il me semble qu'à ne pas connaître les langues mortes on acquiert comme de nouvelles forces.

> [There is no proof that by a simplified method, by the specific study of French texts, one might not give little French citizens a taste for French as quickly and as well [as by classical education]. . . . It seems to me that by not having to learn dead languages, one acquires a new kind of energy.] (12)

Elsewhere, Petit repeats the recurring argument that Latin and Greek are too sacred to be exposed to so many: "Je les estime trop belles pour que tant de Philistins se pressent au pied de leurs autels et tentent de leur rendre un culte indigne d'elles" [I believe they are too beautiful to allow so many Philistines to crowd around their altars and take part in a cult that is unworthy of them] (25). Yet by placing French on the same level as the classical languages, Godefroy and Petit are recognizing it as equally sacred. The movement toward democratization symbolized by the elevation of French literature to the same level (or higher) as classical literature is therefore also a movement toward sacralization of French. Democratization and sacralization are inherently irreconcilable. Frary's straightforward challenge to classical education and the polemic that he initiated then had to make way for a much more complicated discussion. In basic terms, the question became: how does the demotic (French) become the equal of the hieratic (Greek and Latin), without losing all-important the ability to distinguish between the two modes?

Gustave Lanson, the foremost opponent of the rhetorical camp in literary studies, wrote a chapter entitled "Contre la rhétorique et les mauvaises humanités" (Against Rhetoric and the False Humanities) in his polemical book *L'Université et la société moderne* (The University and Modern Society; 1902). He argued that classical education as it existed in the *lycée* was detrimental, "non pas parce qu'on y apprend le grec et le latin, mais parce que l'étude 'littéraire,' celle qui ne regarde que la hardiesse du jeu des idées ou la beauté de leurs formes, y domine trop absolument" [not because one learns Greek and Latin there, but because "literary" study, the one that considers only the daring play of ideas or the beauty of their form, is far too dominant there] (57). This attack on rhetoric, which some would interpret as an attack on reading,[5] is also an attack on the primacy of the ancient over the modern: "Ce système . . . nous l'avons hérité des jésuites qui l'avaient reçu des humanistes de la Renaissance. Il consiste essentiellement à traiter les anciens comme si le dépôt des idées générales de l'humanité était chez eux seuls" [This system is one we inherited from the Jesuits, who received it from the Renaissance humanists. It consists mostly in treating the ancients as if they alone were the depository of the general ideas of humanity] (57). The literariness that reigned over the classical era and the Renaissance is simply not the literariness of the modern world: rhetoric, once capable of producing a Rabelais or a Montaigne, todays leads to nothing more than "un art de parler bien sans penser" [an art of speaking well without thinking] (58). Lanson was not directly proposing to place French literature above the classics in the curriculum. His appeal for a scientific approach to literature, rather than a rhetorical approach, was really nothing more than a revival of the pedagogy of the early collège de Sorèze: read as many texts in their entirety as possible with the goal of understanding them rather than imitating them. Implicit in Lanson's argument, of course, is that this technique will work best for French literature, which the average student who is not destined for the *professions libérales* can be expected to read and understand far better than any other.

CHAPTER 9
FOR LITERATURE: THE "CRISIS OF FRENCH"

Unlike the primary schools, in which one taught French literature with truncated, distorted, homogenized literary texts from the canon, or ones created ad hoc, to inculcate a nonliterary *morale laïque*, the secondary schools of the Third Republic were dominated by the principle of literature, in all its variety and integrity, as a foundation for pedagogy. The centrality of *études littéraires* (the term that competed with *études classiques* to designate literary studies) made the secondary school into a site of conflict. For centuries, the badge of accession to the upper classes was instruction in (though not necessarily knowledge of) Latin. As a result, the *querelle* lingered on in the form of a tacit assumption that classical culture stood for culture *tout court*. The challenge for French literary studies was therefore simply to accede to the status of pedagogical discipline, and then to develop a method.

Literary Pedagogy in the Lycée

As one can easily judge by the Frary polemic and its repercussions, the challenge to the educational establishment was nothing less than a challenge to the assumption that literature deserves any special status beyond that of one academic discipline among many. In spite of many concessions and attempts to co-opt the arguments of people such as Frary, the challenge failed. Literature had a special role to fill, and that privilege stood fast. Sometimes, the arguments used the same basic terms as the opposition, such as Olivier Gréard, the *vice-recteur* of the Paris *Académie*, who wrote in 1884 that while utilitarianists may be justified in relegating the arts to the margins of general education, literature stands apart. Unlike other art forms, literature includes science; and, more controversially yet, Gréard claims that unlike other arts, literature is ultimately concerned with truth, not esthetics (73–4).

In 1884 E. de Calonne, a professor at the *Lycée Saint Louis*, published a guide to the French *baccalauréat* for the benefit of students: *Recueil de compositions françaises en vue du baccalauréat ès lettres* (Collection of French Compositions for Preparing the Baccalauréat in Literature). The composition exercise, which does not provide the student with a literary passage to explicate or comment on, has traditionally been considered one of the hardest exercises on the *baccalauréat* because it is so open-ended. It was a culminating phase of the rhetorical tradition in secondary education in that it required the student finally to exercise his or her own creativity, though often in the "voice" of a canonical author. Some sample questions that Calonne provides, and which were typical of what one could have expected in the exam itself, range from the almost philosophical ("Pourquoi la langue française est-elle universelle?" [Why is the French language universal?] 60), to the almost surreal ("Corneille, ministre de Napoléon Premier" [[Imagine] Corneille as a minister for Napoleon I] 201). Many of them allow the student to overcome the potential obstacle of having to speak in his or her own voice by the conceit of writing a letter in the voice of one of France's great writers.[1] A typical example of the latter: "Réponse de Molière à Olivier Patru,[2] qu'on supposera l'avoir engagé à cesser d'être comédien et directeur de théâtre, pour voir l'Académie française lui ouvrir les portes" [Molière's answer to Olivier Patru who, you will imagine, has urged him to cease being an actor and theater director so the the Académie française will open its doors to him] (18).

The exercise consisting of making the student write a pastiche of one of the great writers of the French tradition is one of the more surprising aspects of secondary education. *Louis-Le-Grand* professor Félix Hémon's *Cours de littérature, à l'usage des divers examens* (Literature Course for Use in [Preparing] the Various Exams; 1889), a guide similar to Calonne's, gives straightforward *dissertation* topics ("Expliquer les caractères différents que revêt l'histoire en passant de Villehardouin à Joinville, Froissart et Commines" [Explain the various aspects taken on by history from Villehardouin to Joinville, Froissart and Commines] 51) as well as composition topics that appear to encourage a great deal of freedom ("La flotte des croisés qui reviennent d'Orient est en vue de la terre de France; peindre leurs impressions diverses" [The armada of crusaders returning from the Orient is within sight of France; describe their various impressions] 47). These exercises in creative writing seem to be at the antipodes of the strictly regulated *explications* and *dissertations* upon which students spent most of their training, and are the immediate descendants of the rhetorical tradition of Greek and Latin compositions, the emphasis on the student's skill at imitating models. French composition is therefore one of the first and most important signs of the recognition by the school of the importance of the literariness inherent in the national language.

The Reforms of 1891

In 1891, *enseignement spécial* became *enseignement moderne*. Although the change in terminology did not have immediate consequences on the structure and methodology of secondary education, it helped pave the way for the reform of 1902, when the "*bac classique*" and "*bac moderne*" were declared officially equivalent.[3] As a result, the year 1891 saw a resurgence of the debate between the French and Latin camps.

Just as in *la question du latin*, the academic establishment in this new phase of the conflict revealed itself as being mostly pro-Latin and conservative. Few voices from the Sorbonne could be found that were willing to speak in favor of the tendency to place French on a par with Latin. Ferdinand Brunetière, consistent with his strong opposition to most trends in contemporary French literature, was one of the most outspoken supporters of Latin. In the *Revue des Deux Mondes* he defended the need for Latin in order to acquire French, with an interesting claim regarding the primacy of Latin over modern foreign languages:

> Rien que pour prendre possession du matériel de la langue, du vocabulaire ou de la syntaxe élémentaire, il y fallait plus que de la mémoire. . . . [E]videmment les langues étrangères ne sauraient ici suffire. . . . [T]raduire du Lessing en français ou du Voltaire en allemand, c'est aller du même au même.
>
> [If only to take possession of the material of language, of elementary syntax or vocabulary, . . . more than memory was required. . . . Obviously foreign languages are not adequate for this. . . . To translate Lessing into French or Voltaire into German is to go from same to same.] (216)

The positions in this debate are so emotionally driven and motivated by faith that it seems uncharitable to point out their logical flaws. Nevertheless, the above quote is exceptional in that regard, and deserves closer scrutiny. Undoubtedly, the reason for Latin's value as a tool for learning French is its similarity to French, the fact that certain aspects of French grammar and syntax such as direct and indirect object have their origin in Latin (or Greek). At the same time, modern languages that replace classical languages in the *spécial/moderne* track cannot perform a similar function because they are too similar to French (or virtually identical, as Brunetière rhetorically overstates, in a manner reminiscent of Condorcet's claim on page 39 that all European languages were turning into French). So, is Latin valuable because it is genetically similar to French, or inalienably different? The irresolvable contradiction is the very root of the mission of national education: to blur the dividing line between sameness and difference, and declare the foreign and strange (Latin) as native. Classical and modern languages are alternately and reciprocally similar to and different from French, and these qualities are negative or positive depending on the context.

Brunetière's point about the acquisition of French language recurs in the same article in reference, this time, to literature. Speaking of the authors of the French seventeenth century, he wrote:

> [C]e sont les plus Français (*sic*) de nos écrivains, ceux en qui l'on reconnaît le moins de traces de l'étranger; et, tout universels qu'ils soient, ce sont pourtant ceux dont les qualités les plus rares échappent le plus aisément à quiconque n'est pas de leur race.
>
> [They are the most French of our authors, those in whom one recognizes the fewest traces of foreignness; and universal though they are, they nevertheless are those whose rarest qualities are most easily missed by anyone who is not of their race.] (221)

These authors are the most French because they display the least amount of influence from other languages and traditions, except of course for the Greek and Latin authors. But Brunetière just finished stating that modern foreign languages, at least the European ones, are the "same" as French, so would it not be logical to fear their influence less than that of the classical period? In addition, the qualities of the most universal of all French authors (suggested by "*tout universels qu'ils soient*") that are "rarest," understood here in the sense of most valuable, are precisely those qualities that a stranger to the French race and language would least be able to appreciate.

The point here is not to make fun of Brunetière, whose contradictions gain some coherence when placed in the context of the late-nineteenth-century culture wars.[4] What is important is that the defense of Latin, which merges into a defense of the latent authenticity of French, is again and again a matter of foreignness being transformed into nativeness. Just as the Gauls in G. Bruno's textbook were both radically alien in their physical appearance yet central to the genetic makeup of the French "race," Latin is the incomprehensible other that lies at the very center of France's collective subjectivity. The notion of a French "race," which is difficult to defend even according to the standards of nineteenth-century ethnography, can only emerge from such a conceptual confusion, or rather sleight of hand. The notion of French "culture," I argue, is no different.

The Philosophers and the Crisis of French: Fouillée and Bergson

In *Les Philosophes de la République* (Philosophers of the Republic; 1988), Jean-Louis Fabiani deplores the fact that philosophers in late-nineteenth-century France squandered the opportunity to make a larger impact on the field by diverting their energies to the debate over education: "La philosophie [pendant la Troisième République] est la discussion du couronnement des études secondaires" [Philosophy [under the Third Republic] consisted of a debate over the final stage of secondary education] (10). What was bad for philosophy, however, was good for education: "Il est significatif que les gestionnaires réformateurs du ministère de l'Instruction publique aient été des philosophes: Ferdinand Buisson pour l'enseignement primaire, Elie Rabier pour l'enseignement secondaire, et surtout Louis Liard pour l'enseignement supérieur" [It is significant that the managers who reformed the ministry of public instruction were philosophers: Ferdinand Buisson for primary education, Elie Rabier for secondary education, and especially Louis Liard for higher education] (21).

In addition to these academics who became the theorists and "manager-reformers" of the pedagogical mission of the Republic, there are the philosophers who saw it as part of their duty simply to comment upon education, and especially the relative importance of French in the curriculum. Claude Digeon's oft-cited book *La Crise allemande de la pensée française* (The German Crisis of French Thought; 1959) gives further reason for the intense mobilization of the philosophical establishment in the debate over secondary pedagogy: while the feeling of inferiority toward Germany's educational system was strong, and contributed to the prestige of Protestantism in pedagogical theory and of Kant in the ideology of *laïcité* in the preparation for the *baccalauréat*, it also produced a backlash against the growing influence of Germany. This backlash not only led to the creation of an antirationalist and regionalist (rather than universalist) ideology among proto-fascists such as Maurice Barrès, but also to a more mainstream search for an alternative to the universalism that had characterized republican thought since the Revolution. According to Digeon, Hippolyte Taine in philosophy and Fustel de Coulanges in history were the most important figures in the search for an "authentic" French thought free from foreign influence, leading in turn to a crisis in the philosophical justification of republicanism: in the context of the defeat, the latent contradiction between "*patrie*" and "*humanité*" could no longer be so easily ignored (537). As Fabiani states, there is almost no member of the philosophical profession who did not become embroiled in this crisis, from which I will now select two examples: Alfred Fouillée, the husband of the author of *Le Tour de la France par deux enfants*, and Henri Bergson.

Fouillée's contribution to philosophy consisted of a reconciliation between positivism and spirituality, a concern that by itself is evidence of his suitability as a "house philosopher" for the ideologues of a moderate Third Republic intent on preserving its role as guardian of spiritual values. Robert Good's excellent summary of Fouillée's ideas shows him bent on protecting the Republic from the critics who charge it with Kantian idealism by founding a new morality that reconciles the mind and the body, thought and action. Interestingly, he believed that this golden age, in which human society will have profoundly internalized the moral basis for action (and for the advent of which he calls in his most famous work, the 1907 *Morale des Idées-Forces*), will come about through a "feminization" of society, a process that Good sees as inspired by Fouillée's wife and her primary school textbooks (1996: 53–7). Fouillée's writings on questions of national education were almost as numerous, and ultimately perhaps more influential than his "purely" philosophical work. He published *L'Enseignement au point de vue national* (Education from the National Perspective) in 1891 (not coincidentally, the year of the resurgence of the French–Latin conflict due to the creation of *enseignement moderne*), a book that is a model of rhetorical restraint and a sublime expression of the need to overcome the raging issues of the day by hovering over them at great altitude. It would simply be unscientific, he argues, to see the choice between Latin and French as an "either-or" proposition, as did Frary and his opponents. "Dans la nature, il n'y a d'évolution que par une répétition continuelle combinée avec un progrès gradué" [In nature, there is evolution only through continual repetition combined with incremental progress] (138). Darwin's law of natural selection applies to culture as well: "La tradition classique, qui a ce privilège d'être en même temps nationale, puisque notre littérature est inspirée des anciens, est donc le naturel soutien de notre génie littéraire et artistique" [The classical tradition, which has the privilege of also being national, since our literature is inspired by the ancients, is therefore the natural support of our literary and artistic genius] (147). The biological metaphor allows one to see the strengths of the French language as merely the survival of the same strengths that one can still discern in the literature of the distant past. Greek and Latin, therefore, are not only like a religion in that their relationship to French is similar to the relationship between Catholicism and republicanism, they are in fact sources of religious authority (albeit in a positivistic sense) outright:

> Leur vertu mystique, si on entend par là une influence latente parce qu'elle est profonde et vitale, vient de tous ces liens invisibles qui nous rattachent à l'antiquité et qu'ont noués, renoués vingt siècles. Vertu toute naturelle et non surnaturelle, analogue à celle de l'hérédité, de la race, de la nationalité.

> [Their mystical quality, if one understands by that an influence that is latent because it is vital and deep, comes from all those invisible threads that attach us to antiquity and that twenty centuries have tied and retied. It is a completely natural quality, not supernatural, analogous to the quality of heredity, race, and nationality.] (150)

Since Fouillée's words are, after all, contributions to the continuing debate over how much Latin, if any, should be required for the *baccalauréat* and in school generally, he argues that Frary and his utilitarian arguments are far too radical:

> M. Raoul Frary aura beau dire qu'il comprend toutes les cultures, sauf celle du bois mort, la littérature latine n'est pas un bois mort, elle est une des principales racines mères dont la sève vient encore se mêler à celle de l'arbre entier et contribuer à sa floraison perpetuelle.

> [Mr. Raoul Frary can well say that he understands every culture except the culture of dead wood, Latin literature is not dead wood: it is one of the main tap roots ["mother roots"] the sap of which still mixes with the sap of the entire tree, contributing to its continuous flowering.] (158)

The strategic adoption by the school of a civic religion explicitly modeled on the Catholic tradition allowed it to negotiate among the competing arguments of the religious, secular, Latin, and French camps. On one level, the substitution of civic religion for Christianity is simple: "De même que, pour le croyant, tout devoir est un devoir envers Dieu, de même, pour celui qui aime la France, tout devoir devient un devoir envers la France" [Just as for the believer, every duty is a duty toward God, for the person who loves France, every duty becomes a duty toward France] (282). The missing element in this substitution—the supernatural authority of

God, which has no apparent counterpart in the unavoidably historical nature of the *patrie*—can nevertheless be found, and is to be found in the national language. Fouillée's major contribution to the cult of French language and literature is summed up in one sentence: "Considérée philosophiquement, la grammaire a sa moralité" [Considered philosophically, grammar has its own morality] (305). The question of whether French grammar is any more "moral" than that of any other language is not addressed, nor is the question of the appropriateness of substituting "France" for God instead of any other country. Quite possibly Fouillée's assertion is no different from the formulation of Ralph Albanese, who wrote: "la correction et la clarté constituent les normes d'une langue qui se veut chargée d'une mission universaliste" [correct [grammar] and clarity constitute the norms of a language that considers itself charged with a universalist mission] (1992: 29). The French language is moral because it is clear, it has to be clear because it is moral.

Fouillée was a harsh critic of the methods of Lanson, revealing once more the division in the pedagogical theories of the Sorbonne that Antoine Compagnon analyzed so thoroughly. "[L]'esprit doit être un instrument, non un magasin d'antiquités . . ." [The mind must be an instrument, not an antique shop] (314), and "Ce n'est pas, tout au moins, en racontant l'histoire de la peinture qu'on fera des peintres" [It is not by telling the history of painting that one will train painters] (323). These arguments repeat in a republican context the fundamental tenet of Jesuit rhetoric: that instruction must result in skill, not erudition, and that the student's mind, like a chrysalis, must develop without getting larger, that is, fuller, "*bien faite*" rather than "*bien pleine*" in the words of Montaigne (378–9). Attention to grammar, and therefore to language's potential as an instrument of knowledge and analysis, is more important, or at least more fundamental, than knowledge itself.

> Si le fondement religieux s'ébranle, sachons bien qu'il n'y a absolument qu'un moyen, un seul, d'y suppléer: c'est le culte des sciences morales et sociales, le culte de la philosophie, surtout d'une philosophie à la fois positive et idéaliste. . . . [I]l faut compenser l'évidente diminution des croyances religieuses dans notre pays par la culture croissante du sens esthétique, du sens moral et social. L'éducation, de moins en moins théologique en France, sera philosophique ou ne sera pas.
>
> [If the religious foundation gives way, let us be sure that there is only one way and one way only to compensate for it: it is the cult of moral and social sciences, of philosophy, especially of one that is both positive and idealist. . . . We must compensate for the obvious decline of religious faiths in our country by the increasing cultivation of esthetic, moral, and

social sensibility. Education, less and less theological in France, will be philosophical or nothing.] (400–1)

The development of the "esthetic, moral and social senses" or faculties, as described by Fouillée, represented the most sophisticated means devised to that point of granting to secular education or *laïcité* its credentials. Perhaps for the first time, the aspects of religious education that had traditionally served as a means of social distinction, enabling the upper classes to demonstrate, when needed, their superiority, were now applied to the enterprise of national education: in republican France, every citizen is a member of the aristocracy.

Henri Bergson, whose reputation is not as dependent as Fouillée's on participation in the cadre of "philosophers of the Republic" that Fabiani analyzed, nevertheless found it necessary, like everyone else, to weigh in on the issue of the proper use and function of literary studies in national education. In a speech given to the *Académie des Sciences Morales* and reprinted in the *Revue de Paris* in May 1923, "Les études gréco-latines et l'enseignement secondaire" ("Greek and Latin Studies and Secondary Education") he came out strongly in favor of some dependence on Classical languages in the secondary school curriculum, but not in a manner that one could possibly mistake for a throwback to pre-republican education. It is instructive to compare his support of Latin with that of Fouillée.

Bergson used his past experience as a philosophy professor both in the class of *terminale* in a *lycée*, and in a *collège d'enseignement spécial*. The difference, of course, is that in the *lycée*, all students had to study Latin, and in the *collège*, almost none did.

J'ai pu ainsi les comparer entre eux. Le résultat de cette comparaison a été très net: la supériorité des élèves de l'enseignement classique était frappante. Ils avaient suivi, je le reconnais, un cours d'études plus long et plus régulier. Mais cela ne suffisait pas à expliquer la différence, qui était moins encore une différence de degré, si je puis m'exprimer ainsi, que de nature. Il est resté évident pour moi qu'il y a une connexion étroite entre la culture gréco-latine et l'art de composer et d'écrire, comme aussi entre la connaissance du latin et le *sentiment* du français.

[I have therefore been able to compare them. The result was very clear: the superiority of students in classical education was striking. They had followed, I admit, a longer and more ordered course of study. But that did not suffice to explain the difference, which was not so much of degree, so to speak, as of kind. I remain convinced that there is a close connection between Greco-Latin culture and the art of writing and composition, as well as between knowledge of Latin and *feeling* for French.] (6)

So far, one sees a strong correlation between Bergson in 1923 and Fouillée in 1891. Both philosophers believe in the organic unity of French and Latin, and the need for Latin in order to achieve real mastery of French.

Where Bergson differs, however, is in his concession that a universal national education based on Latin is simply not feasible. Even though "classical" qualities are most clearly apparent in literature, they emerge at every level of French society, regardless of educational background: "[D]e proche en proche, de haut en bas, se sont toujours transmises à la partie moins cultivée de la nation les qualités, habitudes, exigences intellectuelles qui se manifestent par l'ordre, la proportion, la mesure, et qui se résument dans l'esprit de précision ou esprit classique" [From person to person, from top to bottom, the characteristics, habits, intellectual standards revealed by order, proportion, moderation, that are found in the precise or classical spirit, have always been transmitted to the least cultivated part of society] (10). Deep knowledge of grammar may be required for members of the *professions libérales*, but the classical tradition expresses itself nonlinguistically in the range of other activities carried out by French citizens. If literature is the domain of an elite, its qualities are nevertheless apparent at all levels of society: in buildings, gardens, cooking, and virtually any other national artifact.

According to Bergson, therefore, the state is responsible both to a new "aristocracy" of linguistic competency, as well as to competing elites that did not exist (or not to the same extent) in previous historical eras:

> Une solide étude classique, grecque et latine, pour ceux qui représentent plus spécialement aux yeux du monde l'esprit français; une éducation secondaire sans grec ni latin, très élevée mais de caractère pratique, pour ceux qui auront à développer la richesse du pays. . . . Une division du travail s'impose, qui n'entraîne pas sans doute une spécialisation prématurée, mais qui assure de bonne heure le recrutement d'une double élite, celle de la pensée et celle de l'action.

> [Thorough classical study in Greek and Latin for those who most clearly represent the French spirit in the eyes of the world; secondary education without Greek or Latin, of a very high standard but practical in nature, for those who are to develop the wealth of the nation. . . . A division of labor is necessary that probably does not imply premature specialization, but that guarantees early on the recruitment of a double elite, one of thought and one of action.] (17–18)

The real differences between Bergson's arguments and those of Raoul Frary are subtle. Frary argued as well that Greek and Latin should be relegated to the status of (obscure) academic discipline among many others, while the majority of the population spent its time and energies learning modern languages and science. The disagreement between the two is limited to the fact that Bergson still considered Latin fundamental to certain professions other than *professeur de lettres*, presumably ones in which subtlety of expression is most important: diplomacy, jurisprudence, and most academic disciplines, to name the most obvious. Nevertheless, Bergson's authoritative intervention in the still ongoing debate is significant for the way in which it takes into account, almost to the point of assimilating, the once-radical arguments put forward by Frary and his fellow left-wing utilitarians. The period framed by Fouillée and Bergson's statements is one dominated by the evolution of the republican discourse on the relative importance of Latin, and of literary studies in general, in an attempt by its authors to negotiate with their enemies, while desperately holding on to the central principle of *continuity*: continuity with the pedagogical tradition established by the Church, and with the classical roots of the French language and literature. Without such continuity being paramount, I argue, the covert function of education as a political agent would cease to exist.

The question of where Bergson stood in relation to the policies of the Third Republic is still open to debate. In a recent article, Gilbert Chaitin reads Bergson's spiritualism, with its emphasis on the intuitive experience of the here and now, as a "cryptic attack on the Opportunistic Third Republic" (812), a French attack on the German philosophy that was considered the basis for educational reforms. Indeed, there is an entire tradition of right-wing intellectuals who characterized the Third Republic as not only universalist (as it had not ceased claiming to be ever since the Declaration of the Rights of Man), but more specifically, Kantian. Charles Renouvier's 1872 article "La doctrine républicaine" made an explicit link between neo-Kantian philosophy and republican ideals of law and individual rights (Chaitin 1999: 799), and served to reinforce the tendency to equate the Republic with a particular brand of universalist Enlightenment thought. Though he recognizes Bergson's clear dissociation from the proto-fascist and fascist versions of a kind of glorification of the contingent, illustrated by Maurice Barrès's doctrine of "*la terre et les morts*" (the land and the dead) and later by the Nazi slogan "*Blut und Boden*" (blood and land), Chaitin nevertheless situates him squarely in the right-wing opposition to the Republic.

Although I find Chaitin's argument convincing, I think it needs to be modified when one takes into account not only Bergson's purely philosophical work, but also his forays into the burning issues of the day, such as his statement on the role of Latin. In his ability to echo both Frary and Fouillée, and to preserve for Latin a limited (even marginal), yet at the same time paradoxically privileged position in the hierarchy of disciplines, Bergson in fact contributed to the work of the republican pedagogues, for whom it was necessary to affirm simultaneously values, stances, and traditions that are apparently irreconcilable: God and *laïcité*, universalism and particularism, Latin and French. The official position of the Republic is that it constantly manages this impossible task by transcending the irreconcilable: it stands above sectarian tensions rather than engaging with them, an ethereal attitude that feeds the ire of the anti-Kantian (and, in the case of the extreme Right, anti-parliamentarian) opposition. The truth, however, is that the Republic does not rise above antagonisms, it merely encompasses them, albeit in modified form. The key concept, and one that Bergson demonstrates in his article, is assimilation: no text, artwork, doctrine, or individual lacks the potential to become part of the national community. The problem is how to make the process of assimilation work so that the community does not explode into a random assembly of monads with no other common status than the purely arbitrary and abstract designation of "French." The universalist paradigm, whereby Frenchness is identified with a capacity for reason and balance that all humans share (but few choose to exercise), is an attractive lure but a dangerous one.

Assimilationism is the term I propose as an alternative to, or variation on the universalism so often associated with the Republic. The racial and sociological connotations of the term are entirely appropriate. In France today, "*assimilation*" is a buzzword that occurs frequently in discussion about the responsibilities of society toward immigrants and more importantly, the responsibility of immigrants toward society. Nowhere is the process more intensively promoted than in the school. In her introduction to a recent anthology of texts on the contemporary relationship between the Republic and the school, the famous jurist Elisabeth Badinter wrote: "Grâce à [l'école], des générations d'enfants pauvres ou immigrés se sont intégrés à la société française et ont pu y faire leur chemin, en respectant les valeurs de la République" [Thanks to [the school], generations of poor or immigrant children have been integrated into French society where they have been able to find their path, while respecting the values of the Republic] (7).

Assimilationism, as Badinter indicates, is as strong now as ever, and the origin of the school's assimilationist function to which she refers can be found precisely at the time when the Republic officially claimed its rights over the institution of national education. The term "*droit à la différence"* [the right to difference] was briefly in vogue in the 1980s, when President François Mitterrand suggested that there might be a moral and legal obligation for society to let immigrants join the national community (meaning, ultimately, acquiring French citizenship for themselves or their children) without requiring them to sacrifice their identities as North Africans, Muslims, or other "non-French" designations. *"Droit à la différence"* promised an alternative to traditional assimilation, the latter term very much defined historically by its application to European Jews: "assimilation" designated the process by which one must at the very least sacrifice some external signs of Jewish identity and, at most, submit to baptism and relinquish all identifiably Jewish cultural practices, in exchange for a relative degree of acceptance by the larger community. Unfortunately the debate in France has shifted away from *"droit à la différence"* to concentrate exclusively on the one-way process of assimilation, involving the alien individual on the one hand and the national community on the other.[5]

The consensus that the "right to difference" has no legitimate basis is nothing new. Seen as a requisite step in the process of acquiring citizenship, it applies not only to people, but also to artifacts. Literature and art must also undergo a transformation, meaning a sacrifice of alien characteristics, in order to gain access to the national cultural canon. Unlike immigrants, of course, artifacts cannot change their religion, language, or even nationality: a text translated into French will rarely gain status as a product of the national culture—it will retain a relatively large degree of "difference." Where the parallel between individuals and artifacts is most clear is the production of Francophone texts. Just as the French nation was built on a sort of internal colonization such as laws forbidding the use of regional languages and dialects in the schools, and other measures that abrogated regional cultural practices, the reserves of cultural capital in France are the result of a process whereby individual works, both past and present, are strategically "de-alienated" by a number of institutional structures, the school first and foremost.

The greater the difference between the assimilated object and the assimilating body, the more effectively the body has demonstrated and even proven its capacity to assimilate. In the context of the Third Republic, I argue that the capacity to assimilate is one of the cornerstones of political legitimacy. It is this capacity to assimilate, requiring a constant practical demonstration in order to prove itself, that I argue is the real basis for republican ideology, and makes Bergson into a "fellow traveler" (at least) of the Republic when he grants legitimacy to both the utilitarian and conservative positions on Latin in the curriculum.

The term "assimilation" implies a transformation of the entity being assimilated, and to a lesser degree of the entity doing the assimilation; but what kind of transformation? Rabelais's image in *Gargantua* of reading as another form of eating poses the problem clearly; for if the body of Gargantua the eater, and the intellect of Gargantua the reader, do indeed change in the course of both the literal process (eating) and the figurative process (reading), he nevertheless remains recognizable, and maintains and even strengthens his own identity. The food does not: it is digested, becomes flesh and feces. What about the text? Here, the image of ingestion breaks down, even though reception theory has taught us that the practice of reading has an effect on the text understood as an object, which therefore can be said to have an identity contingent upon place and time. But "reading" does not adequately describe what happens in the particular classroom under national education, as Fabiani states in reference to the teaching of philosophy: while the subordination of philosophy to discussions of its role in education helped guarantee the viability of school reforms, philosophy suffered from becoming nothing more than a method for the controlled dissemination of philosophical concepts and texts. "[L]es philosophèmes sont extraits de leur contexte et remontés dans le dispositif scolaire, espace pacifié et non-contradictoire" [Philosophemes are taken out of their context and set into the educational apparatus, a pacified space devoid of contradictions] (48), precisely the process undergone by literary texts during the same period. In both the teaching of philosophy and literature, we see the same adaptation of the Catholic method of transforming one alien corpus of texts (non-French Scripture) into another one (passages taken out of context, glosses and homilies in the vernacular), or techniques for occulting the text altogether (such as the core of the traditional Latin Mass): mystification under the deceptive guise of pedagogy. The literary criticism of the Third Republic, therefore, can be said to have suffered the same fate as philosophy. Both disciplines were headed for a crisis, at least partly attributable to the disengagement of their practitioners from direct involvement with the fundamental questions of their disciplines: the nature and function of philosophy, the nature and function of literature.

The gallicization of the curriculum cannot be summarized by a series of specific evolutionary changes. Frary's arguments disappeared under a chorus of protests. In 1885, it is not surprising that the Jesuit model, which was coming back strongly at the time, so thoroughly defeated the progressive tendencies of the French camp. What is more surprising is to see the very same questions come up over and over during the next

40 years, as if the entire debate had not progressed, in spite of the increasing control of the republican state over educational philosophy.[6] The reforms of the *baccalauréat* of 1902 that "relativized" classical studies by creating an option in the curriculum that did not include them at all, and made French literature into the universal cultural experience of all secondary school students by default, also aroused a tidal wave of opposition. The regular revival of classical studies at the start of the twentieth century crystallized around two events: first, a small but influential critique of public educational policies that became known as *la crise du français*, and second (and more importantly), the aftermath of World War I.

1910:"La Crise du français"

According to its supporters, Latin had the power to initiate the individual into mastery of language and culture, while French by itself did not. This point came through very clearly in a famous series of articles published in the journal *L'Opinion* in 1910 by Henri Massis and Alfred Tarde under the pseudonym Agathon: *L'Esprit de la nouvelle Sorbonne* (The Spirit of the New Sorbonne), and set the French-Latin conflict once more into motion.[7] The immediate targets of Agathon's polemic are professors of the new disciplines of sociology and literary history (Emile Durkheim and Gustave Lanson foremost among them[8]), whom they blame for undermining the institution of classical education, thereby causing a decline in the quality of spoken and written academic French. The decline to which they refer came to be known in the press as *la crise du français*, and became a national obsession. What is most significant for our purpose is that in the public perception, the academic establishment was associated with the dominance of French over Latin. This suggests a shift in the academic hierarchy, as well as a greater degree of consistency between public policy (via the ministry of Public Instruction) and the beliefs of the cadre of academics that the Republic had always tried to enlist in its support. As we will see, the reality was somewhat more complex than the Agathon polemic suggested.

The "*nouvelle Sorbonne*" functioned as a scapegoat for all the perceived ills resulting from the educational reforms of the previous 30 years. A simplified version of Agathon's argument is that the quality of *dissertations* at the university and *lycée* levels (more than today, the *baccalauréat* was considered an integral part of the university cycle of studies) had declined drastically because of the inappropriate emphasis on the content, or *fond*, that literary history required. In other words, the Jesuit emphasis on rhetoric, as well as on Latin composition and oration rather than literature had been sacrificed, to the ultimate detriment of the French language. Once again, the defeat of 1871 is made responsible for the utilitarian trend in education, and for the fact that slogans such as "*génie de la race*" and "*culture classique*" no longer carried the same authority. Agathon preempted the accusation of a return to elitism by denying the school its democratic claims:

> [J]e ne connais rien de plus antidémocratique que cette doctrine soi-disant flatteuse pour le peuple, je ne connais rien de plus humiliant pour les primaires que cette aumône intellectuelle qui leur est donnée d'un air supérieur, que cet abaissement des études qu'on juge indispensable afin de leur en faciliter l'accès.

> [I know of nothing more undemocratic than this doctrine that is supposed to flatter the people, nothing more humiliating for primary school children than this intellectual alms given to them with an air of superiority, than this lowering of [standards of] class work that is deemed necessary in order to grant them access to it.] (125–6)

Gustave Lanson, the person most closely associated with the advent of literary history as academic discipline, had been careful not to imply that schoolchildren needed to be taught literature as a series of dates and source studies, and famously developed the technique of the *explication de texte*, which brought rhetorical exercises back into the school, in order to make sure that the discipline of literary history proper remained in the university where it belonged. But the damage had already been done, and Agathon's followers were merciless in accusing the university of having replaced the practice of producing classical form with the pursuit of useless knowledge. Maurice Barrès, ever since his election to the National Assembly as a boulangist in 1889, was one of the biggest defenders of the rhetorical exercise of French as a manifestation of *génie de la race*. His letter of support to Agathon is reprinted in the published collection of their articles:

> [J]e ne puis pas ne pas entendre la plainte de tant de jeunes qui, dans la Sorbonne d'aujourd'hui, sont rebutés par la sécheresse, par le défaut d'enthousiasme, par un enseignement qui ne fait jamais appel ni à l'imagination, ni à l'émotion intérieure.

> [I cannot keep myself from hearing the complaint of so many young people in today's Sorbonne who are repelled by the dryness, the lack of enthusiasm of a pedagogy that never appeals to the imagination, nor to interior emotion.] (356)

In mentioning emotion, Barrès exposes one of the biggest issues at stake in the debate over education in the Republic. When people defended "classical culture" against the attacks of the new regime, they did not simply mean the primacy of Latin over French, or of form over content. They also meant the importance of the sacred, always dependent upon faith and therefore a matter of feeling more than reason, of the irrational power of individual conversion over the so-called rational tyranny of the collective.

It has been relatively easy to discredit the positions of Agathon and Barrès, because history in the interim has proven them wrong. The appeal to emotion that is part of the call for a return to pre-1882 pedagogy and to a spiritually and physically united "prelapsarian" French nation became one of the most effective weapons of fascism in the first half of the twentieth century, as Barrès demonstrated. In 1911 his ideas held great appeal, not just for the conservative elite, but for a wide range of French citizens. In fact, the eagerness with which the Republic associated itself with rationalism undoubtedly shocked many people who saw too much of a gap between the liberating universalist rationalism of the *Déclaration des Droits de l'Homme* of the First Republic and the political opportunism, and more cynical claims to rationalism, of the Third.

Georges Batault, writing in the *Mercure de France* about the *crise du français* (July 1911), presents the republican viewpoint in a discussion of two private organizations that had been established to counter the regime's educational reforms, Jean Richepin's *Ligue pour la culture française* and Eugène Montfort's *Les Amis du Latin*. Speaking of these two anti-Republican organizations, he wrote: "C'est à une conviction, à une croyance que nous avons affaire et rien ne sert de la discuter; comme toutes les croyances elle est irrationnelle et enracinée, c'est à la fois une vérité mystique et une vérité affective" [We are dealing with a conviction, a faith, and there is no point in discussing it; like all beliefs, it is irrational and rooted, at once a mystical truth and an emotional one] (64). People who represented the Republic either officially or unofficially usually shrank from a direct attack on the tenets of the Church. Since most voters were practicing Catholics, any direct attack on their faith would have been politically suicidal. The theological debate, which the First Republic had carried out in the open (which no doubt contributed to its early demise), had now been transferred to a different plane. One could only indirectly address matters of "faith" and "sacredness" by speaking in a code whereby the true referent of those terms, God, remained hidden. Instead, Latin, and the various circumlocutions for "literariness" that Kuentz (1981) identifies as the genuine object of contention, becomes the central issue by proxy.

By 1910, the academic establishment, in spite of the monolithic designation "*la nouvelle Sorbonne*," was increasingly divided on the subject of Latin's role in secondary education. The famous linguist Michel Bréal, for example, came out strongly in favor of classical education in the *Revue des Deux Mondes* (1910), the periodical that had clearly become an unofficial forum for the debate since the years following the publication of Frary's book. Emile Faguet also weighed in on the side of Latin, a surprising fact given that he was closely associated with Lanson and the literary history movement. The purpose of his contribution to the *Revue des Deux Mondes* ("La crise du français et l'enseignement littéraire à la Sorbonne" [The Crisis of French and Literary Education at the Sorbonne] 1910) was first of all to defend against specific accusations by Agathon and others that the academic establishment "[sacrifie] absolument l'éducation du goût à la connaissance des faits d'histoire littéraire" [completely sacrifices the education of taste to the knowledge of literary historical facts] (289). His defense of literary history is, at first, very straightforward. Asserting that "impressionnistic criticism" (criticism without erudition) is fine as long as the person doing it is "a man of genius," thereby clearly suggesting that it cannot serve as the basis for any pedagogy, Faguet goes on to state that the French need literary history precisely because it goes against their deeper nature:

> [I]l ne faut point incliner volontairement du côté où déjà l'on penche, mais plutôt au contraire. Or le penchant du Français est du côté des idées générales et de la rhétorique brillante. Ce n'est donc pas ces inclinations qu'il faut favoriser, flatter, caresser et entretenir sur le budget de l'Etat. C'est affaire d'industrie privée.

> [One must not lean voluntarily towards one's inclinations, but do the opposite. In fact the Frenchman's inclination is towards general [abstract] ideas and brilliant rhetoric. One must not therefore encourage, flatter, caress and sustain such inclinations with public funds. It is a matter for the private sector.] (300)

But Faguet's argument is against the rhetorical school of literary studies, and emphatically not against the proponents of classical education. The same argument that French people need to be taught "against the grain," so to speak, also requires them to go through the arduous apprenticeship of Latin, so as not to wallow complacently in their native language (290). If there is a "crisis of French," it is not because students learn too much literary history instead of reading literary texts, but because they are not forced to learn Latin. The Sorbonne under Lanson is thereby acquitted of the charge of subverting the quality of French in schools and universities by ignoring the centrality of Latin: the neglect of Latin was a political error of the education bureaucracy, not a matter of academic orthodoxy by the Sorbonne.

The effect of the defeat in 1871 was to fuel the attack on classical education by the utilitarian faction, an attack the Republic managed to contain. The effect of the victory of 1918 was exactly the reverse. Martha Hanna points out in *The Mobilization of Intellect: French Scholars and Writers during the Great War* (1996), that the practical skills that utilitarians promoted in the wake of 1871 became overshadowed by the more valuable skills necessary for national survival: heroism, self-sacrifice, and the conversion of grief into determination through the "culture of mourning" so clear in the works of the Ancients (146–7). The classical revival, marked as early as 1915 by increases in enrollments in the Latin/Greek curriculum of the *baccalauréat* and by the renewed popularity of seventeenth-century theater, especially of Corneille (143), arose from the surge in conservative nationalism that seized the country as well as the sense that the French population was rediscovering its anti-Germanic roots.

According to Hanna's book, however, what is even more remarkable than the renewed popular support for classical studies during and after the war was the alacrity with which republican scholars interpreted the revival of the classical spirit as an embracing of republican values. On February 12, 1915, for example, the Sorbonne convened a celebration of "Latin culture" with guests and speakers from Greece and all the major Latin countries in Europe, in an ambitious attempt to forge an international coalition based upon common values of "harmony and balance, whether in aesthetic judgments or international adjudication, . . . reason over brute force, clarity over mystical obfuscation, . . . quality of expression over . . . quantity of production" (156–7). The wartime embrace of classicism by the Republic did not, however, placate the right-wing proponents of Latin and Greek, and most likely was not intended to do so. The arguments of Massis and Tarde survived the war intact. At this juncture, as at so many others during the long history of republican pedagogy, one must be very careful when ascertaining the precise role played by the Republic itself in education debates. Just as the early Third Republic was not anti-Catholic, the more mature Republic of World War I and beyond was not anticlassical or pro-French in any easily understood sense of the terms. What is most important to realize is that the pro-classical stance of the Republic and that of its right-wing opponents were two very different species of argument. The complicated task of the Republic was to incorporate enough Latin into the curriculum to preserve the status of the discipline as a foundation for all types of learning, and at the same time to incorporate enough of the benefits of Latin instruction into the teaching of French to ensure that all levels of education have access to the moral benefits of such instruction. The question inherited from the Revolution—how to teach morality without Christ—was not substantially different from the other fundamental question underlying republican pedagogy: how to transmit the value of Latin without reference to Latin language or literature.

The 1922 Reform

A proposal to extend the hours devoted to Greek and Latin in the *lycées* was debated in the National Assembly in 1922. The primary opponent of such a measure was the Deputy Louis Marin, whose speech on the floor of the *Assemblée* provides a remarkable summary of the ideas of Raoul Frary and his followers. Marin argues, in a manner once again reminiscent of the arguments by such as Perrault and La Fontaine in the *Querelle*, in favor of emancipation from the tyranny of the past: "[D]e grands génies sont nés qu'il faut fréquenter pour d'autres qualités que les qualités classiques: aucune éducation ne peut se faire sans Shakespeare et Lamartine" [great geniuses have been born that one must get to know for other qualities than classical ones: no education is possible without Shakespeare and Lamartine] (8). Not content to ascribe value to nonclassical and even to non-French literature, Marin goes so far as to claim that classical civilization is inferior to what man has produced since, because its methods were simpler and too narrowly rational: "Si [les classiques] sont arrivés à ces modèles étonnants, plus vite et plus haut, c'est que les méthodes employées ont été les mêmes" [If the classics achieved such astonishing heights more quickly, it is because their methods had been the same] (8). Clearly, our century needs its own, more evolved model: "Notre culture nationale faite directement sur des auteurs de notre race, ayant les qualités de notre race, avec notre génie propre" [Our national culture, created directly from authors of our own race, with the qualities of our race, our own genius] (16).

Marin's speech provoked a chorus of reactions, many of which came from the biggest names in the intellectual pantheon of the time. Henri Bergson's speech at the *Académie des Sciences Morales* discussed at the beginning of this chapter was just one of those voices, and there is no mistaking the size of the stakes: the teaching of Latin was no less than "la question à laquelle est suspendu l'avenir de la haute culture en France [ainsi que] l'accroissement de notre influence à l'étranger" [the question on which depends the future of high culture in France [as well as] the increase of our influence abroad] (5–6).

Maurice Barrès, who in 1922 was still a member of the Chamber of Deputies representing Paris, intervened right in the middle of Marin's speech on the floor:

> La plupart des choses que nous admirons légitimement dans les civilisa-tions orientales, par exemple toute cette culture persane si charmante et parfois profonde qui a compté d'admirables poètes comme les Saadi et les Djelal-ed-din-Roumi [*sic*[9]] et toute la tradition des mystiques lyriques, eh! Ce sont des prolongements à peine voilés de la tradition hellénique et des suites de la fermentation alexandrine.

> [Most of what we legitimately admire in oriental civilizations, for exam-ple, the charming and sometimes profound Persian culture that includes poets such as Saadi and Jalal ud-din Rumi and the entire traditon of mystical poets, well! They are the barely-disguised continuation of the Hellenic tradition and the consequences of the Alexandrian fertilization [of the East].] (Quoted in Marin, 1922: 18)

Barrès's interruption of Marin is relevant on several levels. His own ostentatious erudition (few deputies would have been able to name not one, but *two* classical Persian poets, and the complete name of Jalal ud-din Rumi, although either Barrès or the secretary of the Chamber did garble it somewhat) was, in a sense, the multiculturalism of the era. The claim that Saadi and Rumi are to be "legitimately" admired only insofar as they extend into the Orient the influence of Classical Greece is the condition, for Barrès as well as for literary studies of the era, for the exis-tence of a "multicultural" perspective, which is of course monocultural at its root. The implied conclusion of Barrès's argument is at once conventional and surprising: just as the literature of the Orient is valu-able insofar as it expresses Occidental (Greek) culture, so is French liter-ature valuable only insofar as it reflects those same roots. To Marin's claim that Rome is not the origin of France or of French culture, Barrès opposes the claim that French culture is only Roman, or at most Greco-Roman, and nothing else. As late as 1922, Marin and others were still fighting for the emancipation of French literature from its classical legacy, and the gradual compromise reached by the state was that if French could stand on its own, then it is only because it is "like" Latin, not radically distinct from it in any way.

The fact that Bergson, Barrès, and so many others believed in the qualitative difference between those who were educated in Latin and/or

Greek and those who had only French should not lead to the conclusion that they advocated classical education for everybody. The position of the defenders of Latin is a complicated one: Latin must be the preserve of an elite, but it should be mandatory for that elite. The *question du latin* was a debate over the nature of the education of the elite, meaning a single, homogenous group. By the 1920s, it seems that it is far more acceptable to imagine a plural elite encompassing specialized groups of men unencumbered by Latin, whose responsibility is to be leaders of science and industry.

For others, Bergson's delicate balance between an elite of thought and an elite of action meant giving too much credit to an entirely modern language-based pedagogy. Léon Blum, a cultural conservative in spite of his left-wing politics, took a much stronger position in the pages of the equally conservative *Revue de Paris* in May 1923: "La section B,[10] où l'éducateur Berlitz tient lieu d'Homère et de Platon, produit de tels fruits que les professeurs de langues vivantes la renient, après lui avoir donné le jour" [The B section, in which the Berlitz instructor replaces Homer and Plato, produces such fruits that language professors disown them after having brought them to light.] (360)

One very important difference between the debate in 1885 and in 1922, of course, is that Frary and his opponents were still under the influence of the defeat of 1871, whereas Marin put forth his arguments in the context of the redeeming victory of 1918. To the extent that the "utilitarians" such as Frary derived some of their arguments from the defeat, and the perceived need to model French education on an international, and even a Prussian paradigm, they had lost considerable ground. Blum alludes to this when he condemns the influence of Germany on the French educational system after 1871, and calls for a return to classicism in the context of the elimination of "la dernière trace des conceptions pédagogiques empruntées à Guillaume II" [the final trace of educational concepts borrowed from Wilhelm the Second] (1923: 383): "au moment où les nations latines, groupées contre la politique germanique, semblent seules capables de guider l'Europe dans la paix, renoncerions-nous à l'éducation latine qui nous a mis à leur tête?" [as the Latin nations, allied against Germanic policy, seem to be the only ones capable of guiding Europe in peace, would we abandon the Latin education that put us in charge of them?] (385).

It was, in many ways, a call for the return of the old Jesuit pedagogy and its emphasis on rhetoric, against the Lanson-inspired imposition of literary history with its concomitant emphasis on empirical knowledge over style and intuition, against the primary school practice of "*leçons de choses*," and even against the attempt to reduce La Fontaine's fables to parables of lay morality. After all, the purely anecdotal evidence provided by "Agathon" and their supporters consisted largely of the growing complaints by teachers over the decline in the written quality of the essays written for the *baccalauréat*, complaints that have existed as long as there have been exams. Of course, no scientific study had been made that could verify such a decline, or separate it from the fact that the numbers of students sitting for the *bac*, and their percentage of their age group, increased steadily every year. What *is* new about the widespread reaction that Massis and Tarde epitomized is the appeal for a more profound understanding of the French literary tradition; after all, the Jesuits taught the arts of self-expression primarily in Latin, while relegating literary texts, both classical and French, to the status of illustrations of rhetorical devices. The closely guarded secret of republican pedagogy, as I have tried to argue, is that the attack on Jesuit pedagogy was a disguised attempt to appropriate the same techniques to its own ends: to teach the *idea* of literature, and the cult of high classical style, instead of literature itself. Now, for the first time, a segment of the public expressed dissatisfaction with both branches of modern pedagogy: the rhetorical, with its roots in Jesuit instruction, and the historical, with its roots in positivism.

The question of the continued relevance of the Jesuit model is raised much more recently by Gérard Genette, in a famous essay originally published in 1966 in the history journal *Annales* titled "Rhétorique et enseignement" (Rhetoric and Education). Genette argues that rhetoric did not disappear from literary pedagogy, contrary to popular belief. What disappeared is a particular kind of rhetoric, and the changes in the field of literary pedagogy brought about by the reforms of the late nineteenth century reflected changes in the literary field. Romanticism, according to Genette, founded a conception of literature based in history rather than rhetoric, and thereby liberated the institution of literature from its status as "applied rhetoric" that had prevailed ever since the term "*littérature*" first emerged during the Renaissance. Literary pedagogy, however, continued to consist of instruction in rhetoric, meaning the rhetorical analysis of classical texts, followed by their imitation, until Lanson and the rest of the university of establishment gradually substituted for it literary history. Of the three elements of classical rhetoric: *inventio* or the search for ideas and arguments; *dispositio*, or composition; and *elocutio*, or the choice and arrangement of words and figures of discourse, the pedagogical emphasis, inherited from the Jesuits, was on the last: "l'accent mis sur le style ne peut que renforcer le caractère littéraire (esthétique) de cette formation" [the emphasis on style can only reinforce the literary (esthetic) aspect of this education] (Genette 1969: 27).

The greatest change brought about by the republican school, according to Genette, is that while traditional literary pedagogy was based on imitation, and there was thus a continuity between the texts that students studied and the ones they produced, literary history inaugurated the era of the *dissertation*, which is a text about literature, not one that aspires to resemble literature. From a rhetorical standpoint, the consequence of this change has been the shift from a pedagogy based on *elocutio* to one based on *dispositio*. The "value" of the *dissertation*, that quality which justifies receiving a high mark from the teacher, is not the student's literary style, which in fact is to be avoided at all costs. Instead, it is the ability to take the syntagmatic structure of the poem or text fragment under examination and transform it into the paradigmatic structure of the student's own text. The term "paradigmatic" in this case refers to the ideal student's ability to organize his or her essay in such a way as to create the impression that various levels of the original text, not obvious to the naked eye, are unfolding on the page in almost organic fashion (33).

Genette refrains from making any clear judgment as to the value of the profound change in rhetorical emphasis in the field of literary pedagogy. He does however conclude his essay by remarking that the study of literature lost its "poetic" dimension (the rhetoric of *elocutio* in students' repeated attempts to practice their own versions of classical literature) ironically at the same time that literature itself was gaining a "critical" dimension. In other words, the works of writers began to take literature itself as their subject, rather than alluding to a reality outside the text, and therefore became discourses "on" literature. So, pedagogy and criticism lost their literary dimension while literature gained a critical one, and it all happened in the late nineteenth century (42). It is not clear whether this change has been to the advantage of literature and its institutions, to their detriment, or neither—though Genette, like Barthes in his essay "Réflexions sur un manuel" (1971), appears to be mourning the loss of criticism's poetic dimension more than he celebrates the acquisition of literature's critical one.

A broader perspective on the rhetorical–historical conflict is provided by Antoine Compagnon's already mentioned book *La Troisième République des lettres: de Flaubert à Proust* (1983). Although it begins with the historical fact of republican literary pedagogy (especially as exemplified by Lanson), it is ultimately a work of literary criticism, or even metacriticism: like so many others, Compagnon is fascinated by the problem of literariness, and how both critics and authors addressed the problem during the Third Republic, when so much depended on the solution. Time and space prevent us from going over his dense argument in detail, but several aspects of it stand out as being particularly relevant.

To begin with, Compagnon situates the obsession of Third Republic academics with pedagogical concerns within the broader context of the history of literary theory, in particular of history *as* literary theory. When Gustave Lanson, inspired by figures such as Charles Sainte-Beuve and Hippolyte Taine, and abetted by colleagues such as the historian Charles Seignobos justified the creation of the discipline of literary history, he did so in reaction against a rhetorical criticism (exemplified by Ferdinand Brunetière, among others) seen as intuitive, "impressionistic," in a word: unscientific. The attack on subjective criticism gave legitimacy to the transformation of literary criticism into a sub-genre of history, which in turn became the ideological justification for turning the school into the laboratory for the creation of a national culture. In simple terms, Lanson, in spite of his famous advocacy and codification of the close-reading exercise of *explication de texte*, solved the problem of literariness primarily by reducing it to a manifestation of national virtues such as classical lucidity and balance (Fouillée and Bergson's "morality of grammar"), and other factors that constitute the specificity, and also superiority, of French culture.

In the wake of Lanson, Compagnon states that the discipline of criticism lost its claim on the esthetic: "la critique littéraire qui se veut désormais historique, n'est plus un genre littéraire" [literary criticism that henceforth claims to be historical is no longer itself a literary genre] (Compagnon 1983: 23); by avoiding the esthetic component of literariness, criticism surrendered its own literariness. Compagnon sees the expulsion of literariness, both as the object and characteristic of criticism, and hence of literary pedagogy, as a crucial regression in the history of the French literary field. Roland Barthes's reaction against the still-Lansonian Sorbonne literary establishment of the 1960s (symbolized by his response to Raymond Picard's attack on Barthes's book on Racine) was nothing more or less, according to Compagnon, than a return of the literary into the fields of criticism and pedagogy.

The reaction of the university of the Third Republic against "impressionistic" literary criticism, against history that was insufficiently distinct from literature (such as Michelet), and against the rhetorical pedagogy of the Jesuits, was all of a piece. Compagnon demonstrates that the long-overdue arrival of French literature into the highest reaches of the academy took the form of an aversion to literary style in academic discourse as well as to the philosophical question of literariness. The creation of a science of literature on which the entire range of educational levels could depend was only possible, ironically, at the sacrifice of the literary. Barthes was only one of a chorus of voices rebelling against the Lansonian status quo, and it is not surprising that he and his contemporaries felt compelled to speak out on the role of literature in the school.

What becomes evident, regardless of the manner in which one approaches the subject of literary pedagogy, is how much it matters to people what literature is. The Barthes essay "Réflexions sur un manuel" was originally on the program of the Cérisy *Décade* on "L'Enseignement de la littérature" in July 1969. The conference at Cérisy, attended by Gérard Genette, A.J. Greimas, and other luminaries associated with the structuralist vogue of the period, and published by Serge Doubrovsky and Tzvetan Todorov under the title *L'Enseignement de la littérature* (The Teaching of Literature; 1971), was one of several concerted attempts in the late 1960s and 1970s to use the tools of modern criticism on the subject of literary pedagogy. Others included the issue of *Littérature* in October 1972 titled *Le Discours de l'école sur les textes* (The Discourse of the School on Literary Texts), quoted several times in this book, and the issue of *Poétique* from 1977 laconically titled *Enseignements*. The mood of these essays on the pedagogical branch of the literary field alternates between the sanguine and the melancholic. Barthes's answer to the question posed in 1975 by the journal *Pratiques*, "Peut-on enseigner la littérature?" [Can One Teach Literature?] was a militant one, and bears quoting: "il ne *faut enseigner que cela*" [one must teach nothing but] (1981: 224). And yet, not only did he face the army of sociological critics who saw the text as inseparable from its institutional setting, and therefore a pretext for the transmission of everything *except* for what might somehow legitimately be posited as being intrinsic to "literature" as opposed to other forms of discourse, he also faced the judgment that Greimas made at the same Cérisy meeting at which Barthes read his *Réflexions sur un manuel*: "On ne sait pas de quoi est spécifique le phénomène littéraire" [No one knows what constitutes the specificity of the literary phenomenon] (Greimas 1971: 97). Literary pedagogy is perhaps unique among academic disciplines in that nobody knows its true object. As teachers of literature, we may be condemned to convey to our students at most a literary sensibility, the ability to say, as Justice Potter Stewart once did in reference to pornography, that I may not be able to define it, but "I know it when I see it."

The difficulty of defining "literariness" has of course not dampened the enthusiasm of those who have made the teaching of literature their profession. If anything, it has had the opposite effect, for what I argue are at least two reasons. First, the problematic nature of "literariness" puts the status of literature as an autonomous entity into doubt. Although this may weaken literature's position relative to disciplines that deal with "real" things such as the sciences, and also disciplines such as history, it strengthens the commitment of its practitioners in the same way that religious faith can be a stronger motivation than empirical knowledge. The defenders of creationism, who have no evidence for their beliefs other than tradition, are therefore able in certain situations to challenge the defenders of evolution, who possess ample physical evidence for their beliefs. To be perfectly banal: faith moves mountains, and it is on such strength that our discipline depends, at least in part. Second, in addition to the faith evidenced by people who happen to be more enamored of books than the average population, there is the social function of literature as transmitter of value, the area of cultural studies in which Bourdieu has set the standard. This is something quite differ- ent from religious or quasi-religious faith, which is belief in absolute value. It is instead the recognition that value is characteristic of all human communities, and that modes of cultural representation both preserve and produce a constantly evolving hierarchy of values, whether defined according to an absolute, religious principle or a relative, economic one.

So the meaning of "literariness" is elusive, and this elusiveness in turn paradoxically strengthens the resolve of the literary pedagogue; perhaps in part for that reason, Greimas did not seem in the least concerned by his acknowledgment that the specificity of the literary phenomenon is unknowable. Far from casting a pall on the discipline of literary studies, such a realization gives it purpose. The title of Greimas's talk was "Transmission et communication," and he approached the teaching of literature as the imperative to communicate cultural values successfully, in other words to transmit them: "Le programme de l'enseignement . . . doit être construit de la même manière que le programme du voyage à la Lune: il doit avoir une finalité qui seule lui permet de se constituer en programme" [The curriculum . . . must be designed in the same way as the trip to the Moon [Greimas spoke only days after the Apollo XI mission landed on the Moon]: it must have a purpose that alone allows it to constitute itself as such] (73). The gratuitous, glory-for-the-sake- of-glory aspect of the Moon missions provided Greimas with a perfect image for the ends of literary pedagogy. To justify those ends by some high-minded purpose would be to miss the point entirely. In fact, Greimas believed that the only human activity comparable in its communicative efficacy to literary transmission was probably advertising, the least "ideal" or disinterested form of communication there is (80).

Ability to achieve certain ends is that which will eventually prove the value of a literary text: "Les formes prises en elles-mêmes sont innocentes, c'est leur finalité qui les valorise ou dévalorise" [Forms in and of themselves are innocent: it is their ultimate purpose that endows or strips them of value] (82). Greimas pushed his thesis to an extreme by suggesting that transmission, or successful communication, is the hallmark both of "good" literature and "good" pedagogy; in both cases, it produces in the reader and student the impression that something unteachable, un-transmittable, has nevertheless been conveyed.

Greimas ends his contribution to the colloquium a little abruptly, without any clear sense of whether the "end" of literary pedagogy has anything to do with the content of the literary text. It is not clear whether literary value is something that is transmitted via the text in the pedagogical situation, or whether it is simply (ideally) the product of the pedagogical situation itself that must be endlessly constructed in order to exist. He leans toward the latter, though one can discern in his conclusion a kind of Beckettian tension: literature (literariness) must be taught . . . it cannot be taught . . . it will be taught.

The repeated injunction that literature "must be taught," whether emanating from Barthes and Greimas or from sociological critics like Renée Balibar, points away from the nineteenth-century opposition between rhetoric and erudition, toward a "third way." This new direction is not simply a throwback to Jesuit pedagogy, both because it rests on all of the insights into the question of literariness of the last century, and because it defines French literature as a work-in-progress, not as a mere proxy of the fossilized classical (Latin) corpus.

Compagnon's book *La Troisième république des lettres* concludes that the search for a "third way" began as the debate between rhetoric and history in the pedagogy in the Third Republic was still raging. For Compagnon, the unrecognized inventor of a truly viable literary pedagogy was none other than Marcel Proust, in a stance that Compagnon provocatively assigns to him and terms "against reading" (221). Contrary to popular belief, Proust was not a great reader; that is, he did not read as much, or not as systematically, as the term "great reader" implies. Proust satirized erudition (the sin of Sainte-Beuve) as well as the fetishization of individual books or works of art (the sin of Charles Swann). But the greatest sin of all was "idolatry," "une confusion de la vie et de l'art" [a confusion of life with art] (Compagnon 1983: 229) that leads people to make the gravest mistakes in life, such as Swann's love for Odette because she resembled a figure in a Botticelli painting. The similarity between Proust's rejection of the idolatry of works of art, and the First Republic's repeated warning against a pedagogy that would teach children to attend to words instead of things, is striking. The Proust of Compagnon's analysis and the revolutionary pedagogues shared the same distrust of religion's tendency to invade the domain of the esthetic. Some republican ideologues were openly atheist, and saw any manifestation of religious sentiment as something to suppress in a truly modern and enlightened society; others wanted simply to put religion back in the churches and temples where it belonged, and end the growing confusion between religion and other cultural categories. Proust was one of the latter.

The saving grace of reading (an activity, as Compagnon admits, that Proust did not believe was always inherently flawed) was that as an exercise it could prepare the individual for the truly important task in life: to write. The writing of a book, in the Proustian sense, is the author's reconciliation and fulfillment in language of two separate and incomplete experiences, reading and living.

> La référence insistante [chez Proust] au "livre intérieur," au "livre essentiel," au "seul livre vrai," qui est partout et nulle part, masque la relation sinon aux autres livres du moins aux auteurs, à la cour de la littérature et surtout à la littérature de cour.

> [[Proust's] constant insistence on the "interior book," on the "essential book," on the "only true book" that is everywhere and nowhere, disguises its relationship if not to other books, then at least to authors, to the court of literature, and especially to the literature of the court.] (Compagnon 1983: 251)

The "court of literature" refers here to the autonomous literary institution that Flaubert and Mallarmé so fervently believed in, and "literature of the court" to the centuries of elitism and incomprehension (bad or insufficient reading) to which the literary corpus had been subjected: two institutional models of literariness that Proust rejected.

What then is the relevance of Proust's redemption of the act of reading by subordinating it to the imperative to write, to the question of literary pedagogy? Although Proust did not follow the lead of many of his contemporaries by entering the debate over questions of pedagogy, or even including them in his novel (*La Recherche* is in fact unusual in how much space it devotes to the time spent by the school-age narrator outside of the classroom—on summer vacation, at home, on the streets—rather than inside of it), Compagnon argues that he was the first and perhaps the best theoretician of reading beyond the categories that pedagogues had traditionally used.

Compagnon continues to explore Proustian writing as a solution to the absence of literariness in literary pedagogy. Around 1900, there was yet another polemic that mobilized public opinion, though not as completely as *la question du latin* or *la crise du français*, called "*la question Taine*" (311). Hippolyte Taine had the reputation of having overcome his lack of natural ability as a writer by dint of unremitting discipline and hard work. The "Taine question," therefore, was implicitly a pedagogical one: are great (and even good) writers born, or are they made? Is it a question of birth, or of schooling? That this was a debate over pedagogy is almost too obvious: if writing is innate, then teaching it is a waste of time, and the only valid purpose of literary pedagogy is to separate the wheat from the chaff in order to create a republican mirror-image of the aristocracy: an elite based upon talent (birth) rather than education. If it can be taught, then it must be taught in the same way to everyone. The debate manifests the French nineteenth-century's inability to escape from the tension between an aristocratic and a democratic principle of social organization and pedagogy. Proust's great insight, according to Compagnon, is to have exposed the sterility of the "Taine question" itself:

> [I]l change le problème, il déplace la question; elle ne porte plus sur l'origine du style, des causes de la création—le génie ou le labeur?—, mais sur les singularités d'une phrase.
>
> [It changes the problem, it shifts the issue: it is no longer about the origin of style, the causes of creation—genius or labor?—, but about the singularities of a sentence.] (314)

Proust's concept of writing as defined by Compagnon, which was similar to (and no doubt influential upon) Barthes's definition of the "writerly," is a far cry from textual fetishization of all kinds, including the standard pedagogical myth that the author is somehow "present" in the text. It is true, according to such a model, that writing constitutes the individual's struggle to come to grips with the real, and in that sense writing is the unique creation of a particular sensibility. Yet the reader does not read the text in order to "commune" with its author, but rather to find the strength to become an author in turn. The fulfillment of human existence is in the writing process, an activity that must not represent the submission of the individual to a preexisting model or models, but his or her overcoming of those models. It is, ultimately, a victory of particularity, of deviance, of the unique contingencies of a person's situation in time and space over the universal.

That is how Proust claims victory, both over Flaubert's aristocratic view that real authors are born as such, and that their texts are vessels for pure art, and the view that Taine both espoused and exemplified, that authors are made and that their texts are historical documents, without any artistic value that cannot be explained by empirical methods. The source of literariness is to be found in "the singularities of a sentence"; not in the quasi-religious notion that style derives from God's grace, nor in the historical notion that it derives from the author's particular circumstances, but in the writing process itself.

Compagnon's insight into Proust suggests a solution to the problem of the ideological character of every institution, even—especially—the school. For centuries, humanity has been searching for a truly liberating pedagogy. In their way, the schools instituted by Luther and Melanchthon, as well as those proposed by Masuyer and Lepeletier de Saint-Fargeau, were stages in the search for a pedagogy that would finally place the interests of the individual over those of arbitrary authority. It is unrealistic to expect that the school will ever reverse that order, or that it will cease to be the means by which the past invests itself with the power of religion. On a certain level such a reversal would be undesirable, since the tyranny of education is in part the necessary, ritual sacrifice of particular self-interest on which the survival of society depends. In the specific case of the pedagogical discipline of literary studies, however, it is perhaps salutary to regard literariness, the quality that critics have tried in vain to isolate, as finally residing not in the text but in each individual, waiting to be awakened. Proust's (and Compagnon's, and Barthes's) paean to writing as a way out of the pedagogical dilemma can serve as an apt provisional conclusion to this book.

Conclusion

The Spirituality of French Literature

The theory and practice of literary study within the rigid structure of French national education is a complex topic to which this book may serve at best as an introduction. Many issues alluded to in the previous chapters simply have not received the scholarly attention they continue to require. Among these are the failed attempt by radicals of the First Republic to create a national literature modeled on a regenerated French language; the sexual prohibitions, modeled on those of the clergy, imposed by the Third Republic on the pedagogical profession, especially its female members; the partnership between the French government and private publishing houses that not only provided textbooks for the republican school, but also printed the best-selling polemical and theoretical treatises that followed the advent of pedagogy as an object of scientific inquiry and political debate; the gap separating the French literary canon of higher education from the narrower and more distorted canon of primary and secondary education; and many more. Most important of all, perhaps, is the centrality of the School in contemporary analyses of institutionalized practices of reading or not reading literary texts, whether from the sociological perspective (especially Bourdieu and his disciples), or from the tradition of close reading (Barthes, Genette, Greimas, and others). The field of French literary studies is poised to undertake a more extensive discussion of many of these issues.

I have tried to accomplish two tasks in this book, one fairly reasonable, another ludicrously ambitious. In addition to providing a partial history of the institution of literary pedagogy from its Enlightenment roots to the Third Republic, I have tried to maintain some focus on the profound question on which all literary study depends: the nature of literariness, the quality that distinguishes literature from other kinds of discourse, and in turn founds the discipline of literary study. To attempt to come to grips with literariness is a much greater task than the already broad historical ambition to account for the role of literature in the primary and secondary schools of the Republic. Because literary study in all of its guises constitutes a practice, and therefore a set of rules and assumptions that guides the practitioner, however, I believe that one can learn much about literature by observing those who value it most.

Part II of this book described the "evangelical" aspect of the republican educational enterprise as demonstrated by the historical, theoretical, and prescriptive writings of its foremost academic supporters, and by the textbooks published in their wake. Part III focused on the relative status of French and Latin language and literature in the secondary school system as a further example of the republican search for legitimacy through continuity with the literally evangelical tradition on which national education was modeled. It concludes with more general comments on the parallel between the separate concepts of sacredness and literariness, which nevertheless share a common resistance to empirical analysis. That sacredness and literariness are both deductive in nature, first principles whose reality is perceived by faith rather than physical experience, is not the only characteristic they share. What I have tried to show is that both divinity and literariness operate within institutional frameworks, even though they may resist being defined by those frameworks alone: in the case of modern France, those are the Roman Catholic Church and the institution of public education, respectively. To repeat a claim made in the Introduction: viewed structurally, the functions of sacredness and of literariness are indistinguishable.

The Third Republic was a founding moment in the history of an ongoing practice,[1] and the continuity between the late nineteenth century and the *ancien régime*, in this as well as other aspects of society, must not hide the fact that diverse cultural practices (as, e.g., the catechism in the Church and *récitation* in primary schools) may very well appear similar, yet it matters a great deal in what context they occur. To give one small illustration: in a 1968 handbook on how to write a French literature *dissertation*, Philippe Sellier wrote the following:

> La véritable formation est celle qui apprendra à réfléchir, à ordonner des idées, à les exprimer, quel que soit le sujet proposé, ou s'il s'agit d'un texte, à le comprendre, à en déceler les beautés, à dialoguer avec l'artiste, *qui y demeure présent*.

> [True education will teach how to think, organize ideas and to express them, no matter what topic is assigned, and in the case of a text [to be analyzed], to understand it, to uncover its beauties, and to converse with the artist *who remains present in it*.] (1968: 3, emphasis added.)

In a single sentence, Sellier succeeds in summarizing the two primary means by which literary pedagogy evolved directly out of a religious, and more specifically Christian view of the pedagogical function of the word: first, that the purpose of instruction is to develop one's innate moral capacities that *laïcité* traditionally equates with the ability to reason (*réfléchir, ordonner*); and second, that the purpose of reading is to experience the "real presence" of the author, just as the physical Bible contains the divine presence. Whether access to the divine is gained through the Bible's talismanic function, in which its mere proximity to the worshiper (on the altar, e.g.) manifests God's presence, or through the act of reading, is a question that has divided Catholics and Protestants for centuries, and which the republican school fails to answer. Indeed, the inability of literary pedagogy to decide between rhetoric and history, and between interpretation and erudition, is a symptom of the larger dilemma between a top–down, dogmatic transmission of values, and a more modern (democratic) system in which individuals bear the responsibility for their own salvation. I have argued that the French school, by and large, has adhered to the first (dogmatic) model, while claiming to adhere to the second one.

If the republican school was indeed a "false break" with the dogmatically religious institution it purported to oppose, then it follows that the pedagogical practices of the school were similarly continuous with preexisting ones. Historians and literary critics have already spent considerable energy analyzing the shift from religious education (the catechism, biblical history) to its secular form (*morale laïque*, French history). One of the fundamental studies in this area remains Phyllis Stock-Morton's *Moral Education for a Secular Society: The Development of Morale Laïque in Nineteenth-Century France* (1988). I have instead focused on the teaching of literature as an important part of the illusion that the republican school instituted a new educational paradigm. The substitution of the "*leçon de morale*" for the catechism, and of a "sainted history of France" (to quote once again Eugen Weber's formulation) for the characters and events of the Bible, was after all crude and artificial. The teaching of literature, by contrast, presented a much subtler appearance of change. For one, it did not simply serve as the secular version of a traditional sacred practice: the teaching of literature did not replace the teaching of Scripture, simply because French literature had already been a part of the primary and especially the secondary curriculum since at least as far back as the eighteenth century. It would be more accurate to say that the study of Scripture (and of texts inspired by it) was traditionally confined to the catechism, and that the demand for secular moral texts to replace Scripture was only indirectly related to the teaching of literary texts. In fact, we have three separate and interrelated foundations for linguistic and moral pedagogy at the primary and secondary level, the relative importance of which changed over the centuries since the Reformation placed popular education onto center stage: religious education ranging from the ability to read scripture to the purely passive memorization of articles of faith, Latin prayers, and so on; the institution of *morale laïque* that replaced religious education in the national schools of the Third Republic; and literary studies, occupying a vaguely delineated intermediary space between the other two.

The division of texts into the categories of sacred and secular is also present at the methodological level within the field of literary pedagogy itself. Daniel Bergez in 1989 published a sophisticated handbook on *L'explication de texte littéraire* (The School Exercise of Literary Analysis)[2] in which he claimed that the oral exercise of *explication* that had been institutionalized in the French secondary and higher education in the 1880s was the survival of two ancient traditions of exegesis, "l'une grecque et mettant l'accent sur la rhétorique, les figures du discours, et l'art du bien dire, l'autre juive et tendue vers la signification globale" [one Greek, emphasizing rhetoric, figures of speech, and elocution, the other one Jewish, and aspiring to global meaning] (4). The pedagogy that the Republic inherited from the Church in turn was an amalgam of Greek and Jewish traditions; Bergez's attribution of the pedagogical imperative to seek a "global meaning" in the text to the influence of rabbinical exegesis is highly original. The student's work upon the French literary text is therefore constrained on one side by the scholastic emphasis on linguistic function, and on the other side by the need to posit a "beyond" of the text that provides the occasion for endless speculation as to its covert but authentic meaning. Both the neo-Aristotelian medieval university and, much later, the Protestant return to Scripture against the tradition of paraphrase that prevailed in the Church, restored balance to a tradition that had erred too far in the direction of never-ending interpretation on the model of Talmudic and cabalistic practices (4). Jesuit pedagogy was the product of both of these reforms. By the end of the nineteenth century, according to this account, the pendulum had started to swing back toward less dependence on rhetoric, and an acknowledgment that the literary text carries within it a transcendent meaning that the student can experience, even if he or she cannot name it directly.

Pedagogues of the Third Republic from Compayré to Lanson insisted over and over that the role of literature in the school had been defined by

Jesuit pedagogy, and that it was this tradition that required revolutionary change. By charging the *Ratio Studiorum* with the greatest sins of Catholic education, they were able to create the impression of a genuine break from tradition by the republican school much more effectively than by advocating a relatively mechanical switch from one set of moral principles (Catholic virtues) to another (civic morality), and from one mythology (Biblical history and Scripture) to another (French history and literature). This is one of the more significant paradoxes that the study of literary pedagogy reveals: in spite of, or perhaps because of, the fact that literature had always been part of the pedagogical process, and that even the content of the canon changed only superficially in the transition from the Catholic to the republican school, the discipline of literature provided the Republic with the ideal opportunity to claim independence from the authoritarian, Church-based power structure whose legitimacy it sought to replace. Crudely put, the greater the superficial change in pedagogical practice (such as the shift from a religious to a secular catechism), the smaller the actual change in pedagogical philosophy; conversely, the smaller the change (from an exclusively Latin-dominated, rhetorical transmission of "literary" values, to a Latin- and French-dominated, attenuated rhetorical approach), the greater the potential for competition against, as opposed to imitation of, the preexisting model.

In fact, a truly significant change did occur. French literature, through the institution of national education, had usurped from Latin the role of social divider, of emblem of "High" culture, and had transformed the alienating aspect of classical studies into a national ideology in which the overcoming of the "foreign" within the national literary tradition became a defining characteristic of citizenship. If, during the Revolution, French was indeed a foreign language to the majority of potential citizens, in the Third Republic, through the teaching of literature, it retained a figurative "foreignness" that made it the perfect model for the foundational principle of assimilation: to be French, one had to be "born again" into the nation, and the school was the site and the instrument of that rebirth. The challenge is to attempt to measure the importance of this change, so as to determine whether the shift from a religious monopoly to a state monopoly over the spiritual business of the nation was really the replacement of one belief system by another, or simply the evolution over time of an intrinsically coherent belief system, from the increasingly privatized realm of participation in organized religion to the increasingly public realm of participation in civic life.

One cannot find a more sincere nor more urgent plea for the relevance of the *explication de texte* as a pillar of general education as well as a privileged tool for literary analysis than Pierre Clarac's book *L'Enseignement du français* (Teaching French), published in 1963 as a kind of pedagogical testament informed by 60 years of experience as a student and teacher. The great critic and *Inspecteur d'Académie* wrote an eloquent conservative defense of the *explication* that touched upon all the reasons that allow it to transcend its practical function as a method for learning French. In the realm of literary pedagogy, Clarac saw many opportunities for sin. He wrote that it is unforgivable, for example: "de profaner une page sacrée, de prétendre la juger de haut, de l'aborder sans préparation ni humilité" [to desecrate a sacred page, to dare to judge it from above, to approach it without preparation or humility] (44). "Pour saisir la composition d'un poème en vers ou en prose, il faudrait d'abord en découvrir le centre, ce centre d'où rayonnent les thèmes qui se croisent et se combinent avec une liberté souvent merveilleuse. Or, découvrir le centre du texte, cette 'idée générale' . . ., ce sera la conclusion et la récompense de l'explication" [In order to understand the composition of a prose or verse poem, it is necessary first to discover its center, from which radiate themes that intersect and recombine with an often marvelous freedom. In fact, to discover the center, this "general idea" . . . will be the conclusion and the reward of the exercise] (84–5). "Le respect de l'unité du texte s'impose à nous absolument. . . . [L'ordre du texte est] profondément révélateur des intentions de l'écrivain" [Respect for the unity of the text is absolutely required. . . . [The order of the text] is profoundly revealing of the author's intentions] (93). At the beginning of every class, the teacher must give a reading of the text to be analyzed, in order to give the students "le 'choc' nécessaire et, au seuil de l'enquête, de les mettre en état de grâce. . . . Les analyses de détail, les remarques particulières n'ont, en effet, de sens et de vertu que si elles convergent vers une résurrection intégrale du texte" [the "shock" necessary at the threshold of the enterprise to place them in a state of grace. . . . Analyses of detail and individual comments indeed have meaning and quality only if they converge towards a complete resurrection of the text] (100). Clarac uses the language of Catholic ritual in the above passages and throughout his book to such a degree that it loses its figurative meaning, and one is forced to conclude that it is the testimonial of a literally priestly vocation.

Several times in the course of his polemic, Clarac referred to "les problèmes de l'heure" [the problems of the hour] (1), by which he meant the threat of nuclear war (the Cuban Missile Crisis was unfolding as he wrote). The conventional view of the clerical role that Clarac adopted is of someone removed from such problems, and the activity of writing about literature is at best a retreat from historical violence into the atemporal. But Clarac concludes his book with a startling claim:

> Souvent, en écrivant ces notes, j'ai dû m'arracher à l'obsession des menaces qui pèsent lourdement sur la France et sur le monde. Mais pour un professeur, penser à son métier ce n'est pas un moyen spécieux de fuir le présent, ses devoirs et son angoisse. En enseignant aux hommes de demain à distinguer le vrai du faux, le bien du mal, le beau du laid, il prépare, dans le mesure de ses forces, un meilleur avenir.

> [Often while writing down these words I have had to tear myself away from the obsession of the threats that weigh heavily on France and the world. But for a professor, to think about his craft is not a way of escaping from the present, from his responsibilities and fear. By teaching the men of tomorrow how to distinguish truth from falsehood, beauty from ugliness, he is preparing to the best of his ability a better future.] (147)

Clarac's concluding statement is much more than a moving reminder that for decades, the threat of nuclear annihilation gave every human occupation, especially academic ones, an even more acute air of absurdity. By claiming that the study of literature "prepares a better world," Clarac is doing nothing less than granting his profession redemptive power. A generation of "men of tomorrow" nourished on the ritual of the *explication* will have seen the light, and they will dismantle the doomsday apparatus that drains our lives of meaning. The figurative "better world" of Christianity that the faithful will know through death and resurrection has become literalized in Clarac's argument that, through the resurrection of literary texts, our lives will not simply be better (richer, more interesting), but that they will be saved. The magnitude of the threat of nuclear war has finally allowed secular salvation to compete in moral importance with its religious forebear. Much as Clarac deplores the existence of the Bomb, he implicitly acknowledges that it has the virtue of finally absolving literary studies of being nothing but a secular surrogate for the true spiritual task of humankind; nuclear war has finally made literary pedagogy into a sacred enterprise, literally and no longer figuratively.

A comparison between Jesuit and republican literary pedagogies is the subject of an article by Jean-Claude Chevalier titled "La pédagogie des collèges jésuites" (The Pedagogy of Jesuit Schools; 1972), a contribution to the milestone issue of *Littérature* titled *Le Discours de l'école sur les textes*. Viewing the republican pedagogues' virulent attacks on Jesuit pedagogy as a form of denial (he thinks they doth protest too much),

Chevalier argues that the cornerstone of literary pedagogy in the *lycée*, the "explication de texte," whether extolled by the historian Lanson or the rhetorician Brunetière, was in fact directly descended from the Jesuit exercise of *praelectio*. According to Chevalier's interpretation of the *Ratio Studiorum* and of its application in Jesuit schools up to and including the era of the Third Republic, *praelectio* was invented as a method of identifying and commenting upon the "precept," moral rule, or truth content of a given text. Such "truth" was considered "à la fois sûre, présente, et inatteignable" [at once certain, present, and unattainable] (Chevalier 1972: 121), a clear expression of the "invisible presence" or "presence in absence" found in religious rituals, a faith in the presence of what cannot be seen or heard, that guarantees the authenticity of a sacred text (echoing the pedagogic rule quoted from the dissertation manual by Phillippe Sellier at the beginning of this chapter, "l'artiste . . . demeure présent [dans le texte]" [the artist remains present in the text]). In other words, the method of interpretation practiced in the Jesuit school was formally indistinguishable from the ideal pedagogy that is the Catholic Mass: certainty that the truth resides in the text, coupled with the impossibility of revealing that truth except indirectly, through commentary upon the text. In a reflection of the principle of inaccessibility of the "truth" or "presence" that founds the canonic status of the text that to this very day, the perfect score of twenty over twenty, "*vingt sur vingt,*" is almost never awarded to students in the traditional humanistic disciplines of the *baccalauréat* and other exams, and even a "*dix-huit*" (eighteen) is extraordinary.

The status of the "truth" of the text determines the role of the author (intercessor between God and the reader), and of the reader who is "une cire à imprimer, un vase à prendre les bonnes odeurs. . . . [L]'élève est métamorphosé dans ce discours institué par l'école" [a [drop of] wax to be stamped, a vase to gather the sweet smells. . . . [T]he student is metamorphosed in the discourse instituted by the school] (122). But the *praelectio* is not limited to the purely passive conversion of the student through the discovery of belief in the presence of truth (but not of the always elusive truth itself) in the text. In fact, the text on which the *praelectio* functions is ultimately a pretext for the student's own commentary, the real purpose of the exercise. Pedagogically speaking, the text is therefore subordinate to the personal discourse of the student, a fact that allowed the Third Republic pedagogues to accuse the Jesuits of disregarding literature in favor of "exercises of style." Chevalier observes a survival of the techniques of the *praelectio* into the 1880s and beyond, although it is not simply a case of a continuation of Jesuit pedagogy under the guise of its simulated suppression. These techniques not only survived, they enjoyed a revival that one cannot explain entirely by the renewed militancy of Catholic pedagogues in the face of republican reforms. The work of le Père de Jouvancy, a professor at Louis-le-Grand who in the late seventeenth century had developed methods for adapting the *Ratio Studiorum* into the classroom titled *De la Manière d'apprendre et d'enseigner* (On the Manner of Learning and Teaching) and *L'Elève de rhétorique* (The Student of Rhetoric), was reprinted in 1892 bearing the subtitle "Enseignement des Jésuites" (The Teaching of the Jesuits) by none other than Hachette, the same company that had benefited commercially, along with Belin and a few others, from the creation of a mandatory national curriculum.[3] It was not uncommon for Hachette and other companies to publish works perceived as critical or antithetical to the pedagogic movement of which they were a part; it could also be that Jesuit pedagogy gained new respect from the same academic establishment that had been so intent upon its delegitimization. The role of the school in identifying an elite and granting it a *savoir faire* that labels it as inherently distinct from the lesser classes is the explanation given by Marxist and other left-wing critics of republican education's tendency to revert back to pedagogy's *ancien régime* complicity with Church and aristocracy. Chevalier echoes that very same Marxist sociological analysis of the school that posits a two-faced pedagogy: a democratic one for public display only, and a clandestine, aristocratic one. In the atmosphere of an ostensible return to literature (and literary history) against the tradition of the Jesuits, their rhetorical legacy was to survive in secret in order for the new educational organization of the school to ensure, even better than the "old school" did, the creation of the managerial class that capitalism required in the late nineteenth and twentieth centuries (128). But is that all there is, and were the pedagogues of the Third Republic as plainly hypocritical as they are portrayed? I argue that while social distinction is always one of the unavowed purposes of all education, something else is also at work.

There is no lack of official statements, especially in the years when *la question du latin* seemed to retreat once again into the background, at least temporarily, that not only affirm the superiority of French literature, but also make the reading of literature (instead of reading "around" literature) into the central mission of the school. In October 1890, the *ministre de l'Instruction publique* Léon Bourgeois attached a memorandum to the list sent to the various *académies* of authors to be studied for the *brevet supérieur*. It is clear from the urgent tone of the memorandum that Bourgeois was responding to increasing concerns that students were not reading enough literature, practicing instead the famous (and to this day unabated) phenomenon of *bachotage*, the memorization of facts and received ideas.

> Aucune rédaction de devoir, aucune analyse littéraire, aucun cahier d'histoire de la littérature, ne fera autant pour le développement de leur esprit que ces heures consacrées à étudier dans le texte-même, les chefs d'oeuvre du génie français. . . . [P]eu à peu, [cette étude] éveillera en eux des idées et des sentiments, qu'ils n'auraient jamais acquis sans ce noble commerce avec l'élite de notre race.
>
> [No writing assignment, no literary analysis, no book of literary history will accomplish as much for the development of their minds than the hours spent studying the text itself of the masterpieces of the French genius. . . . [L]ittle by little, [such study] will awaken in them ideas and feelings that they would never have acquired without this noble exchange with the elite of our race.] (Quoted in Ecole Normale de Saint Cloud *La Pédagogie du français au XIXe siècle*, 1973: 159)

The significance of Bourgeois's memorandum, for our purposes, is its unusually candid appeal in favor of the activity of reading, placing him in the noble lineage of pedagogues, beginning with the proponents of reading over oration in the eighteenth century, who truly can claim to have perpetuated the field of literary studies. While terms such as "génie français" and "élite de la race" admittedly place his statement in an ideological context that is miles away from the practice of close reading as we would define it today, the privileging of "le texte-même" clearly expresses a reformist spirit that republicans too often denied.

The growth of state responsibility over spiritual matters, finally, is reflected in the difference between the pedagogical literary canon (texts used for the various secondary and post-secondary exams), and the broader canon of educated taste. While it is true that the school simply followed tradition when determining what texts to include in its curricula, as an institution it became increasingly concerned with excluding certain texts that had achieved canonical status outside of the school. Scholars have studied the relationship between the institution of education and the literary canon by analyzing the content of the secondary school literature curriculum from a longitudinal perspective, assessing the relative canonic strength of authors by following the evolution over time of the number of pages they occupy in the most commonly used anthologies. Roger Fayolle did just that, using the example of Baudelaire, the original "marginal" poet whose career is a study in the gradual conquest of autonomy by the literary field that Bourdieu described, and perhaps one of the first writers to whom one could apply the principle that modern art has achieved a reversal of the free-market system of valuation (the less popular an artist is, the better he or she is; in economic terms: the lower the demand, the higher the price). Fayolle took the most widely circulated secondary school literature anthologies from the year of the first major educational reforms of the Third Republic (1880) to the year when he researched his article: "La poésie dans l'enseignement de la littérature: le cas Baudelaire" (Poetry in Literary Education: The Case of Baudelaire 1972). As one might have predicted, Fayolle discovered that Baudelaire became increasingly popular or, perhaps more accurately, tolerable to the editors of textbooks (who themselves took their cue from the "*programmes*" or reading lists for the major exams that the ministry releases every year) as time went on. His figures deserve close scrutiny, however, because that is not the only conclusion one can draw from them.

Fayolle identifies in his article several important dates: he writes that 1880, the start of his survey, was the year that the educational establishment finally required French literature exams to cover the nineteenth century, a reform that Jules Simon had called for and never achieved during his stint as Minister in 1870; 1902, the year of the creation of a Latin-free *baccalauréat*, was also when the Ministry responded to criticism of the *lycée*'s emphasis on literary history by encouraging faculty and students to focus on reading larger and larger numbers of literary works; 1918, finally, was the year in which Baudelaire became a truly central figure in the curriculum, enjoying a much greater increase in his allotted "space" in the anthologies than at any other time before or since (48–55). Fayolle's statistics are divided into four periods; here is how Baudelaire fares during each of those periods against the poet, Victor Hugo, whose work was perennially number one in terms of pages allotted in the anthologies (adapted from Fayolle 1972):

Time period	Poets	Rank	Percentage of pages
1880–1900	Hugo	First	15.8
	Baudelaire	Thirty-sixth	0.3
1900–20	Hugo	First	14
	Baudelaire	Twentieth	1.2
1920–40	Hugo	First	11.75
	Baudelaire	Fourth	6.4
1940–72	Hugo	First	10.25
	Baudelaire	Second	9.3

Two other paradigmatically "marginal" yet canonic nineteenth-century poets Fayolle mentions are Verlaine and Rimbaud, both of whom are completely absent from anthologies until well into the twentieth century. Like Baudelaire, they both enjoyed an *"extraordinaire promotion"* (with 1918 also presumably a breakthrough year), Verlaine going from eighteenth to fifth to fourth in the last three periods of Fayolle's analysis, and Rimbaud having the greatest differential, going from forty-fourth to eighteenth to eighth.

What, if anything, do these statistics prove? For Fayolle, they demonstrate that the French educational system has shown an ever-increasing reliance on genuine literary study, as opposed to the traditional dialectic of rhetoric and literary history that dominated the late nineteenth and early twentieth centuries, and that this is evidenced by greater attention to poetry in general, as well as by much greater diversity in the variety of poetic *exempla* promoted in the school. Indeed it seems that the institution of secondary education has been able to reflect, with a time lag of several decades, the process of autonomization that literature itself had undergone. Consequently one can almost speak of a power of the literary field over the educational institution, rather than vice versa, one that contrasts with the easy assumption that begins and ends with the enlistment of literature for the sake of nation building as characteristic of the early half of the Third Republic.

It is not surprising to see Hugo in first place throughout the period of Fayolle's survey, though the extent and duration of his domination are remarkable. To my knowledge, Fayolle has not published a follow-up to his study, so I do not know whether Baudelaire has finally overtaken Hugo in the last decades of the twentieth century. It would certainly be worth finding out, and discussing the consequences either of Baudelaire's extraordinary accession to first place among the poets of the republican school, or the even more extraordinary durability of Hugo, if the order of the top two has not changed.

The most fascinating aspects of these statistics, however, are their illustration of a process to which I have already referred time and again: assimilation. When applied to literature, the term is often used in the guise of ingestion and digestion as a metaphor for the act of reading, of acquiring knowledge from outside of oneself that subtly and permanently alters one's identity; ultimately, it is about the acquisition of wisdom, as in Bakhtin's discussion of the banquet imagery in Rabelais: "Man's encounter with the world in the act of eating is joyful, triumphant; he triumphs over the world, devours it without being devoured himself. The limits between man and the world are erased, to man's advantage" (1984: 281). When we examine the figures showing Baudelaire's progressive assimilation by the educational literary canon, the term "assimilation" connotes another related process, this time at the level of the institution rather than the individual. Moving from the individual to the institution, the meaning of the term changes. The triumph experienced by the individual in the process of reading, of acquiring wisdom (in a word: learning) does not apply, or at least not in the same way, to the academic institution that allows itself to be occupied by an ever-increasingly *different* corpus of texts (different, i.e., from the "standard" corpus elevated by the institution to the status of symbol for the indefinable term "literariness": in the case of the French school, that corpus is seventeenth-century neoclassical verse). The figurative act of eating is triumphant for the individual not only because of the pleasure it affords, but because it allows the eater (reader, learner) to become more and more him or herself as he or she gradually absorbs ever-larger portions of the inherently alien world. In the Rabelaisian humanist context, the more varied the food—the more different, one might say, it is from mother's milk—the better.

While for the institution, the process of assimilation is certainly a victory of sorts (bringing Baudelaire into the fold is a bit like welcoming a prodigal son, or rather like naturalizing a foreign-born citizen), it is not clear who benefits from this victory, and how. For Baudelaire and other anti-classicists like Verlaine and Rimbaud, for the list of writers that could go on indefinitely, and include all those who are still today validated by Bourdieu's reverse-market definition of cultural value,[4] inclusion in the pedagogical canon, as distinct from the broader literary canon with which it overlaps, is not an unqualified boon.

"Canonicity" is also a mixed blessing in Barbara Johnson's book on Baudelaire, *Défigurations du langage poétique* (Disfigurations of Poetic Language; 1979). According to Johnson, there are in fact two Baudelaires: "un 'premier' Baudelaire consacré et vulgarisé par l'enseignement . . . un 'second' Baudelaire plus obscur mais peut-être plus poétiquement fécond" [a "first" Baudelaire consecrated and popularized by education . . . a "second" Baudelaire, more obscure, but perhaps more poetically fertile] (15). The "second" Baudelaire is not the one enshrined in the anthologies and curricula of secondary education; in fact, the assimilation process that he undergoes at the hands of the school is actually a form of disfiguring violence that ensures that the "real," untamed Baudelaire will always remain at a safe distance, like a tempting but poisonous fruit. In the specific case of Baudelaire, the assimilable texts are naturally his verse, as opposed to his prose poetry: the Baudelaire of the (pedagogical) canon consists of the poems that do not threaten the received definition of poetry. As to his *Poèmes en prose*, the disgust of the contemporaneous critic at Baudelaire's image of eating his lover's hair in "Un hémisphère dans une chevelure" ("Quand je mordille tes cheveux élastiques et rebelles, il me semble que je mange des souvenirs" [When I nibble on your elastic and rebellious hair, it seems as if I am eating memories]) is the universal first reaction to any cultural artifact the esthetic nature of which one has not already experienced, and therefore assimilated. In Barbara Johnson's brilliant formulation: "En esthétique comme en gastronomie, le goût est une question de dégustation, et l'habitude est plutôt une insensibilisation à l'étrangeté qu'un affinement de la perception" [In esthetics as in gastronomy, taste is a matter of *dégustation*, and habit is more a gradual loss of sensitivity to the strange than it is a refinement of perception] (39). The word "dégustation" (usually meaning simply "sampling" of food or wine, but quite untranslatable in this context) is the perfect metaphor for cultural assimilation: the "taste" of the alien must disappear, the assimilated food must be "de-tasted" (*dé-gusté*) before the diner is able to "keep it down" and make it a part of him- or herself. Rather than a sign of increased sophistication (the ability to appreciate a wider spectrum of flavors), the ability to absorb strange foods or other foreign artifacts is a function of one's acquired insensitivity or blindness to their foreignness.[5]

But are we giving the state too much credit? Is it not paranoid to accuse of collaboration with the self-interested, assimilationist policies of the state those academic bureaucrats responsible for state taste, who devise the lists of authors to be included on the *baccalauréat*? True, they opened the doors of the schools to the avant-garde by misrepresenting it, but in so doing, were they not simply maintaining a fine balance between the divergent pedagogical duties toward inclusiveness on the one hand, and intelligibility on the other?

It would be much easier to view the work of the academics enlisted by the Ministry and the authors of pedagogical works (who were often the same people) as benign, if it was clear that they saw the world of literature as intrinsically autonomous; in other words, if they refrained from interfering in the world of literary production except insofar as the creation of a literary curriculum necessarily and inevitably affected it. In fact, the links between the state, the academic community, and the field of literary production were even stronger than it appears, as the following example of government involvement in the literary field attests: before the end of the Second Empire, in 1867, poet Théophile Gautier was commissioned by the education minister Victor Duruy to write a report on the current state of poetry in France that appeared in 1868 as part of a larger *Rapport sur le progrès des lettres* (Report on the Progress of Literature). In 1903, Catulle Mendès was called upon to do the same, and produced *Le Mouvement poétique français de 1867 à 1900, Rapport à M. le Ministre de l'Instruction Publique et des Beaux-Arts* (The French Poetic Movement from 1867 to 1900, Report Submitted to the Minister of Public Instruction and Fine Arts). Mendès's report is actually a brief essay on modern poetry followed by a dictionary of sorts, an alphabetically arranged list of poets accompanied by critical commentaries of varying length depending on the poet's importance. These two reports, though part of the public record and distributed in bookstores (they were published by the *Imprimerie Impériale* and the *Imprimerie Nationale* respectively), were not intended for the edification of the masses. Since at the time, the cultural portfolio was part of the ministry of public instruction, it is perfectly normal that the government sought to keep itself informed of what was going on by asking a poet to report on the state of poetry. There is no evidence that these reports ever received much attention, or that the French government commissioned any other such report before 1867 or after 1903. Quite possibly, they were a way of providing some extra income for aging artists whom the state felt duty-bound to support. Yet regardless of the real motivation behind these reports, and the specific uses to which they may have been applied, their very existence raises questions. The commissioning of these reports was an official act, and reflected the principle that the government had a right, and even a duty, to establish a list of "important" contemporary poets. Who knows what benefits may have accrued to those on the list, and what it meant to be left off? Perhaps nothing in practice; in principle, however, it matters for the producers of culture to be living in a society in which such a list exists, despite the lack of any guarantee that the list itself is even the slightest bit objective.[6]

The counterpart to literature's role in national education is the role of national education in literature. One of critic Renée Balibar's most important contributions was to discern the effect of the two-tiered structure of French literary pedagogy that evolved from the establishment of national French in the wake of the Revolution upon the production of authors educated under that system. An early example she mentions is Flaubert, an author concerned with maintaining a clear distinction between literary French and the "language of the tribe," to use Mallarmé's expression, and she subsequently examines Camus, an author concerned with eliminating that same distinction. In principle, one could proceed on a case-by-case basis and examine the influence of specific pedagogical practices on every French or Francophone author whose educational experience can be more or less reconstituted, based on biographical and historical data such as school records, juvenilia, and the ideas and methods of particular pedagogues. Balibar has shown in her analysis of Péguy that such an approach is far more fruitful than the discredited historical materialism of Renan or Sainte-Beuve that had already been denounced by Lanson from the scientific perspective, and by Proust from the artistic perspective: attention to pedagogy redeems literary history.

Literary historians in France at the turn of the century based their new science on the study of extratextual evidence, primarily history and biography. Although this evolution first took place in the university and not in the school, it set the tone for the field of literary studies at all levels: by surrendering any claim to the irreducible, sacred literary "core" of the text, literary historians participated in the definition of one of the founding principles of the school of the fledgling Third Republic, and in the appropriation of the function of cultural transmission by constituted bodies of the state. The question of whether one accepts the existence of a sacred, inviolable dimension to the literary text, thereby defining the limits of the field of literary studies, is central to the role of literature in the French school.

In addition to the issue of whether literariness should be a pedagogical concern, there is a narrower but no less fruitful avenue of research into the effect of the school on literary production. The end of the nineteenth and beginning of the twentieth centuries in France saw an increase in literary works that featured the school, whether in a positive or negative light. Many of these works are propaganda, and therefore merit attention as part of the historical archive, such as *Une Année de collège à Paris* (A Year of Secondary School in Paris; 1883) by A. Laurie, the pen name of Paschal Grousset, one of Jules Verne's collaborators. The crucial passage in Laurie's novel describes the *concours général* exam in terms both militaristic—each *lycée* sends its students to the exam room dressed in its particular uniform—and religious:

> Sept heures sonnent. Les deux battants s'ouvrent avec un grand bruit de barres de fer et de gonds criards. La salle du concours nous apparaît, béante comme une église, entre les murs blancs percés de hautes fenêtres.

> The bell rings seven o'clock. The double doors open with a great noise of iron bars and screaming hinges. The contest room appears before us, gaping like a church, between the white walls pierced by high windows. (212)

A *locus classicus* of the glorification of the national school (albeit set during the fall of the Second Empire) is Alphonse Daudet's short story "La Dernière classe" (The Last Class) from *Contes du lundi* (1873), depicting a classroom that had been hastily evacuated during the French retreat from Alsace, a text that quickly found its way into school anthologies of the Republic. On the opposite end of the political spectrum is Jules Vallès's *Jacques Vingtras* trilogy and its ominous progression from *L'Enfant* to *Le Bachelier* to *L'Insurgé* (The Child, The Graduate, The Insurgent; 1879–86), published just as the Republic was trying to absolve the school once and for all of the charge that it was a tool of elitist oppression. Other voices on the Left were much more sympathetic to the liberating, egalitarian ambitions professed by national public education: Zola's last work, the unfinished *Les Quatre Evangiles* (The Four Gospels), culminates with a fictionalized account of the Dreyfus Affair titled *Vérité* (Truth; 1903) that features a schoolteacher as the martyred, innocent victim. Louis Pergaud's *La Guerre des boutons* (The War of Buttons; 1912) romanticizes the school as a site for the productive interaction of childhood freedom and social authority, a dialectic that takes a more metaphysical and esthetic turn in Alain-Fournier's *Le Grand Meaulnes* (The Wanderer; 1913), and a satirical one in Colette's *Claudine à l'école* (Claudine at School; 1900). The tension between the centralized Francophone culture of the state school and the heterogeneous cultures within the national boundaries are frequent themes of regionalist literature such as Pierre-Jakez Hélias's *Le Cheval d'orgueil* (1975), about growing up in Brittany at the turn of the last century.

An area of inquiry that is only beginning to emerge is the articulation of two antagonisms: the one between *métropole* and *périphérie* found in the works of regional authors, and the similar duality in the works of Francophone writers from the former colonies.[7] Foundational texts from the waning era of French colonialism such as Camara Laye's *L'Enfant noir* (The Black Child; 1953) and Joseph Zobel's *Rue Cases-Nègres* (Sugar-Cane Alley; 1950), representing West Africa and the West Indies respectively, are among the first Francophone texts to achieve canonical status in France, and like so many others (e.g., Kateb Yacine's 1956 *Nedjma* for North Africa), they use the experience of French national education, from which Francophone literature first emerged, as a structuring theme of the narrative and object of more or less direct attack.[8] In addition to these obvious examples, there are countless allusions to the Church-like function of the school throughout French literature of the last century, suggesting an unprecedented degree of obsession on the part of writers with the institutional conditions of their own apprenticeship. *Yale French Studies* devoted an issue to French education in 1958 that naturally gravitated to the pedagogic paradigm and/or image of the school in literary works including Cocteau's *Les Enfants terribles* (1929), Giraudoux's *Simon le pathétique* (1918), and Louis Guilloux's *Le Sang noir* (1935). The list could go on indefinitely. Perhaps because thematic criticism has been out of fashion for decades, very little has been published on the school in literature, much less than on literature in the school. Still, it is surprising that critics have not responded as strongly to the pedagogical experience as have literary authors.

Literariness is cultural identity is religion, metaphorically speaking. The problems of defining the characteristics of each one are alike, as are their respective dependencies on faith. Whenever such figurative associations emerge out of disparate material, there is a tendency to preserve the metaphoric status of the relationship by pointing to the distance, the difference separating the two terms. Literally speaking, art is emphatically not religion, a primordial distinction that gives the metaphor of art as religion its strength. In his article "On Schools, Churches and Museums" in the aforementioned *A New History of French Literature* (1989), Denis Hollier wrote of the early-twentieth-century mourning of the loss of sacredness of religious art in Maurice Barrès's *La Grande pitié des églises de France* (The Great Compassion of the Churches of France; 1914) and in Proust's article in *Le Figaro* on "La Mort des cathédrales" (The Death of the Cathedrals; 1905) (Hollier 1989: 834). Both writers warned against the danger of losing sight of the specifically religious nature of sacred architecture, and of confusing the categories of the esthetic and the sacred.[9] In a way, Barrès and Proust were fighting rearguard actions: the point of Hollier's article is the emergence in the twentieth century of a public cult of art, epitomized by André Malraux's status as the first minister of Culture in 1959 and his subsequent "museification" of the French cultural landscape (836). The artifacts of French culture became, more than ever before, sacred objects. As Barrès, Proust, Péguy, and others warned, the consequence of this development is not only the loss of identity of churches, when they become nothing more than beautiful art galleries, but a corresponding loss of identity of art as well. Churches lose by becoming museums just as museums lose by becoming churches. If we take our cue from these voices (admittedly reactionary ones, even in the case of Proust) of a century ago, then we may have at least a starting point for further investigation into the specific nature of art: in spite of appearances, art is not the same as religion, and we must begin by freeing ourselves of the persistent illusion that it is.

It is not easy to dissociate art, the broader category of culture and the narrower one of literature, from their acquired religious status. Nowhere is this fact more apparent than in the almost universal tendency to believe in the assimilating, that is to say salvational, powers of each: culture develops into an institution (becomes "national culture"), and the institution becomes the center of a cult. Historian Fernand Braudel's valedictorian work *The Identity of France* (1986, trans. 1989) contains two revealing allusions to the assimilating function of culture through education. One is the formulation of the need for the French nation to create itself by quite literally disciplining the difference out of its far-flung provinces and citizens; he refers in the first volume to the French nation's need to domesticate, so to speak, the margins of its territory over time. Only from the perspective of recent studies in colonialism and postcolonialism (including the prototypical colonialism that accompanies the very act of nation building in a country, like France, that has traditionally enjoyed huge cultural and linguistic diversity) have such historical analyses undergone significant challenge since the French Revolution. Braudel's second allusion, however, goes straight to the heart of the assimilationist dilemma as it arises in the context of contemporary French social policy. He recounts listening on the radio to "a young Algerian girl . . . describing her unhappiness, her feelings of anger and the constant problems she had to face. And she said all this in such perfect and elegant French (there must be something to be said for French schooling) that I suddenly had the cheerful and no doubt absurd feeling that, for her at least, success was just around the corner" (II: 210). "No doubt absurd," indeed: one must give Braudel credit for recognizing that perfect fluency and even elegance of expression do not alone constitute evidence of successful assimilation.

Let us end with a concrete example of artwork that affirms its own uniqueness by co-opting the spiritual magic that the French school borrowed from its Catholic model. In a talk on the creation of the image of national unity under Jules Ferry titled "La Formation de l'hexagone républicain" (The Formation of the Republican Hexagon; 1985), historian Eugen Weber alluded to one of the more bizarre, monumental legacies of the era of the Third Republic, the famous "*Palais idéal*", a structure built between 1879 and 1912 by Ferdinand Cheval, known to posterity as "le facteur Cheval" [Cheval the mailman] (just as fellow primitive artist and public employee Henri Rousseau was known as "le douanier Rousseau" [Rousseau the toll collector]). This impressive and completely inexplicable secular cathedral created by a modestly educated civil servant in his hometown in the department of the Drôme is covered by a large number of inscriptions: it is literally a monument of words. Weber claimed that these inscriptions prove that inhabitants of the French countryside, traditionally so diverse and so profoundly indifferent to the political and philosophical debates going on in Paris, by the end of the nineteenth century had finally started to think of themselves as French. It is important to remember that the assimilation of the *paysan* (a social status that Cheval proudly asserted several times in the writings that cover his masterpiece) into the nation did not take place as a direct result of the revelation by the school of the Republic's spiritual authority. Much more important as a factor of assimilation, according to Weber, was the increased standard of living: French people embraced their nation through the shrewd pursuit of their material interests, not through any political belief, esthetic conditioning, or philosophical idealism. But Weber takes his analysis one crucial step further: once people saw their material circumstances improve through increased interaction with the forces of the Republic, and the concomitant growth of the market in food, wine, and durable goods, they *also* began to assimilate the "images et paroles de cette bonne république" [images and words of that good republic] (Weber 1985: 236). The way to the hearts of French citizens was through their stomachs. However literal the means of assimilation of and into the national culture may have been, however, the results were profoundly spiritual in nature.

Weber quotes several of Cheval's architectural inscriptions to show how similar they are to the precepts of "*morale laïque*" that formed the backbone of the elementary school textbooks that proliferated in the last quarter of the nineteenth century, such as the following:

> Le travail fut ma seule gloire
> L'honneur mon seul bonheur.
>
> [Work was my only glory
> Honor my only happiness.]
>
> Par cela, j'apprends à tout âge
> Qu'en se montrant persévérant
> Laborieux, rempli de courage
> On arrive à tout sûrement.
>
> [Thus I learn at every age
> That by being steadfast
> Hard-working, filled with courage
> One surely can achieve all.] (Quoted in Weber 1985: 236)

Indeed, these homilies that Cheval composed himself and incorporated into his dream palace are strikingly similar to the "*morales*" that introduce each chapter of G. Bruno's *Le Tour de la France par deux enfants*, the most famous vessel for the dominant values of the Republican school, such as: "On estime toujours ceux qui travaillent" [People always respect those who work] (1930: 37) or "Il n'est guère d'obstacle qu'on ne puisse surmonter avec de la persévérance" [There is no obstacle that one cannot overcome by perseverance] (1930: 15). It is important here to recognize that the mundane bread and wine of increased rural prosperity that accompanied the extension of the Republic's reach into the farthest corners of France miraculously transubstantiated into the presence of the literary, and that they did so as a result of the individual initiative of a man who had never studied in a *lycée*. "The literary" is the appropriate term: for Weber omitted to mention one other significant aspect of Cheval's monumental words, beyond their similarity to the new pedagogical liturgy contained in the textbooks of the Republic. They are written in verse.

NOTES

Introduction

1. On the profound and often militant loyalty of many French Jews to the Third Republic as a consequence of their emancipation, see Pierre Birnbaum, *The Jews of the Republic: A Political History of State Jews from Gambetta to Vichy* (1992, trans. 1996).
2. In France in the 1980s, the possibility for individual citizens to preserve some degree of cultural autonomy in the midst of the dominant population was enshrined in the expression "*droit à la différence*" [right to difference]. The notion that such autonomy constitutes a fundamental human right was immediately challenged, not only in France, but also in every developed nation in which immigration is an important demographic factor. One cannot discuss the term "assimilation" without also discussing the degree of difference, if any, the assimilating body can tolerate. I will return to this problem as it occurs in literary canon formation as well as the larger social context in part III and in the conclusion.
3. The spelling of "Church" (referring specifically to the institution of the Roman Catholic Church) with an upper-case "C" and "state" with a lower-case "s" serves the same function as the distinction above between "Scripture" and "scripture" as a metaphor for literature: the second term in each pair refers to a purely human creation, and is therefore a common rather than a proper noun.
4. In history textbooks after the creation of national education, Charlemagne's role as a builder of schools took on increased importance. The implication is clearly that education had been an affair of state ever since the beginning of France's history as a nation. The fact that education in the Carolingian period was tied to the process of evangelization, and in the republican period to the process of creating French citizens, is a difference that ultimately did no harm to the ideologues of the Republic: in a predominantly Catholic country, reminding people that the roots of modern education were evangelical only contributed to the belief that the school is a hallowed institution, even when the overtly religious component of education has almost disappeared.
5. The much-debated Protestant affiliation of major figures of Republican pedagogy, most notably Ferdinand Buisson, Félix Pécaut, and Jules Steeg, is examined in part II, chapters 3 and 4.

6. For years, the most cited authority on the mythical and even mass-delusional aspects of nationalist ideology has been Benedict Anderson's *Imagined Communities: Reflections on the Origins and Spread of Nationalism* (1983). In my experience, it presents some of the strongest arguments that universalism plays an important role in the development of specific nationalist ideologies.

7. I use this term ("exceptionalism") to evoke the expression that is now current in French public debate: "*l'exception française*," the argument that certain sectors of the French economy—such as the audiovisual media—should be exempt from free-trade agreements. It is the argument that protectionism is justified, not when jobs or prosperity are in danger, but when a segment of the nation's cultural production risks being overwhelmed by foreign competition. In other words, cultural identity is above the law.

8. It is hard to resist comparing France and the United States in this regard. The pretensions to universality that are fundamental to American ideology are, in part, similar to (and even inherited from) French ones: when the Pledge of Allegiance ends with the words "with liberty and justice for all" it means all *people*, not "all Americans." The status of all human beings as "potential Americans" is in that way no different from the principles of French citizenship, inasmuch as French cultural and political values are offered as the salvation for people everywhere (and for many years, this civic–evangelic process did indeed occur beyond the original boundaries of the state, first in the colonial provinces, then in the attempts in other countries—Italy, Latin American republics, and others—to recreate the French Revolution on native ground). In practice, however, stark differences between American and French universality emerge: historically, the United States has been a land of immigration because it is large enough, not only geographically but culturally and politically, to contain multiple and incompatible world views: the mosaic rather than the melting-pot, integration without assimilation. The same process is reflected in the academic trend to be as inclusive as possible of diverse ethnicities, sexualities, and other group identities in the syllabi of Humanities courses. France, on the other hand, has remained largely faithful to its original claim of providing all humanity with one acceptable, coherent system of values. To put it simply: America is the land of integration, in which communities are allowed, at least in principle, to coexist while remaining largely faithful to their specific cultural identities, and France is the land of assimilation, in which aspiring citizens are welcome in principle, provided they merge with the preexisting national community. This difference between the United States and France would seem fairly irrelevant if it were not so often invoked in France as an important philosophical disagreement between the two cultures, such as in the editorials in *Le Monde* or *Le Nouvel Observateur* (see, e.g., Jacques Julliard, "Les États Désunis d'Amérique" (The Disunited States of America), 1991).

9. The emphasis on literary pedagogical practice rather than on the intrinsic characteristics of literary texts has been a focus of French criticism from the beginning of its ascendancy in literary studies, as papers from the landmark conference on "*L'Enseignement de la littérature*," published in 1971 by Serge Doubrovsky and Tzvetan Todorov, attest (see part III, chapter 9).

10. The theory that literariness depends largely on figures of speech, and that it is therefore the antithesis to unadorned, straightforward, and effective communication was fairly common in the eighteenth century, a golden age for the science of rhetoric. As we will see, this early attempt to come to grips with the concept of "literariness" played an important role in the First Republic, when several proponents of national education called for a complete regeneration of French language and literature through the banishment of figures of speech and other mystifying, distorting, aristocratic techniques.

11. The conflict between literal and figurative, secular and sacred, political and religious is indeed the proper framework for the analysis of the republican pedagogical approach to language. Though such confrontations are philosophical, one must not overlook the huge practical issues at stake in the decision to institute an ideal, transparent national language. Nothing illustrates those issues better than a passage from a letter written by Racine on November 11, 1661 to his friend La Fontaine. Relating a misadventure that occurred during a trip to the provinces, Racine complained of the difficulty in making himself understood by the servants of the inn where he slept, who placed a portable stove under his bed, when he had asked them for a chamber pot: "Vous pouvez vous imaginer les suites de cette maudite aventure, et ce qui peut arriver à un homme endormi qui se sert d'un réchaud dans ses nécessités de nuit" [You can imagine the consequences of this damned incident, and what can happen to a sleeping man who uses a stove for his nighttime needs] (quoted in Caput 1972: 297).

12. Ralph Albanese, one of several American experts on French literary pedagogy, has suggested in a personal communication that the unconditional acceptance of "*raison d'Etat*," or the right of the state to invoke its own (secret) interests in order to override other legal or moral concerns, is a direct outgrowth of the cultivation and cult of "*raison*" itself.

Chapter 1   The Taboo Against Literature in the School of the Republic

1. See, e.g., the reference to George Washington as a member of the "*Panthéon Républicain*" in part II, chapter 3. In this luxuriously published edition of republican propaganda by François Enne (1874), Washington is glorified in part because, rather than being inclined toward letters, he developed skills as a land surveyor: his ability to make maps of the real world was considered morally superior to other people's skills at navigating the virtual world of literary expression. Condorcet's proposal to include "*arpentage*" or land measurement in the curriculum therefore survived as a kind of symbol of the popular common sense of the Republic, concerned with actual space, as opposed to the elitist fantasy and "virtual space" associated with the literary misuse of language.

2. Traces of this contradiction survived in the ideology of the Third Republic, which also appeared alternately as "religion" and "antireligion." But Jules

Ferry and his academic supporters, as we will see, had a major advantage over their revolutionary precursors: their historical perspective on the First Republic allowed them to hide the more radical sources of republican ideology such as Condillac (whom Claude Nicolet [1982] describes as the founder of republican secularism through his materialist "désacralisation et . . . naturalisation de la pensée" [desacralization and naturalization of thought], 118) behind the more moderate figure of Condorcet, and the tradition of republicanism as it survived during Empire and Restoration.

3. For more on the relationship between Protestantism and the science of pedagogy under the Third Republic, see part II, chapter 3.

4. A more accurate translation would read: "the new society established its belief upon a spiritualized recasting of ideas that had established *the society* violently."

5. One can say that the creation of the Third Republic was nonviolent, since it existed only as a result of the failure of royalists and Bonapartists to unite sufficiently to impose a restoration or a Third Empire. This gave the republicans the opportunity to claim that their advent to power was the result of an almost organic process, rather than a violent upheaval, a claim challenged by Marc Fumaroli in *L'Etat culturel: Essai sur une religion moderne* (The Cultural State: Essay on a Modern Religion; 1991). The main argument against this view came, interestingly enough, from the left of the political spectrum: those who had the best case against the Republic's claims to have been born out of a peaceful process were the Paris Communards, whose bloody suppression was one of the first acts of the embryonic republican regime. By granting amnesty to all surviving participants of the *Commune* in 1879, President Jules Grévy acknowledged the need to erase the last remaining evidence that the Republic owed its existence to anything other than historical inevitability.

6. The distrust of eloquence (much stronger in the revolutionary figures discussed in the previous chapter than it is here) can be attributed at least in part to the influence of Rousseau. An important area of inquiry that is wide open, it seems to me, is the way in which Rousseau's call for transparency in language, in strong contradistinction to the valuation of imagery and wit in written and especially spoken discourse, lent authority to the republican campaign against Jesuit (rhetorical) pedagogy, and for the institution of a sacred national corpus. A related subject is the tension, already obvious in Rousseau, between writing as a privileged means of communication because of its abstraction from the social corruption inherent in conversation, and writing as a less sincere, because less spontaneous, form of discourse than speech (one thinks of the many "*esprit de l'escalier*" "stairwell wit" passages in the *Confessions* and elsewhere in which Rousseau, ostensibly deploring his lack of *repartie*, secretly congratulates himself for not having the ability to score points in conversation, which, after all, is only a sign of one's enslavement to a particularly noxious type of rhetoric). The debate over literature in the school during the various French Republics is partly a consequence of Rousseau's almost total banishment of literature from early education in *Emile*, a book that continued to dominate educational policy debate until well after the Revolution.

7. Charles Coutel, in his introduction to a 1989 reprinting of Compayré's work, describes it as *"[un résumé de] toutes les contradictions possibles dans les définitions de la mission de l'école"* [a summary of all possible contradictions in the definition of the school's mission] (II: 39). In brief, the moderate faction (Condorcet, Charles Romme) confronted the radical one (Le Peletier), and synthesis arrived through the intervention of Talleyrand. But all substantive proposals, in particular those emanating from Condorcet's *Comité d'Instruction Publique* came under attack and failed to see enactment into law. Compayré's work, therefore, is one of rehabilitation, of recognition of the sacrifice of the "true" founders of national education, as well as an attempt to see their debates as part of a coherent process leading ineluctably to the laws of the 1880s.

8. Condorcet's last work, written after he was sentenced to death during the Terror, was a *Manuel d'arithmétique*, a final attempt to salvage his educational vision long after the National Convention tabled his proposals.

Chapter 2   Beyond Condorcet: The Revolutionary Attack on Literature

1. Among Petit's publications that did not result directly from his functions as deputy from the department of l'Aisne, and shows his strong interest in the effect of language reform on literary production, is a pamphlet titled *Des changements que l'amour de la vérité produira dans la poésie et dans l'éloquence* [Of the Changes that the Love of Truth Shall Produce in Poetry and in Eloquence; 1792], in which he develops further the principle that all literature up until the present is tainted by its origins in privilege, and that literary value, as it had been understood up to that point, was incompatible with truth.

2. In 1793, Paris fashion had not yet given birth to the *"incroyables,"* whose speech and dress expressed the most extreme form of artificiality; they were associated with the *Directoire*, beginning in 1795. Petit's condemnation of the *"républicains monarchisés"* and their ridiculous *"brinborions"* would seem to prefigure the caricaturesque styles to come, however.

3. The "journal de classe," defined in Buisson's *Dictionnaire* as "la préparation écrite et plus ou moins développée du travail de chaque jour de l'instituteur" [the written and more or less developed preparation [perhaps better understood as "record"] of the teacher's work of each day] (quoted in Giolitto 1983–84: 234) actually became required in 1866, and soon attracted a great deal of controversy. Intended to serve as a means of controlling the quality of instruction, it was perceived by teachers as a burden and an abuse of administrative authority. By 1881, it was no longer required, though Buisson's *Dictionnaire* was one of several means by which the pedagogical establishment expressed its regret that the initiative was not successful. Clearly, it had been a central tenet of republican pedagogical policy until the resistance of the teachers became simply too strong (Giolitto 1983–84: 243–7).

Chapter 3   The Evangelism of National Education

1. The fact that there was a legal office of "Cultes" resulted in part from the 1801 *Concordat* between Napoleon and the Church. In exchange for the Vatican's agreement not to challenge France's ownership of Church holdings confiscated during the Revolution, the French government agreed to take on part of the remuneration of priests and other expenses. In effect, therefore, Catholicism was as close as France ever came to a state-sanctioned religion, before the official separation of Church and state in 1905 (Gaillard 1989: 477–8). The French government of course no longer subsidizes religion directly; however, religious affairs and the term "cultes" are still in the government's purview, now as part of the Ministry of the Interior.

2. Much of the preceding information is drawn from the webpage of the French Ministry of National Education, where it is fleshed out in far greater detail.

3. The foremost literary example of the reaction against Kantian idealism in the school is Maurice Barrès's novel *Les Déracinés* (The Uprooted) of 1897, in which a lycée teacher of philosophy named Bouteiller serves as the embodiment of the abstract, centralized, and tyrannical Republic. Had Ferry not mentioned Kant as a founder of *morale laïque*, it is possible that French right-wing extremism at the end of the century would have taken on a quite different complexion.

4. The matter of Ferry's own religious beliefs, or lack thereof, parallels the history of French republican ideology. Claude Nicolet writes in *L'Idée républicaine en France* (1982) that the greatest—and ultimately unresolved—difficulty in elaborating a republican ideology lay in the inadequacy of positivism as a founding principle. Strictly speaking, positivism even in its extreme Comtean form excludes axiomatic starting points and teleological endpoints, making it not only an "anti-religion," but casting doubt on the validity of republican "first principles" such as the Declaration of the Rights of Man or of ultimate goals such as "liberty, equality, fraternity" (188). These philosophical contradictions did not prevent Ferry and others from behaving as if positivism and republican dogma were reconcilable, however.

5. Actually, Péguy's memorable phrase is constantly misquoted. In his novel *L'Argent* (Money; 1961, first ed. 1913), he creates a vivid portrait of the public school teachers fresh from their *brevet de capacité*, some of whom were still in their teens. He calls them "hussards noirs," "hussards de la République," and "hussards noirs de la discipline" (1115), but never "hussards noirs de la République." What is important, of course, is not his exact words so much as the military (and not clerical) analogy that the black uniforms of the young teachers suggested to Péguy's imagination.

6. The infamous "Article 7" of the laws on education proposed by Ferry in 1879 stipulated that all schoolteachers had the right to belong to a "*congrégation autorisée*." The Jesuits were the main "non-authorized" congregation to practice education, and were therefore subject to this law when it was finally passed, after much debate, along with the educational decrees of March 29, 1880.

7. The Hachette publishing house was, without a doubt, one of the greatest private beneficiaries of the educational policies of the Third Republic. Not

only did Hachette publish many of the very popular historical and socio-logical essays and polemical texts that served partly as propaganda for the republican school, it also provided many of the textbooks for the rapidly increasing national school population. Another beneficiary was Belin, publisher of G. Bruno's *Le Tour de la France par deux enfants*, which became the biggest success in French school publishing history (see part two, chapter 2). The history of the relationship between the publishing industry and the national school has yet to be written.

8. Jean Macé's private *Ligue nationale pour l'enseignement*, founded in 1866, was an important force in the nationalization of education. Known primar-ily for his populist tendencies, Macé also took Germany as a source of inspi-ration and framed his call for educational reform in the rhetoric of spiritual regeneration. Françoise Mayeur points out that this eventually led to his downfall, when the policies he proposed were shown to be consistent with Freemasonry (268–70). Whether Positivist, Protestant, or Masonic, it seems that talk of state-sponsored educational reform could only exist in denominational terms.

9. Textbooks of the Third Republic (and no doubt from later periods in French history) often instruct the schoolchild on the virtue of losing rather than winning, as if winning signified at best nothing more than superior brute strength (and by implication, inferior spiritual and intellectual quali-ties), and at worst, some form of cheating. I believe the effects of this type of instruction survived for a long time in France under the guise of what I call the "Poulidor complex": in the 1960s, there were two great French cyclists, Jacques Anquetil and Raymond Poulidor. Anquetil won the Tour de France five times, and was considered almost unbeatable on any given day. Poulidor, by contrast, never won the Tour, and earned the affectionate moniker "l'éternel second" [the eternal runner-up]. Poulidor was adored by the French public, while Anquetil never fully gained its trust. The French victory in the 1998 soccer World Cup may have been a watershed event, putting a symbolic end to this strange reversal of values.

10. The last pamphlet published by Hureaux to be shelved in the Bibliothèque Nationale is a summary of his life-long quest, and gives some indication that by that point he had become excessively enamored of his idiosyncratic spiritual vision. It is titled *Le Livre de vie, oeuvre universelle de lumière et de justice. La chute du monde d'iniquités dans l'abîme, le salut et la gloire de la France républicaine, des républiques et de l'humanité libre par l'avènement du christianisme scientifique* (The Book of Life, Universal Work of Light and Justice. The Fall of the World of Iniquities into the Abyss, the Salvation and Glory of Republican France, of the Republics and of Free Humanity through the Advent of Scientific Christianity; 1888).

11. The lack of a well-organized national education system such as the one enjoyed by Prussia was one of the main reasons given for the defeat in the years immediately after it occurred. Since then, of course, all manner of historical analysis has arisen, some of which has trickled down to the class-room. The theory that the French troops were made overconfident because of their faith in the technological superiority of their "Chassepot" rifles was

current 20 or 30 years ago, as I mentioned anecdotally in the Preface, and was presented as at least as important a factor as the relative lack of education of the troops.

12. The ritual of beginning each day with a *leçon de morale*, rooted in the primacy of religious instruction mandated by the *loi Guizot* of 1833 and reinforced by the *loi Falloux* of 1850, is consistent throughout the history of French primary education. My personal experience confirms that in 1969 the elementary school day began (at least once a week) with the careful presentation and recopying in the *cahier du jour* of a particular moral precept that served as the basis for a lesson; the late 1960s were, however, the end of an era in French education.

Chapter 4   The Fathers of Pedagogical Science, Gabriel Compayré and Ferdinand Buisson

1. When Compayré wrote his essay, the Jesuits were still one of the largest contingents of school teachers in the Catholic Church. Although they had been eliminated from the schools by the application of Ferry's "*Article 7*" in 1880, they were to return as a result of concessions made by the Republic to the principle of private education, and by 1890 25 of the 27 Jesuit schools that had been shut down were back in full strength (Bush 1975: 126).

2. See, e.g., the article by George Chase, "Ferdinand Buisson and Salvation by National Education" (1983), which presents the failure of the Reformation in France as a precondition for the success of republican educational policy.

3. The *Revue Pédagogique*, along with Buisson's dictionary, was the signal of the birth of a new science. There is a cloud over the birth, however. Not only were the theories and histories of pedagogy often written with the scientifically suspect purpose of undergirding Ferry's initiatives, the *Revue* began a *deuxième série*, with the numbering of issues starting again at one, in the year 1882, four years after its inaugural issue. Buisson's dictionary also began to appear in 1882, a fact that is hardly a matter of coincidence. While it was no doubt justified by administrative or budgetary reasons, this relaunching of the journal at the time Ferry's laws were being debated made the relationship between the science and politics of pedagogy very explicit indeed.

4. The practice of selection was most evident in the inclusion of only certain of La Fontaine's Aesopic fables into the pedagogical canon.

5. Such exclusion operates today by the activation of a principle which had always been latent in modern French law: citizenship itself is the one right which is not universal. In fact, it amounts to a privilege. In the history of the French Republics, anybody born on French soil could become a citizen, with all the rights and responsibilities thereof. Over the years, that right under republican law has alternated between a simple privilege of birth that required no further initiative on the part of the individual, to a status that had to be confirmed at the time the aspiring citizen reached majority. Since the 1990s, the latter principle has been in effect: children of foreign parents born on

French soil have to petition for citizenship after their eighteenth birthday. The law poses an interesting dilemma for such individuals, since full access to "universal human rights" as guaranteed by French law is conditional upon French citizenship, which for this particular minority has more and more the appearance of a privilege extended by the state. Since privileges are basically arbitrary, they can be granted or withheld with little need for justification (since an objectively justifiable privilege is actually a right).

6. More recently the principle of *laïcité* has played an important role in the debate over the right of the public schools to forbid the wearing of the Islamic veil (actually a headdress that veils the hair) by girls in French public schools. Jean Boussinesq has published in the *Points* collection a small book entitled *La laïcité française* (1994) that reviews the legal history of the separation of Church and state in France, and its application to the current crisis. Implicit in his exposition is the idea that by presenting the legal texts upon which the banning of the veil is justified, the issue will be clearer to the public. In other words, the law itself having been revealed, the justification for the banning of the veil becomes clear and no longer debatable. Under the guise of bringing more clarity and "un accès pratique aux textes législatifs et réglementaires qui touchent de près ou de loin à ce problème" [practical access to the statutory and regulatory texts that touch directly or indirectly on this problem] (7), Boussinesq in fact argues in favor of the state by citing the *Code*, one of the primary responsibilities of a prosecutor in a French court of law. There are, however, many balanced presentations of the veil affair which take the issue of individual freedom of religion and expression into account, such as *Le foulard et la République* by Françoise Gaspard and Farhad Khosrokhavar (1995).

7. Much has been made of the influence on Jules Ferry of his wife's Protestantism, and the fact that 8 percent of the government staff in 1880 was Protestant. Certainly, the affinity between Protestantism and republican pedagogy was of enormous consequence to Compayré, Buisson, and many of their colleagues, as we have seen. A far more important influence on Ferry himself, however, was the extreme positivism of Auguste Comte, with its blend of materialist philosophy and moral idealism. Ferry himself was more rationalist than Christian in his beliefs, joining the Freemasons in 1875 and claiming positivism as the greatest influence on his public positions. Louis Legrand (*L'influence du positivisme dans l'oeuvre scolaire de Jules Ferry* 1961) and Claude Nicolet (*L'Idée républicaine en France: Essai d'histoire critique* 1982) provide ample analysis of his relationship to positivism as one of the dominant ideologies to compete with Christianity in the nineteenth century.

Chapter 5 The Suppression and Expression of Literature in Primary Education: Evolution of the Manuel de français

1. The designation of authors who are most useful to the enterprise of primary education was a radical step in the integration of literature into elementary

school pedagogy. As such, it marks a major shift away from the suspicion of literature that characterized the educational policies of the Revolution. Of course, the creation of such a list of authors was made easier by the fact that the state had already been involved in the creation of an "official" canon at the secondary and tertiary level least since the Napoleonic era. Daniel Milo points out that in 1802, when French literature began to appear in the curricula of universities and *lycées*, and despite the backlash it caused in favor of Latin, the term "classical" in reference to French literary works of the seventeenth century came into usage (531).

2. For a modern critique of the point of view illustrated by Bonnefon, see Edgar Tripet's article "Langue, littérature et pouvoir," already mentioned in the Introduction.

Chapter 6   The Theme of Assimilation in Primary School Textbooks

1. Bigot's *Le Petit Français* is the one example in this study of a very important genre of primary school textbooks designed to teach the mandatory subject of *instruction morale et civique*, for which a set amount of time was reserved each morning. These are, by and large, part of a separate genre from the literary anthologies or compendia of practical knowledge that I analyze here. They were attempts to teach *morale laïque* directly by making it the primary requisite for citizenship in the new republic, and often put legal duties such as voting and paying taxes on the same level occupied by Christian values of charity and devotion. Catholic schools created their own competing textbooks on civil morality, and the best analysis of this particular publishing phenomenon and the social conflicts it produced is in Yves Déloye's *Ecole et citoyenneté: l'individualisme républicain de Jules Ferry à Vichy* (School and Citizenship: Republican Individualism from Jules Ferry to Vichy 1994).

2. Louis Liard's "moral" anthology of French literature is related, on a fairly deep level, with a contemporary anthology: William Bennett's *Book of Virtues*, which also implicitly links literary value to moral insight. The difference, of course, is that Liard and others were explicit and unabashed in their substitution of the criterion of morality for the less easily defined one of literariness. Bennett, by contrast, does not claim that his book is an anthology of the best literature, only that great authors tend to express moral precepts better.

3. The anecdote and its accompanying illustration show Vercingétorix in a very positive light, considering that he is in the process of surrendering. Two things come to mind. First, there is a parody of the same scene in the *Astérix* comic books by René Goscinny and Albert Uderzo: a towering, handsome Vercingétorix hurls his weapons at the feet of a tiny Caesar who cries out in pain, since the weapons appear to have landed on his toes. One can safely assume that Goscinny and Uderzo created that scene because they had already known it as schoolboys, though probably not in Augé, which had pretty much gone out of print by the 1920s. G. Bruno was another source for the Vercingétorix episode, but it had clearly made its way into many schoolbooks, Augé simply being one of them.

4. A good number of the poems in Augé's textbook are clearly written for a primary school audience. The question of whether any of the authors wrote them for Augé specifically, or had simply written poetry for children that Augé decided to use, is one that I have not explored. In the event that the poems were commissioned, a whole new dimension of the role of the state, mediated through the private publishing houses that provided schools with the physical materials needed in order to apply the directives of the government, upon the "literary field" of the late nineteenth century, would have to be explored.

5. Like Rousseau's comment on *Le Corbeau et le renard*, "Qu'est-ce qu'un arbre perché?" the anecdote of the *Vase de Soissons* became a trite classroom joke as a direct result of the popularity of Augé's book and others in which it appeared so prominently. The teacher asks a student: "Qui a cassé le vase de Soissons?" and the student indignantly replies: "C'est pas moi, M'sieur!" [Who broke the vase of Soissons?—I didn't do it, sir!].

6. There has recently been a minor vogue of films that portray, negatively and positively, the literary potential of language as it was exploited by social elites under the *ancien régime*, such as *Ridicule* and *Wit*.

7. The difference between "dialecte" and "patois," in 1892 as well as today, is one of class: "patois" is specifically the language of peasants, while "dialecte" can encompass a range of social levels—only up to a point, however: there is a degree of respectability one can attain only by adopting the universal dialect of literary French. The pejorative connotations of "patois" that Augé uses are the result of that distinction, not the cause. Therefore the claim still should hold that both terms are, for practical purposes, synonymous.

8. In 1877, the spirit of *revanche* was still very strong, and it is therefore not surprising that the story begins with an allusion to the humiliation of the 1871 defeat. The journey of the two orphans will then become a healing experience, a means of finding their lost homeland—Lorraine—in the newly discovered one of France. As Dupuy (1953) and others point out, however, references to the defeat became increasingly rare as the Third Republic grew stronger. As a result, Mme Fouillée emphasized it less in subsequent editions, giving a more optimistic and strong image of the *patrie*. The 1889 edition that I studied, however, was still very much a product of the defeat; revisions concerning 1871 were nevertheless minor compared to the more concerted efforts to exclude references to organized religion as the work's popularity increased.

9. Five years earlier Daniel Bonnefon, e.g., called the Gauls "nos véritables ancêtres" [our true ancestors] in his popular textbook *Les Ecrivains célèbres de la France* (Famous Writers of France), published in 1872 (2).

10. The image of young children from West Africa studiously repeating the words "nos ancêtres, les Gaulois" makes for a good joke, but is probably not entirely accurate. Françoise Mayeur pointed out in her book on the history of French education (1981) that the national curriculum was, for a very long time, kept out of French colonies altogether, and colonial teachers enjoyed an impressive amount of freedom to develop instructional methods and content. Around 1920, there was a move to make colonial education

more consistent with practices in the *métropole*, later superseded by an attempt to develop materials and methods specifically adapted to local needs and expectations (586–7). In the years since Mayeur's work appeared, there has been a huge increase in the amount of research on the educational system in the French colonies.

11. Jean-Jacques Walz, under the name "le Père Hansi," published a famous series of picture books in the years surrounding World War I that were an iconography of the longing of his native Alsace to become French. He created a striking visual echo of Bruno's description of the Gauls, with his blond and blue-eyed children in their native costumes, struggling to keep the flame of French identity alive under hostile German rule.

12. While visiting the Dauphiné region, André and Julien stay at an inn: "L'hôtellière était une bonne vieille, qui paraissait si avenante, qu'André, pour faire plaisir à Julien, se hasarda à l'interroger, mais elle ne comprenait que quelques phrases françaises, car elle parlait à l'ordinaire, comme beaucoup de vieilles gens du lieu, le patois du midi" [The landlady was a good old woman who seemed so pleasant that André, to make Julien happy, ventured to ask her questions, but she understood only a few French phrases because, like many old people in the area, she normally spoke the southern patois] (161). The tendency of scholars such as Jacques and Mona Ozouf to overlook this passage is a sign that Bruno's ideal of a completely homogeneous nation is so powerful that it has blinded readers to the traces of pre-republican heterogeneity that she nevertheless includes.

13. The Third Republic, even before the period leading directly to World War I, was not pacifist. Concern over *revanche* declined as the government shrewdly shifted public attention to France's colonial enterprise. The 1880s and 1890s were the periods of greatest expansion in Central Africa and Indochina. Though perilous, these military expeditions had the advantage of guaranteed success. The Republic could therefore repel any charge of taking a passive attitude militarily, while concentrating on its cultural war on the home front (see, e.g., Raoul Girardet, *Le Nationalisme français, 1871–1914* 1966).

Chapter 7   Latin as Symbol for the Mysteries of French

1. One would not go very far with a philosophy of literary value that did little more than give positive weight to a text's capacity to remain impenetrable. Taken to its logical conclusion, such a definition would simply equate literariness with obscurity, whereas anyone familiar with the exercise of reading knows that most of the time it occurs, impenetrability is antiliterary and merely the result of bad writing. I hope to make my argument in favor of this (partial) definition, however, by drawing attention to its context: literature is impenetrable in the same way that Scripture is (as text), and that Latin has been (as language) for most of the postclassical era: not muddled and simply obfuscating, but suggestive of great depth. Literary criticism consists in part of the process of excavating and revealing, but the inability ever to reveal all is where criticism ceases to be an exercise in

discovery, and becomes a religious ritual. If Scripture is the trope for the literary text, then Latin is the trope for literary discourse *on* the text.

2. In this chapter and in chapter 8, the term "Latin" is sometimes replaced by "*études classiques*," a term that incorporates Ancient Greek as well. The fact is that Greek, though always present in the secondary school system, was never required of all candidates to the *baccalauréat*. Latin, on the other hand, not only used to be taught to all schoolchildren as a means of learning to read French, it was required at one time or another of almost every student who continued beyond the mandatory minimum school age. The most notable exceptions, i.e., those students who could escape from the clutches of Latin, were the students of *enseignement spécial* beginning in the mid-nineteenth century, and girls. Whether the term is "Latin" or "*études classiques*," therefore, it is really Latin that is in question.

3. De Broglie gave his speech after the golden era of the secular sainthood of the writer, according to Bénichou, was over. Indeed, one detects in de Broglie a shift in emphasis from the contemporary man of letters to the dead one. He was speaking of past human accomplishments, all of which were ultimately made possible by the work of writers. Writers are therefore the foundation of great human achievement, an argument that places their importance in the distant past, rather than ascribing great moral authority to those who are active. Such an argument is consistent with Bénichou's chronology.

4. Incidentally, one notes with interest the disappearance in the program of *seconde* of Jean-Baptiste Massillon, whom Daniel Milo, quoted earlier, mentioned as an author whose reputation had been artificially maintained by the institution of public education.

5. André Chervel documents this evolution: from being a pillar of the textbook publishing industry in the mid-nineteenth century, classical texts and manuals had declined to modest percentages by the early twentieth. Chervel's statistics put the whole debate in perspective, reminding one that the latinists, in spite of their high visibility in the press, were fighting a losing battle, and knew it.

6. Even today, educational reform in France which involves the Latin curriculum is likely to arouse anger. Classical languages have not been required for the *baccalauréat* in many years. Yet the belief still persists that mastery of French is incomplete without a classical foundation, and any attempt to marginalize Classics even further, as has occurred numerous times during the educational reforms of the twentieth century, still brings out protests from a surprising number of people.

7. *Version*, as we have seen, is the term applied to the exercise of translating passages from classical literature into French, and *thème* is the translation of a French text into Latin or Greek; one must also add *composition grecque ou latine*, or the creation of original texts, usually applying traditional rules of prosody and rhetoric. All were (and, for some students, still are) the basic elements of *éducation classique*, although, as the reference to d'Alembert shows, the necessity for all educated people to write and speak Latin or Greek came into question, creating a culture in which competition between

French and classical languages (the latter no longer being treated as "living" languages) steadily declined in intensity.

Chapter 8   Against Literature: The "Question of Latin"

1. The controversy surrounding Frary's book was still very much alive as late as 1891 when the philosopher Alfred Fouillée wrote *L'Enseignement au point de vue national* (Education from the National Perspective, Hachette), a work at least partly motivated by a desire to repel the attacks on traditional classical education.
2. There is no better analysis of the conservative function of education in general, and the French model in particular, than Pierre Bourdieu's sociological critique of pedagogical institutions. The present work is part of an attempt to trace the ideological function of French education to concerns that were specific to the French Third Republic, at a time when its very existence depended upon public policies in the realm of culture.
3. The term "utilitarian" was used against Frary, not only because of its negative connotations in France (connoting Anglo-Saxon principles antithetical to *art de vivre*), but also because of the real tradition of opposition to Latin associated with utilitarianism. In the American colonies from their very beginning, e.g., utilitarian principles drove the development of education away from the classics, since there was so little use for them (Waquet 2001: 215).
4. The term "*casier scolaire*" is modeled on "*casier judiciaire*," or rap sheet. Was Ferdinand Réal aware of this irony? In any case, his vision of a system of academic credentials based on transcripts rather than exams was revolutionary for France then, and still is today.
5. Antoine Compagnon has done a most thorough job of describing the battle between the rhetorical and historical camp as a precursor to the battle between *ancienne* and *nouvelle critique* symbolized by Roland Barthes's polemic with Raymond Picard on Racine in *La Troisième République des Lettres: de Flaubert à Proust* (1983).

Chapter 9   For Literature: The "Crisis of French"

1. The exercise of *composition française* actually makes its appearance relatively early in a student's career, as any number of primary school textbooks demonstrate. The theme of writing a letter in the name of a famous historical figure also occurs early on, which can be interpreted in two separate ways: first, as a guard against the child being too independent and exercising too much of his or her own judgment, and second, as a creative challenge, encouraging the child's individuality by making him or her temporarily take the place of a person who has already earned the right to speak in his or her name.
2. Patru is presented as a "villain" of sorts several times in Calonne's exercises, one of which asks the student to write a letter from Patru to his friend Boileau to dissuade him from writing an *Art poétique* (1). The type of composition Calonne uses here was one of the regular options of subjects for

the *baccalauréat* in French literature, in which a contemporary figure is blind to the reasons for the greatness of his more famous colleagues. It would be interesting to explore reasons why Patru was the patsy in the republican school's cult of the seventeenth century, and what other figures might have served a similar function.

3. I will not dwell here on the important 1902 reforms except to point out the discrepancy between the reforms and their effect on pedagogic practice. Not only did French society resist the official attempt to place French literature on the same level as Latin, even supporters of the reforms such Charles Navarre admitted that the "D" track, the one without obligatory Latin or Greek, was in fact, if not by law, inferior to the others (Hanna 1996: 173).

4. I cannot resist bringing attention to one of Brunetière's opponents in these culture wars, none other than Gustave Kahn, who wrote a review in the *Revue Blanche* in 1901 of the recent crop of *manuels* of literary history by the big guns of the Sorbonne: Doumic, Lanson, and Brunetière. Contemptuous of all of these, Kahn reserves special wrath for Brunetière, whose hostility toward Baudelaire and Gautier (and, by implication, toward their contemporary disciples such as Kahn) is especially objectionable. Brunetière included no living authors in his *manuel*, not even the foes of symbolism, an omission leading Kahn to remark: "Je m'explique peu alors tant d'articles de combat du même Brunetière" [I therefore cannot explain so many of the same Brunetière's war articles [polemical pieces]] (585).

5. The point of placing "assimilation" in a more recent historical context is twofold. First, I want to make at least some claim for the currency of the questions discussed in this book, without however making a full comparison between French literary pedagogy today and one hundred years ago, which would take an entirely different book to accomplish. Second, I believe that relatively recent debates over "*droit à la différence*" give one greater insight into the purpose and limitations of the assimilationist function of the school, since the student body of the Third Republic, the vast majority of which was French speaking and born of French parents, did not call for "assimilation" as much as it does now, with its larger contingent of non-European immigrants, or did during the plurilingual eighteenth century. Elisabeth Badinter, quoted above, came out very strongly during the "*affaire du foulard*" in favor of the right of the "*école laïque*" to forbid the wearing of the Islamic headscarf by young girls in a school in Creil; Mitterrand's wife Danielle was one of the stronger voices in favor of the right of the girls to defy the ban (see Gaspard and Khosrokhavar, esp. 163–70 and 192–200).

6. The lack of progress in the debate between French and Latin was due in part to the intractability in both camps. Very few tried to break out of the stalemate. One example is an article by Marcelin Berthelot, a scientist and former Minister of Public Instruction in the *Revue des Deux Mondes* in 1891. He believed firmly that the goals of the utilitarians, whom he saw as the inheritors of eighteenth-century *encyclopédistes*, could be reconciled with those of the ministry of education, and that exams such as the *baccalauréat* should be eliminated since they distort the experience of the student (347). While his anti-exam stance was so far ahead of its time that it has yet to be taken

seriously, his vision of a "literary" track with mandatory French and Latin, and a "scientific" track with mandatory French only, is quite close to what had already been proposed and was to be made into law, albeit temporarily, in 1902 (374).

7. The creation of a *baccalauréat moderne* with the same status as the classical one in 1902 of course had a major reviving effect on the French–Latin debate as well. What is interesting about the 1910 controversy is that it was not motivated by a particular reform, but rather by a sense of frustration at the tendency of the "*nouvelle Sorbonne*," under the leadership of Lanson, to relegate Latin to the status of narrow academic discipline.

8. Antoine Compagnon situates the *crise du français* in the context of political struggles in French higher education and in the history of academic trends in literary criticism in the first part of *La Troisième République des lettres: de Flaubert à Proust* (1983).

9. The traditional French transcription of the Persian poet's name is Djalal al-din al-Rumi (or Roumi).

10. "*La section B*" refers to the creation of tracks within the *lycée* system in which the mandatory exam in Greek and/or Latin as part of the *baccalauréat* had been eliminated. The 1902 reforms had permanently established such tracks, which never lost their reputation for being the refuge of the least capable scions of the bourgeoisie. Today there is a specific *programme* for Greek and Latin, which very few students elect; the most prestigious track is math and physics, while modern languages, even though they include a strong emphasis on French literature, still suffer from being among the least prestigious, if one does not include the even less exalted pre-professional tracks (computer programming, accounting, etc.), which have gradually been added since the 1970s.

Conclusion

1. Pierre Albertini suggests that 1880 marks the beginning of a chapter in French education that lasts all the way until 1968, after which time the secondary school, and the *baccalauréat* itself, finally ceased to be elitist institutions (3). It is certainly true that there is a surprising continuity in programs, methods, and even content in education, especially literary education, throughout that period.

2. Bergez aimed his text primarily at the student of literature at the university level, and it is therefore more sophisticated than most other works that attempt to present a coherent theory and practice of the *explication de texte*, the exercise on which every exam and *concours* from the *baccalauréat* to the *agrégation* is based. Bergez is one of the very few to have placed the *explication* in the context of the history of textual interpretation, and to have enlisted twentieth-century literary theory (by Barthes, Todorov, Genette, and others) in support of his enterprise.

3. Hachette and other large publishing houses that specialized in classroom materials were not, of course, beholden to the republican regime. Private schools purchased textbooks from them as well, and had been doing so for

many years before the institution of the Ferry laws. One must, however, take account of the fact that the new laws resulted not only in an increase in the growth rate of the school population, but also required the creation of brand new textbooks to fill the mandate to teach "civic and moral instruction," to answer the increased demand for French literature anthologies, and so on. Private schools that insisted on continuing to require religious study in addition to the official curriculum depended increasingly on smaller, specialized publishers for whom the new laws were not such a windfall: for more on Catholic and secular school publishing, see Yves Déloye's *Ecole et citoyenneté* (School and Citizenship; chapters 5 and 6). A further sign of the unholy alliance of the Republic and the publishing industry is that many of the scientific and/or polemical works on education in the late nineteenth century were published by the same houses that relied on textbooks for a large, if not the largest, part of their revenue.

4. The cultural marketplace has of course become even more complicated since the nineteenth century. Now one must contend not only with the phenomenon that "high" art has come to mean art without a large enough public to constitute a viable market for the dissemination of cultural artifacts, and is therefore directly related to the nineteenth-century avant-garde that declared its autonomy in part by declaring its freedom from the market of cultural goods, but also with the fact that previously mainstream culture (plays by Racine, classical music) now struggles to find a market, whereas commercially successful popular culture such as the rap music of MC Solar is every bit as likely as serious avant-garde experimentation to claim a marginal, contestatory role in society.

5. The term "foreign" here is both literal (from outside of France and/or the French language) as well as figurative: the sense that an individual or a cultural community experiences art as something strange, until such time as it has been adequately "domesticated" by the process of individual appreciation or cultural canonization. This dual meaning of "foreign" raises many questions, foremost among them whether it is possible to experience art simultaneously as art (strange) and as cultural expression (familiar), and whether true appreciation of the foreign is possible without "going native," and losing one's inherited cultural identity in the process.

6. One would be correct to assume that asking a poet with a very specific esthetic agenda such as Mendès to make a list of significant poets since 1867 would result in a fairly skewed perspective. The poets featured most prominently in his report are, in alphabetical order: Banville, Baudelaire, Coppée, Desbordes-Valmore, Dierx, Dumas *son*, Gautier, Hérédia, Hugo, Kahn, Lamartine, Leconte de Lisle, Maeterlinck, Mallarmé, Mendès, Merrill, Mistral, Musset, Régnier, Retté, Richepin, Rimbaud, Rostand, Saint-Pol-Roux, Sully-Prudhomme, Verhaeren, Verlaine, Vielé-Griffin, and Vigny. This is really a partial list of the Parnasse poets and the Symbolists, with a few extra thrown in, along with the obligatory Hugo. I do not know what the French Romantics are doing in a list that is supposed to cover the period 1867–1900, but assume that Mendès must have considered them such important influences that they deserved mention. True, he does state that the

"dictionary" part of his report is meant to include the most important poets of the nineteenth century, meaning presumably the entire nineteenth century, but if that is the case, then the omission of any but the very biggest names from the first half of the century is all the more glaring.

7. Issues of education are of course nothing new in the still-nascent field of Francophone literary studies. A recent article suggests a potentially productive direction: the different negative reactions to French national education, depending on whether the recipients are of French heritage or not: Michel Pichot, "Educational Policies of the French Third Republic (1870–1939) in the Village of Guiard, Algeria: Hostility of the French Settlers and Cultural Resistance of Indigenous Muslims" (*Michigan Academician* 1999). Though Pichot does not discuss literature, his article suggests a distinction between French and non-French colonial subjects based on their different experience of the oppressive institution of the school.

8. As is to be expected, many works of Francophone literature that allude to the experience of French colonial education portray it as an instrument of oppression. To say that and nothing more, however, is to remain at a very superficial level. Of the works mentioned above, Zobel's probably shows the French school in the most positive light and Yacine's in the most negative; in both, one can detect the ambivalence of the colonial subject toward dominant institutions. If it were possible to generalize on the role of the school in Francophone literature of the late-colonial era, one could say that these texts often display a high degree of awareness of the dual nature of the French educational promise: it is both a sign of the traumatic separation from the moorings of ancestral culture, and an opportunity to take possession of the French language by an act of *détournement* and use it as a tool of cultural and even political freedom, as does Aimé Césaire in his long poem *Cahier d'un retour au pays natal* (Notebook of a Return to the Native Land; 1939).

9. The turn of the century image of the cathedral as the site of the victory of esthetic norms of value over religious ones was already clearly apparent in the work of Joris-Karl Huysmans. In his journey from a Symbolist belief in mystical estheticism in *A rebours* (Against Nature; 1884) and other works, to a return to the subordination of the esthetic to the religious in *La Cathédrale* (1898), he also illustrates the anxiety, followed by a defensive reaction, that occurs when the first term of the metaphor ("art") begins to overshadow the second one ("religion").

BIBLIOGRAPHY

Primary Sources

Pedagogical Works

Allais, Gustave. *Esquisse d'une méthode générale de préparation et d'explication des auteurs français*. Paris: Delalain, 1884.

Augé, Claude. *Deuxième livre de grammaire, livre de l'élève*. Paris: Larousse, 1891.

———. *Deuxième livre de grammaire, livre du maître*. Paris: Larousse, 1891.

———. *Grammaire enfantine, livre de l'élève*. Paris: Larousse, 1891.

———. *Grammaire enfantine, livre du maître*. Paris: Larousse, 1891.

———. *Premier livre de grammaire, livre du maître*. Paris: Larousse, 1890.

———. *Troisième livre de grammaire, livre de l'élève*. Paris: Larousse, 1892.

———. *Troisième livre de grammaire, livre du maître*. Paris: Larousse, 1892.

Bergez, Daniel. *L'explication de texte littéraire*. Paris: Dunod (Bordas), 1989.

Bigot, Charles. *Le petit français*. Paris: Weill et Maurice, 1883.

Bonnefon, Daniel. *Les écrivains célèbres de la France ou histoire de la littérature française à l'usage des Etablissements d'instruction publique, 9e édition*. N.p.: Librairie Fischbacher, n.d. (1st ed. 1872).

Bruno, G. [Augustine Fouillée, *née* Tuillerie]. *Les Enfants de Marcel: Instruction morale et civique en action*. Paris: Belin, 1887.

———. *Francinet: Livre de lecture courante*. Paris: Belin, 1876.

———. *Le Tour de la France par deux enfants*. Paris: Belin, 1877.

———. *Le Tour de la France par deux enfants*. Paris: Belin, 1930.

Calonne, E. de. *Recueil de compositions françaises en vue du baccalauréat ès lettres*. Paris: P. Dupont, 1884.

Croisset, Alfred, R. Lallier, and Petit de Julleville. *Premières leçons d'histoire littéraire*. Paris: G. Masson, 1889.

Doumic, René. *Histoire de la littérature française, nouvelle édition*. Paris: Paul Mellottée, n.d.

Doumic, René and Léon Levrault. *Etudes littéraires sur les auteurs français prescrits pour l'examen du brevet supérieur*. Paris: Paul Delaplane, 1900.

Franchet, Antonin. *Le Bon Dieu laïque*. Paris: Editions de la Petite République, 1903.

Guyau, M. *La Première année de lecture courante: morale, connaissances usuelles, devoirs civiques*. Paris: Armand Colin, 1899.

Hémon, Félix. *Cours de littérature à l'usage des divers examens*. Paris: Charles Delagrave, 1889.

Lanson, Gustave. *Histoire de la littérature française (1894), remaniée et complétée pour la période 1850–1950 par Paul Tuffrau.* Paris: Hachette, 1967.

Legouvé, Ernest. *L'art de la lecture: nouvelle édition revue et corrigée (d'après l'édition de 1877).* Paris: J. Hetzel et Cie, 1886.

———. *La lecture en action.* Paris: J. Hetzel et Cie, 1881.

———. *La lecture en famille.* Paris: J. Hetzel et Cie, 1882.

Liard, Louis. *Lectures morales et littéraires.* Paris: Belin, 1882.

Marguerin, Emile and L.C. Michel. *Recueil de morceaux choisis en prose et en vers.* Paris: Charles Delagrave, 1882 (1st ed. 1859–60).

Merlet, Gustave. *Etudes littéraires sur les classiques français des classes supérieures.* Paris: Hachette, 1883.

Nisard, Désiré. *Histoire de la littérature française.* 1844. Paris: Firmin-Didot, 1883.

Philibert-Soupé, A. *Analyses des ouvrages français indiqués aux programmes du baccalauréat ès lettres (première partie) des baccalauréats ès sciences complet et restreint, de l'enseignement secondaire spécial, de l'enseignement secondaire des jeunes filles et de l'enseignement primaire supérieur.* Paris: Foucart, 1888.

Rinn, Wilhelm. *Littérature, composition et style.* Paris: Delalain, 1880.

Roehrich, Edouard. *La Chanson de Roland. Traduction nouvelle à l'usage des écoles précédée d'une introduction sur l'importance de la chanson de Roland pour l'éducation de la jeunesse.* Paris: Fischbacher, 1885.

Sellier, Philippe. *La Dissertation française—Le commentaire composé.* Paris: Larousse, 1968.

Sorieul, A. *Mémoire sur la manière d'expliquer les auteurs français dans les classes de grammaire.* Alençon: De Broise, 1873.

Contemporaneous Articles, Books, and Pamphlets on
Education and Related Issues

Agathon [Henri Massis and Alfred Tarde]. *L'Esprit de la nouvelle Sorbonne.* Paris: Mercure de France, 1911.

Alain [Emile Auguste Chartier]. *Propos sur l'éducation.* 1932. Paris: PUF, 1976.

Bader, Clarisse. *Une Question vitale: l'élément religieux est-il indispensable à l'enseignement scolaire dans un état libre?* Paris: Didier et Cie, 1871.

Batault, Georges. "Le problème de la culture et la crise du français." *Mercure de France* 92 (July 1911): 52–81.

Bénard, Léon. *L'Art de lire et d'écouter ou l'éducation littéraire.* 2 vols. Paris: Alphonse Picard, 1878.

Benda, Julien. *La Trahison des clercs.* Paris: Bernard Grasset, 1927.

Bergson, Henri. "Les études gréco-latines et l'enseignement secondaire." *La Revue de Paris* 10 (May 1923): 5–18.

Berthelot, M. "La Crise de l'enseignement secondaire." *Revue des Deux Mondes* 104 (1891, deuxième période): 337–74.

Bezard, J. *La Réforme du latin par les mères.* Paris: Vuibert, 1926.

———. *La Sélection par le latin et la réforme de l'enseignement secondaire.* Paris: Vuibert, 1923.

Blanchard, M. *L'Enseignement littéraire*. Beauvais: E. Laffineur, 1876.

Blum, Léon. "La bataille pour les humanités." *La Revue de Paris* 10 (May 1923): 355–85.

Bourrié, Léon. *De la lecture considérée comme exercice de classe*. Montpellier: Firmin et Cabirou, 1875.

Bréal, Michel. *Quelques mots sur l'instruction publique en France*. Paris: Hachette, 1872.

Broglie, Albert de. *Mémoire sur l'Instruction Publique*. Paris: Fournier, 1842.

Brunetière, Ferdinand. *La Liberté de l'enseignement*. Paris: Perrin et Cie, 1900.

———. "Sur l'origine de l'enseignement secondaire français." *Revue des Deux Mondes* 105 (1891, troisième période): 214–25.

Buisson, Ferdinand, ed. *Dictionnaire de pédagogie et d'instruction primaire, deux parties en cinq volumes et deux suppléments*. Paris: Hachette, 1882–87.

Caron, Ernest. *L'Instruction laïque: lettre à un homme du peuple*. Paris: Victor Sarlit, 1872.

Carré, M.I. "Le Certificat d'Etudes primaires élémentaires." *Recueil des Monographies pédagogiques publiées à l'occasion de l'exposition universelle de 1889* (tome 3). Paris: Imprimerie Nationale, 1889. 443–503.

Compayré, Gabriel. *Etudes sur l'enseignement et sur l'éducation*. Paris: Hachette, 1891.

———. *Histoire critique des doctrines de l'éducation depuis le seizième siècle*. Paris: Hachette, 1879.

———. "Jésuites." *Dictionnaire de pédagogie et d'instruction primaire*, Ed. Ferdinand Buisson. Part I. Paris: Hachette, 1882–87. 1418–424.

Condorcet, Marie-Jean Antoine de Caritat, marquis de. *Ecrits sur l'Instruction Publique*. Ed. Gabriel Compayré. Facsimile of 1883 edition. Vol. I: *Cinq mémoires sur l'Instruction Publique*, ed. Charles Coutel and Catherine Kintzler; Vol. II: *Rapport sur l'Instruction Publique*, ed. Charles Coutel. Paris: Edilig, 1989.

Deltour, F. *Lettre à M. Cuvillier-Fleury de l'Académie française*. Paris: E. Dentu, 1872.

Deville, A. *Un An d'application de la loi du 28 mars 1882*. Paris: Gervais, 1883.

Duboys, Melchior. *Exposé de l'Instruction Publique en France: son histoire, son état actuel*. Pithiviers: Forteau, 1885.

Dumesnil, Georges. "Goût." *Dictionnaire de pédagogie et d'instruction primaire*. Ed. Ferdinand Buisson. Paris: Hachette, 1882–87. 1420–422.

Duplan, E. *L'Enseignement primaire public à Paris*. Paris: Chaix, 1891.

Durkheim, Emile. *L'Evolution pédagogique en France*. Paris: Félix Alcan, 1938.

Duruy, Albert. *L'Instruction Publique et la démocratie*. Paris: Hachette, 1886.

———. *L'Instruction publique et la Révolution*. Paris: Hachette, 1882.

Enne, François. *Le Panthéon Républicain*. Paris: Fayard, 1874.

Escoffier, Emile. *Le Régénération de la France par l'instruction et l'éducation républicaines*. Douai: L. Crepin, 1873.

Faguet, Emile. "La Crise du français et l'enseignement littéraire à la Sorbonne." *Revue des Deux Mondes* (1910, cinquième période): 289–301.

Fouillée, Alfred. *L'Enseignement au point de vue national*. Paris: Hachette, 1909.

Frary, Raoul. *La Question du latin*. Paris: Léopold Cerf, 1885.

Gautier, Paul. "La Bourgeoisie et la réforme de l'enseignement secondaire." *Revue d'enseignement Secondaire et d'Enseignement Supérieur* 15 (1891): 367–72.

Gautier, Théophile. "Rapport sur les progrès de la poésie." *Recueil de rapports sur les progrès des sciences et des lettres en France: Rapport sur le progrès des lettres.* Paris: Hachette/Imprimerie Impériale, 1868. 67–141.

Gerold, Theéodore. "Protestantisme." *Dictionnaire de pédagogie et d'instruction primaire.* Ed. Ferdinand Buisson. Part I. Paris: Hachette, 1882–87. 2461–470.

Godefroy, Fr. *La Gloire de la France: de la part qui doit être faite à l'étude de la littérature française dans l'éducation classique. Discours à l'Ecole de Sorèze, Pâques 1873.* Paris: Adrien Le Clère, 1873.

Gréard, Olivier. *La Question des programmes dans l'enseignement secondaire.* Paris: n.p., 1884.

Guérin. *La Question du latin et la réforme professionnelle de l'enseignement secondaire.* Paris: Cerf, 1890.

Heinrich, G.-A. *Le Procès du latin; observations sur le livre de M. Raoul Frary.* Paris: E. Leroux, 1886.

Hémon, Félix. "Les Auteurs français de l'enseignement primaire." *Recueil des Monographies pédagogiques publiées à l'occasion de l'exposition universelle de 1889* (tome 3). Paris: Imprimerie Nationale, 1889. 379–441.

Hignard, H. *La Question du latin.* Lyon: Vitte et Perrussel, 1886.

Hureaux, Jean-Pierre. *Le Livre de vie, oeuvre universelle de lumière et de justice. La chute du monde d'iniquités dans l'abîme, le salut et la gloire de la France républicaine, des républiques et de l'humanité libre par l'avènement du christianisme scientifique.* Paris: l'auteur, 1888.

———. *L'Oeuvre de la résolution des temps. Le Code moral de la République ou de l'esprit chrétien passé majeur.* Paris: Imprimerie de Duval, 1879.

———. *Les Principes de l'éducation républicaine pour l'enseignement dans les écoles.* Paris: l'auteur, 1878.

Jail, O. *De la décadence des études latines en France.* Discours à la distribution des prix de l'Institut Robin (Vienne) le 27.7.1885. Vienne: Savigné, 1885.

Julliard, Jacques. "Les Etats désunis d'Amérique." *Le Nouvel observateur* 1383 (May 9–15, 1991): 23.

Kahn, Gustave. "La littérature et les manuels d'histoire littéraire." *La Revue Blanche* 24 (1901): 583–91.

Lanson, Gustave. *Essais de méthode, de critique et d'histoire littéraire.* Ed. Henri Peyre. Paris: Hachette, 1965.

Lavoisier, A.S. *Réflexions sur l'instruction publique par le Bureau de Consultation des Arts et Métiers.* [Paris]: n.p. [ca. 1793].

Lepeletier, Michel [Lepeletier de Saint-Fargeau, Louis-Michel]. *Plan d'éducation nationale. Présenté à la Convention à titre posthume par M. Robespierre.* Paris: Convention Nationale, 1793.

Leroy, E. *De l'utilité du latin dans l'enseignement classique. Discours à la distribution des prix au gymnase catholique du Haut-Rhin le 2.8.1887.* Montbéliard: Hoffmann, 1887.

Marguerin, Emile. "Littérature." *Dictionnaire de pédagogie et d'instruction primaire.* Ed. Ferdinand Buisson. Part I. Paris: Hachette, 1882–87. 1594–604.

Marin, Louis. *La nécessité en France d'un enseignement secondaire fondé sur la langue maternelle et la culture nationale à l'exclusion des langues mortes.* Extrait du *Journal Officiel.* Paris: Imprimerie Nationale, 1922.

Marion, Henri. "Le Mouvement des idées pédagogiques en France." *Recueil des monographies pédagogiques publiées à l'occasion de l'exposition universelle de 1889* (tome 1). Paris: Imprimerie Nationale, 1889. 1–83.

Masuyer, Claude-Laurent-Louis. *Discours sur l'organisation de l'instruction publique et de l'éducation nationale en France et réfutation du système proposé successivement par les citoyens Condorcet et Romme.* Paris: Convention Nationale, 1793.

Mendès, Catulle. *Le Mouvement poétique français de 1867 à 1900: Rapport à M. le Ministre de l'Instruction publique.* Paris: Imprimerie Nationale, 1903.

Paris, Gaston. "La Littérature française du Moyen Age et la littérature française moderne." *Revue Universitaire* 5:1 (1896): 221–38.

Pécaut, Félix. "Poésie." *Dictionnaire de pédagogie et d'instruction primaire.* Ed. Ferdinand Buisson. Part I. Paris: Hachette, 1882–887. 2387–392.

Petit, Ed. *Autour de l'Ecole, avec une préface de Jules Simon.* Paris: M. Dreyfous, 1890.

Petit, Michel Edme. *Des changements que l'amour de la vérité produira dans la poésie et dans l'éloquence.* Paris: Imprimerie de la rue des Droits de l'homme, 1792.

———. *Opinion contre le projet des écoles primaires.* [Paris]: n.p. [ca. 1793].

Pigeonneau, H. *Réponse à la question du latin.* Paris: Léopold Cerf, 1885.

Réal, Ferdinand. *La Réforme de l'enseignement secondaire. Lettre au ministre de l'Instruction publique avec lettre-préface de Jules Simon.* Paris: Michaud, 1890.

Renan, Ernest. *Qu'est-ce qu'une nation?* 1882. Paris: Bordas, 1991.

———. *La Réforme intellectuelle et morale.* Paris: Michel Lévy Frères, 1871.

———. *La Vie de Jésus.* Paris: Calmann-Lévy, 1863.

Réville, Albert. "Bible." *Dictionnaire de pédagogie et d'instruction primaire.* Ed. Ferdinand Buisson. Part I. Paris: Hachette, 1882–887. 185–93.

Robert, Charles Frédéric. *Le Salut par l'éducation et le discours de Fichte à la nation allemande en 1807.* Paris: Hachette, 1872.

Simon, Jules. "Discours." *Le Centenaire de Lamartine à Macon.* Paris: Institut de France, 1890. 11–14.

———. *L'Ecole.* Paris: Hachette, 1865.

———. *Opinions et discours.* Paris: Henri Gautier, 1888.

Vessiot, A. *La Question du latin de M. Frary et les professions libérales.* Paris: Lecène et Oudin, 1886.

Wogue, J. "L'Enseignement de l'histoire littéraire dans les lycées et collèges." *Revue de l'enseignement secondaire et de l'enseignement supérieur* 13 (1890): 400–09.

Zevort, Edgar (recteur de l'Académie de Caen). *L'Enseignement secondaire de 1880 à 1890.* Paris: P. Dupont, 1890.

Literary Works

Barrès, Maurice. *Les Déracinés.* Paris: Nelson, 1897.

Camus, Albert. *L'Etranger. Théâtre, récits, nouvelles.* Paris: Gallimard, 1962.

Goscinny, René, and Albert Uderzo. *Astérix le Gaulois*. Paris: Dargaud, 1961.

Laurie, A. [Paschal Grousset]. *Une Année de collège à Paris*. Paris: J. Hetzel, 1883.

Maupassant, Guy de. "La Question du Latin." *Contes et Nouvelles*. 1886. Paris: Albin Michel, 1959–60.

Péguy, Charles. *L'Argent. Oeuvres en prose*, vol. 2. Paris: Gallimard, 1961.

Proust, Marcel. *A la recherche du temps perdu*, vol. 1. Paris: Gallimard, 1954.

Vallès, Jules. *L'Ecolier; Le Bachelier; L'Insurgé*. 1879–86. *Oeuvres*. Paris: Gallimard, 1975.

Zola, Emile. *Vérité*. Paris: Fasquelle, 1903.

Secondary Sources

Albanese, Ralph Jr. "Le Discours scolaire au dix-neuvième siècle: Le cas de La Fontaine." *French Review* 72:5 (April 1999): 824–38.

———. *Molière à l'école républicaine: de la critique universitaire aux manuels scolaires (1870–1914)*. Stanford: French and Italian Studies 72, Anma Libri, 1992.

Albertini, Pierre. *L'Ecole en France: XIXe–XXe siècle*. Paris: Hachette, 1992.

Anderson, Benedict. *Imagined Communities: Reflections on the Origin and Spread of Nationalism*. London: Verso, 1983.

Antoine, Gérald and Robert Martin. *Histoire de la langue française, 1880–1914*. Paris: CNRS, 1985.

Ariès, Philippe. "Problèmes de l'éducation." *Encyclopédie de la Pléiade: La France et les Français*. Ed. Michel François. Paris: Gallimard, 1972. 871–966.

Badinter, Elisabeth. "Introduction." *La République et l'école: une anthologie*. Ed. Charles Coutel. Paris: Presses Pocket, 1991.

Bakhtin, Mikhail. *Rabelais and His World*. Trans. Hélène Iswolsky. Bloomington, IN: Indiana University Press, 1984.

Balibar, Renée, Geneviève Merlin, and Gilles Tret. *Les Français fictifs: Le rapport des styles littéraires au français national*. Paris: Hachette, 1974.

Balibar, Renée and Dominique Laporte. *Le Français national: politique et pratique de la langue nationale sous la révolution*. Paris: Hachette, 1974.

Balibar, Renée. "L'Ecole de 1880. Le Français national: républicain, scolaire, grammatical, primaire." *Histoire de la langue française, 1880–1914*. Ed. Gérald Antoine and Robert Martin. Paris: CNRS, 1985. 255–93.

———. *Histoire de la littérature française*. Paris: Presses Universitaires de France, 1991.

———. *L'Institution du français: Essai sur le colinguisme des Carolingiens à la République*. Paris: PUF, 1985.

———. "O mère ensevelie hors du premier jardin: La poésie des écoliers républicains." *Revue des Lettres Modernes* 959–64 (1990): 125–51.

———. "Le Passé composé fictif dans *L'Etranger* d'Albert Camus." *Littérature* 7 (1972): 102–09.

———. "La Révolution Française et l'Universalisation du Français National en France." *History of European Ideas* 13:1/2 (1991): 89–95.

———. "Les Textes français." *Revue des sciences humaines* 174 (1979): 9–20.

Barthes, Roland. *Le Grain de la voix: entretiens 1962–1980.* Paris: Seuil, 1981.

———. "Réflexions sur un manuel." *L'Enseignement de la littérature: Colloque de Cérisy.* July 22–29, 1969. Ed. Serge Doubrovsky and Tzvetan Todorov. Paris: Plon, 1971.

Béhard, Henri. *Les Cultures de Jarry.* Paris: PUF, 1988.

Bellet, Roger. "L'Image de l'école chez Jules Vallès." *Revue des Sciences Humaines (Lille III)* 174 (1979): 37–59.

Bénichou, Paul. "De la Révolution française à l'éducation sous la Troisième République." *Annales Historiques de la Révolution française* 287 (January–March 1992): 105–29.

———. *The Consecration of the Writer, 1750–1830.* Trans. Mark K. Jensen. Lincoln and London: University of Nebraska Press, 1999.

Bernard, Claude. *L'Enseignement de l'histoire en France au dix-neuvième siècle.* Thèse, Paris VIII. Paris: Librairie Honoré Champion, 1978.

Bertens, Hans. *Literary Theory: The Basics.* London and New York: Routledge, 2001.

Birnbaum, Pierre. *The Jews of the Republic: A Political History of State Jews from Gambetta to Vichy.* Trans. Jane Marie Todd. Stanford: Stanford University Press, 1996.

Bloch, R. Howard. "Naturalisme, nationalisme, médiévisme." *L'Identité française: Colloque à l'Université de Copenhague, nov. 1987.* Ed. Hans Boll Johansen. Copenhagen: Akademisk Forlag, 1989. 62–87.

Bonnet, Jean-Claude. "Naissance du Panthéon." *Poétique* 33 (1978): 46–65.

Boulerie, Florence. "La Littérature pour apprendre le réel? Ambiguïtés du statut de la littérature chez deux pédagogues des Lumières, Rousseau et La Chalotais." *Littératures classiques 37* (Fall 1999): 201–11.

Bourdieu, Pierre and Jean Passeron. *Reproduction in Education, Society and Culture.* Trans. Richard Nice. London: Sage, 1990.

Bourdieu, Pierre. "Champ du pouvoir, champ intellectuel et habitus de classe." *Scolies* 1 (1971): 7–26.

———. *Distinction: A Social Critique of the Judgment of Taste.* Trans. Richard Nice. Cambridge, MA: Harvard University Press, 1984.

———. "L'Ecole conservatrice: les inégalités devant l'école et devant la culture." *Revue Française de Sociologie* VII (1966): 325–47.

———. *The Field of Cultural Production: Essays on Art and Literature.* Ed. Randal Johnson, various trans. New York: Columbia University Press, 1993.

———. "On the Fundamental Ambivalence of the State." *Polygraph 10: Legislating Culture* (1998): 21–32.

———. *The Rules of Art: Genesis and Structure of the Literary Field.* Trans. Susan Emanuel. Stanford: Stanford University Press, 1996.

Boussinesq, Jean. *La Laïcité française.* Paris: Seuil, 1994.

Braudel, Fernand. *The Identity of France.* Vols. I and II. Trans. Siân Reynolds. London: William Collins, 1990.

Breuilly, John. *Nationalism and the State.* New York: Saint Martin's Press, 1982.

Brunet, Etienne. "Le Latin dans la littérature française." *Actes du colloque: La réception du latin.* Angers: Presses Universitaires, 1996. 125–41.

Bush, John W. "Education and Social Status: the Jesuit *Collège* in the Early Third Republic." *French Historical Studies* 9:1 (Spring 1975): 125–40.

Byrnes, Joseph F. "Reconciliation of Cultures in the Third Republic: Emile Mâle (1862–1954)." *Catholic Historical Review* 83:3 (July 1997): 401–27.

Cabanel, Patrick. "Occasion manquée, occasion saisie: les protestants dans l'Ecole républicaine, 1792–1879." *Revue du Nord* 78:318 (October–December 1996): 941–52.

Capéran, Louis. *Histoire contemporaine de la laïcité française*. 3 vols. Paris: Marcel Rivière, 1957–61.

Caput, Jean-Pol. *La Langue française: histoire d'une institution*. Paris: Larousse, 1972.

Carpentier, Claude. "L'Ecole de la Troisième République fait sa généalogie: l'exemple de la *Revue Pédagogique*." *Revue du Nord* 78:317 (October–December 1996): 953–965.

Chaitin, Gilbert D. "From the Third Republic to Postmodernism: Language, Freedom and the Politics of the Contingent." *Modern Language Notes* 114:4 (September 1999): 780–815.

Chanet, Jean-François. "L'Ecole républicaine et la postérité de la Révolution: commémoration, pédagogie, recherches 1879–1914." *Revue du Nord* 78:317 (October–December 1996): 987–1010.

Charle, Christophe. *Elites de la République, 1880–1900*. Paris: Fayard, 1987.

———. *Naissance des "intellectuels" 1880–1900*. Paris: Minuit, 1990.

Chase, George. "Ferdinand Buisson and Salvation by National Education." *L'Offre d'école: Eléments pour une étude comparée des politiques éducatives au dix-neuvième siècle*. Ed. Willem Frijhoff. Paris: Institut National de Recherche Pédagogique, la Sorbonne, 1983. 263–75.

Chervel, André. *Les Auteurs français, latins et grecs au programme de l'enseignement secondaire de 1800 à nos jours*. Paris: La Sorbonne, 1986.

———. "Sur l'origine de l'enseignement du français dans le secondaire." *Histoire de l'éducation* 25 (1985): 3–10.

Chervel, André and Marie-Madeleine Compère. "Les Humanités dans l'histoire de l'enseignement français." *Histoire de l'Education* 74 (1997): 5–38.

Chessex-Viguet, Christiane. *L'Ecole est un roman: Essai sur la relation pédagogique dans la literature européenne*. Lausanne: Editions d'En-bas, 1990.

Chevalier, Jean-Claude. "La pédagogie des collèges Jésuites." *Littérature* 7 (October 1972): 120–30.

Chisick, Harvey. *The Limits of Reform in the Enlightenment: Attitudes Toward the Education of the Lower Classes in Eighteenth-Century France*. Princeton: Princeton University Press, 1981.

Chiss, Jean-Louis. " 'Les Français fictifs,' ou l'analyse d'un lapsus." *Littérature* 19 (October 1975): 118–26.

Choppin, Alain. "L'Histoire des manuels scolaires: une approche globale." *Histoire de l'éducation* 9 (1980): 1–25.

———, ed. *Les Manuels scolaires en France de 1789 à nos jours*. 3 vols. Paris: Sorbonne, 1987.

Cibois, Philippe. "La Question du latin: des critiques du XVIIIe siècle au *revival* du XIXe." *L'Information Littéraire* 52:1 (January–March 2000): 7–28.

Citron, Suzanne. "Enseignement secondaire et idéologie élitiste entre 1880 et 1914." *Mouvement Social* (July–September 1976): 81–101.

Citti, Pierre and M. Détrie. *Le Champ littéraire*. Paris: J. Vrin, 1992.

Clarac, Pierre. *L'enseignement du français*. Paris: PUF, 1963.

Clark, Linda L. "Approaching the History of Modern French Education: Recent Surveys and Research Guides." *French Historical Studies* 15:1 (Spring 1987): 157–65.

Compagnon, Antoine. "Literature in the Classroom." *A New History of French Literature*. Ed. Denis Hollier. Cambridge, MA: Harvard University Press, 1989.

————. *La Troisième République des lettres: de Flaubert à Proust*. Paris: Seuil, 1983.

Coutel, Charles. "La Troisième République lit Condorcet." *Revue du Nord* 78:317 (October–December 1996): 967–74.

Crubellier, Maurice. *L'Ecole républicaine, 1870–1940*. Paris: Christian, 1993.

————. "Généalogie d'une morale: La morale de l'école républicaine." *L'Offre d'école: Eléments pour une étude comparée des politiques éducatives au dix-neuvième siècle*. Ed. Willem Frijhoff. Paris: Institut National de Recherche Pédagogique, Sorbonne, 1983. 253–61.

Cuddon, J.A. *The Penguin Dictionary of Literary Terms and Literary Theory*. 3rd ed. London: Penguin Books, 1991.

Dauzat, Albert. *Le Génie de la langue française*. Paris: Payot, 1949.

Déloye, Yves. *Ecole et citoyenneté: l'individualisme républicain de Jules Ferry à Vichy: controverses*. Paris: Fondation Nationale des Sciences Politiques, 1994.

Demnard, Dimitri. *Dictionnaire de l'histoire de l'enseignement*. Paris: J.-P. Delage, 1981.

Désirat, Claude and Tristan Hordé. "Les écoles normales: une liquidation de la rhétorique? Littérature et grammaire dans les programmes de l'Ecole normale de l'an III." *Littérature* 18 (May 1975): 31–50.

Digeon, Claude. *La Crise allemande de la pensée française (1870–1914)*. Paris: PUF, 1959.

Doubrovsky, Serge and Tzvetan Todorov, eds. *L'Enseignement de la littérature, entretiens du Centre Culturel de Cérisy, 22 au 29 juillet 1969*. Paris: Plon, 1971.

Dubois, Jacques. *L'Institution de la littérature*. Brussels: F. Nathan-Editions Labor, 1978.

Dupuy, Aimé. "Histoire sociale et manuels scolaires: les livres de lecture de G. Bruno." *Revue d'Histoire économique et sociale*. XXXI:2 (1953): 128–51.

Duveau, Georges. *Les Instituteurs*. Paris: Seuil, 1957.

Ecole Normale Supérieure de Saint Cloud. *La Pédagogie du français au XIXe siècle*. Limoges: Centre de Recherche et de formation en éducation, Documents pédagogiques, 1973.

Encrevé, André and Michel Richard. *Les Protestants dans les débuts de la Troisième République (1871–1885)*. Paris: Société d'Histoire du protestantisme français, 1979.

Fabiani, Jean-Louis. *Les Philosophes de la république*. Paris: Minuit, 1988.

Fayolle, Roger. "Les Français fictifs (review)." *Le Français Aujourd'hui* 31 (September 1975): 57–62.

Fayolle, Roger. "Naissance d'une discipline: l'enseignement de la littérature française." *Le Français Aujourd'hui* supplément au no. 45 (March 1979): 4–5 and 8–9.

———. "La poésie dans l'enseignement de la littérature: le cas Baudelaire." *Littérature* 7 (October 1972): 48–72.

Fraisse, Emmanuel. *Les Anthologies en France*. Paris: Presses Universitaires de France, 1999.

———. "L'Invention d'une littérature scolaire: les manuels de morceaux choisis de 1872 à 1923." *Etudes de linguistique appliquée* 57 (1985): 102–09.

Fumaroli, Marc. *L'Etat culturel: Essai sur une religion moderne*. Paris: Fallois, 1991.

Furet, François. "Jules Ferry et l'histoire de la Révolution française: la polémique autour du livre d'Edgar Quinet, 1865–1866." *Jules Ferry fondateur de la République: Actes du Colloque de 1982*. Ed. François Furet. Paris: Ecole des Hautes Etudes en Sciences Sociales, 1985. 15–22.

Furet, François and Jacques Ozouf. *Reading and Writing: Literacy in France from Calvin to Jules Ferry*. Cambridge: Cambridge University Press, 1982.

Gaillard, Jean-Michel. *Jules Ferry*. Paris: Fayard, 1989.

Gaspard, Françoise and Farhad Khosrokhavar. *Le foulard et la République*. Paris: La Découverte, 1995.

Genette, Gérard. *Figures II*. Paris: Seuil, 1969.

Gerbod, Paul. *La Vie quotidienne dans les lycées et collèges au 19ième siècle*. Paris: Hachette, 1968.

Giolitto, P. *Histoire de l'enseignement primaire au XIXe siècle, tome I: L'organisation pédagogique*. Paris: Nathan, 1983–84.

Girard, René. *Things Hidden since the Foundation of the World*. Trans. Stephen Bann and Michael Metteer. Stanford: Stanford University Press, 1987.

———. *Violence and the Sacred*. Trans. Patrick Gregory. Baltimore and London: The Johns Hopkins University Press, 1977.

Girardet, Raoul. *Le Nationalisme français, 1871–1914*. Paris: Armand Colin, 1966.

Goblot, Edmond. *La Barrière et le niveau: étude sociologique sur la bourgeoisie française moderne*. 1925. Brionne: Gérard Monfort, 1984.

Good, Robert. "Good Women and Good Will: Pedagogy Meets Philosophy in the Third Republic." *Women in French Studies* 4 (Fall 1996): 50–9.

Greimas, A.J. "Transmission et communication." *L'Enseignement de la littérature: Colloque de Cérisy*. July 22–29, 1969. Ed. Serge Doubrovsky and Tzvetan Todorov. Paris: Plon, 1971.

Grivel, Charles. "Le sujet de l'école et de la littérature." *Revue de L'Institut de Sociologie* 3–4 (1980): 461–79.

Guillory, John. *Cultural Capital: The Problem of Literary Canon Formation*. Chicago and London: The University of Chicago Press, 1993.

Hanna, Martha. *The Mobilization of Intellect: French Scholars and Writers during the Great War*. Cambridge, MA: Harvard University Press, 1996.

Hause, Steven C. "Anti-Protestant Rhetoric in the Early Third Republic." *French Historical Studies* 16:1 (Spring 1989): 183–201.

Hazareesingh, S. "An Intellectual Founder of the Third Republic: The Neo-Kantian Republicanism of Jules Barni." *History of Political Thought* 22:1 (Spring 2001): 131–40.

Hebrard, Jean. "Ecole et alphabétisation au XIXème siècle (approche psycho-pédagogique de documents historiques)." *Annales: Economies, Sociétés, Civilisations* 35:1 (January–February 1980): 66–80.

Heyndels, Ralph. "Situation et perspectives de la sociologie de la littérature." *Revue de l'Université de Bruxelles* 3–4 (1976): 292–300.

Hirtz, Colette. "L'Ecole normale supérieure de Fontenay; les protestants aux sources de la laïcité française." *Bulletin de la Société de l'Histoire du Protestantisme Français* 135:2 (1989): 281–90.

Hobsbawm, Eric. "Mass-producing Traditions: Europe, 1870–1914." *The Invention of Tradition* Ed. Eric Hobsbawn and Terence Ranger. Cambridge: Cambridge University Press, 1983. 263–307.

Hollier, Denis. "On Schools, Churches and Museums." *A New History of French Literature*. Ed. Denis Hollier. Cambridge: Harvard University Press, 1989. 830–36.

Hordé, Tristan. "L'enseignement de l'histoire littéraire: les instructions officielles au XIXe siècle." *Le français aujourd'hui* 72 (1985): 50–4.

Hyslop, Beatrice Fry. *French Nationalism in 1789 According to the General Cahiers*. New York: Columbia University Press, 1934.

Isambart-Jamati, Viviane. "L'Enseignement de la langue écrite dans les lycées du Second Empire et des premières années de la République." *Revue des Sciences Humaines (Lille III)* 174 (1979): 21–35.

Johnson, Barbara. *Défigurations du langage poétique: la seconde révolution baudelairienne*. Paris: Flammarion, 1979.

Johnson, Douglas. "Jules Ferry et les Protestants." *Jules Ferry fondateur de la République: Actes du Colloque de 1982*. Ed. François Furet. Paris: Ecole des Hautes Etudes en Sciences Sociales, 1985. 73–78.

Julia, Dominique. "Livres de classe et usages pédagogiques." *Histoire de l'édition française, tome II: Le livre triomphant, 1660–1830*. Ed. Henri-Jean Martin and Roger Chartrier. Paris: Promodis, 1984.

———. *Les Trois couleurs du tableau noir*. Paris: Belin, 1981.

Karady, Victor. "Recherches sur la morphologie du corps universitaire littéraire sous la Troisième République." *Mouvement Social* 96 (1976): 47–79.

Kuentz, Pierre. "L'envers du texte." *Littérature* 7 (October 1972): 3–26.

———. "Le modèle latin." *Littérature* 42 (1981): 109–22.

Langford, Rachael. "Revolutionary Times: The Use of the Diary Form to Contest the French Third Republic in the *Jacques Vingtras* Trilogy by Jules Vallès." *Marginal Voices, Marginal Forms: Diaries in Modern European Literature and History*. Ed. Rachael Langford and Russel West. Amsterdam: Rodopi, 1999. 90–106.

Legrand, Louis. *L'influence du positivisme dans l'oeuvre scolaire de Jules Ferry*. Paris: Marcel Rivière, 1961.

Lejeune, Philippe. "L'enseignement de la littérature au lycée au siècle dernier." *Le Français aujourd'hui* 4 (January 1969): 26–37.

Mackey, William F. "*L'Institution du Français* by Renée Balibar (Review)." *History of European Ideas* 13:1/2 (1991): 125–30.

Maingueneau, Dominique. *Les Livres d'école de la République, 1870–1914: Discours et idéologie*. Paris: Le Sycomore, 1979.

Marcoin, Francis. *A l'école de la littérature*. Paris: Les Editions Ouvrières, 1992.

Mayeur, Françoise. *Histoire générale de l'enseignement en France, tome III: de la Révolution à l'Ecole républicaine*. Paris: G.V. Labat, 1981.

———. "Recent Views on the History of Education in France." *European History Quarterly* 14:1 (January 1984): 93–102.

Mayeur, Jean-Marie. "Jules Ferry et la laïcité." *Jules Ferry fondateur de la République: Actes du Colloque de 1982*. Ed. François Furet. Paris: Ecole des Hautes Etudes en Sciences Sociales, 1985. 147–60.

Milo, Daniel. "Les Classiques scolaires." *Les Lieux de mémoire, tome II: La Nation*. Ed. Pierre Nora. Paris: Gallimard, 1984. 517–62.

Muel, Francine. "L'Alphabétisation de Calvin à Jules Ferry." *Annales: Economies, Sociétés, Civilisations* 35:1 (January–February 1980): 66–80.

Nicolet, Claude. *L'Idée républicaine en France: Essai d'histoire critique*. Paris: Gallimard, 1982.

———. "Jules Ferry et la tradition positiviste." *Commentaire* 18 (1982): 306–21.

Ognier, Pierre. *L'Ecole républicaine française et ses miroirs*. Berne: Peter Lang, 1988.

Ozouf, Jacques and Mona Ozouf. *La République des Instituteurs*. Paris: Gallimard, 1992.

———. "Le Tour de la France par deux enfants: Le petit livre rouge de la République." *Les Lieux de mémoire, tome I: La République*. Ed. Pierre Nora. Paris: Gallimard, 1984. 291–321.

Ozouf, Mona. *L'Ecole, l'Eglise, et la République*. Paris: Armand Colin, 1963.

———. *La Fête révolutionnaire—1789–1799*. Paris: Gallimard, 1976.

———. "Unité nationale et unité de la pensée de Jules Ferry." *Jules Ferry fondateur de la République: Actes du Colloque de 1982*. Ed. François Furet. Paris: Ecole des Hautes Etudes en Sciences Sociales, 1985. 59–72.

Palméro, J. *Histoire des institutions et des doctrines pédagogiques par les textes*. Paris: Société Universitaire d'Editions et de Libraire, 1958.

Pichot, Michel. "Educational Policies of the French Third Republic (1870–1939) in the Village of Guiard, Algeria: Hostility of the French Settlers and Cultural Resistance of the Indigenous Muslims." *Michigan Academician* 31:4 (1999): 509–17.

Ponton, Rémy. "Programme esthétique et capital symbolique: l'exemple du Parnasse." *Revue Française de Sociologie* XIV:2 (1973): 202–20.

Poulet, Georges. *La Pensée indéterminée II: du romantisme au début du XXe siècle*. Paris: PUF, 1987.

Prost, Antoine. *Histoire de l'enseignement en France 1800–1967*. Paris: Armand Colin, 1968.

———. "Jules Ferry, ministre de l'Instruction publique ou de l'administration de la pédagogie." *Jules Ferry fondateur de la République: Actes du Colloque de 1982*. Ed. François Furet. Paris: Ecole des Hautes Etudes en Sciences Sociales, 1985. 161–69.

———. "Lecture historique et lecture sociologique des politiques d'éducation." *Permanence et renouvellement en sociologie de l'éducation*. Paris: INRP L'Harmattan, 1992. 203–12.

Pujade-Renaud, C. *L'Ecole dans la littérature*. Paris: Editions ESF, 1986.

Raynaud, Philippe and Paul Thibaud. *La Fin de l'école républicaine*. Paris: Calmann-Lévy, 1990.

Ringer, Fritz. *Fields of Knowledge: French Academic Culture in Comparative Perspective*. Cambridge: Cambridge University Press, 1992.

Sammons, Jeffrey L. *Literary Sociology and Practical Criticism*. Bloomington and London: Indiana University Press, 1977.

Schor, Naomi. "The Crisis of French Universalism." *France/USA: The Cultural Wars, Yale French Studies* 100 (2001): 43–64.

Shklovsky, Victor. "Art as Technique." *Russian Formalist Criticism: Four Essays*. Ed. Lee T. Lemon and Marion J. Reis. Lincoln/London: University of Nebraska Press, 1965. 3–24.

Stock-Morton, Phyllis. *Moral Education for a Secular Society: The Development of* Morale Laïque *in Nineteenth-Century France*. Albany: SUNY Press, 1988.

Texte, J. "L'Hégémonie littéraire de la France au XVIIIème siècle." *Revue universitaire* 5:2 (1986): 163–65.

Thiesse, Anne-Marie and Hélène Mathieu. "The Decline of the Classical Age and the Birth of the Classics." *Displacements: Women, Tradition, Literatures in French*. Ed. Joan De Jean and Nancy K. Miller. Baltimore and London: Johns Hopkins University Press, 1991. 74–96.

Tripet, Edgar. "Langue, littérature et pouvoir." *Qu'est-ce que la culture française?* Ed. Jean-Paul Aron. Paris: Denoël/Gonthier, 1975. 201–09.

Valéry, Paul. *Regards sur le monde actuel et autres essais*. Paris: Gallimard, 1945.

Vossler, Ch. *Langue et culture de la France*. Trans. Alphonse Juilland. Paris: Payot, 1953.

Waquet, Françoise. *Latin or the Empire of a Sign: From the Sixteenth to the Twentieth Centuries*. Trans. John Howe. London and New York: Verso, 2001.

Weber, Eugen. "La Formation de l'hexagone Républicain." *Jules Ferry fondateur de la République: Actes du Colloque de 1982*. Ed. François Furet. Paris: Ecole des Hautes Etudes en Sciences Sociales, 1985. 223–24.

———. *Peasants into Frenchmen: The Modernization of Rural France, 1870–1914*. Stanford: Stanford University Press, 1976.

Weill, Georges. *Histoire de l'enseignement secondaire en France (1802–1920)*. Paris: Payot et Cie, 1921.

Weiss, John H. "The History of Education in 19th-century France: A Survey of Recent Writings." *Journal of Social History* 3:1 (Fall 1969): 154–62.

Yale French Studies: French Education 22 (1958): passim.

Index